Practical Portfolio Performance Measurement and Attribution

Wiley Finance Series

Practical Portfolio Performance Measurement and Attribution

Carl R. Bacon

John Wiley & Sons, Ltd

Other Wiley Editorial Offices

John Wiley & Sons Inc., 111 River Street, Hoboken, NJ 07030, USA

Jossey-Bass, 989 Market Street, San Francisco, CA 94103-1741, USA

Wiley-VCH Verlag GmbH, Boschstr. 12, D-69469 Weinheim, Germany

John Wiley & Sons Australia Ltd, 33 Park Road, Milton, Queensland 4064, Australia

John Wiley & Sons (Asia) Pte Ltd, 2 Clementi Loop #02-01, Jin Xing Distripark, Singapore 129809

John Wiley & Sons Canada Ltd, 22 Worcester Road, Etobicoke, Ontario, Canada M9W 1L1

Wiley also publishes its books in a variety of electronic formats. Some content that appears
in print may not be available in electronic books.

British Library Cataloguing in Publication Data

A catalogue record for this book is available from the British Library

ISBN-10   0-470-85679-3 (H/B)
ISBN-13   978-0470-85679-6 (H/B)

Project management by Originator, Gt Yarmouth, Norfolk (typeset in 10/12pt Times)
Printed and bound in Great Britain by Antony Rowe Ltd, Chippenham, Wiltshire
This book is printed on acid-free paper responsibly manufactured from sustainable forestry
in which at least two trees are planted for each one used for paper production.

This book is dedicated to Alex and Matt

Thanks for the support, black coffee and
suffering in silence the temporary suspension of
normal family life

Contents

About the Author

Carl Bacon joined StatPro Group plc as Chairman in April 2000. StatPro develops and markets specialist middle-office reporting software to the asset management industry. Carl also runs his own consultancy business providing advice to asset managers on various risk and performance measurement issues.

Prior to joining StatPro Carl was Director of Risk Control and Performance at Foreign & Colonial Management Ltd, Vice President Head of Performance (Europe) for J P Morgan Investment Management Inc., and Head of Performance for Royal Insurance Asset Management.

Carl holds a B.Sc. Hons. in Mathematics from Manchester University and is a member of the UK Investment Performance Committee (UKIPC), the European Investment Performance Committee (EIPC) and the Investment Performance Council (IPC). An original GIPS committee member, Carl also chairs the IPC Interpretations Sub-Committee, is ex-chair of the IPC Verification Sub-committee and is a member of the Advisory Board of the *Journal of Performance Measurement*.

Acknowledgements

This book developed from the series of performance measurement trainings courses I have had the pleasure of running around the world since the mid-1990s. I have learned so much and continue to learn from the questions and observations of the participants over the years, all of whom must be thanked.

I should also like to thank the many individuals at work, at conferences and in various IPC committee meetings who have influenced my views over the years and are not mentioned specifically.

Naturally from the practitioner's perspective, I've favoured certain methodologies over others – apologies to those who may feel their methods have been unfairly treated.

I am particularly grateful to Stefan Illmer for his useful corrections and suggestions for additional sections.

Of course, all errors and omissions are my own.

Carl R. Bacon
Deeping St James
September 2004

1
Introduction

> *The more precisely the position is determined, the less precisely the momentum is known in this instant, and vice versa.*
>
> Heisenberg, *The Uncertainty Principle* (1927)

WHY MEASURE PORTFOLIO PERFORMANCE?

Whether we manage our own investment assets or choose to hire others to manage the assets on our behalf we are keen to know "how well" our collection, or portfolio of assets are performing.

The process of adding value via benchmarking, asset allocation, security analysis, portfolio construction and executing transactions is collectively described as the investment decision process. The measurement of portfolio performance should be part of the investment decision process, not external to it.

Clearly there are many stakeholders in the investment decision process; this book focuses on the investors or owners of capital and the firms managing their assets (asset managers or individual portfolio managers). Other stakeholders in the investment decision process include independent consultants tasked with providing advice to clients, custodians, independent performance measurers and audit firms.

Portfolio performance measurement answers the three basic questions central to the relationship between asset managers and the owners of capital:

(1) *What* is the return on assets?
(2) *Why* has the portfolio performed that way?
(3) *How* can we improve performance?

Portfolio performance measurement is the quality control of the investment decision process and provides the necessary information to enable asset managers and clients to assess exactly how the money has been invested and the results of the process. The US Bank Administration Institute (BAI) laid down the foundations of the performance measurement process as early as 1968. The main conclusions of their study hold today:

(1) Performance measurement returns should be based on asset values measured at market value not at cost.

(2) Returns should be "total" returns (i.e., they should include both income and changes in market value – realized and unrealized capital appreciation).
(3) Returns should be time-weighted.
(4) Measurement should include risk as well as return.

THE PURPOSE OF THIS BOOK

The vocabulary of performance measurement and the multiple methodologies open to performance analysts worldwide are extremely varied and complex.

My purpose in writing this book is an attempt to provide a reference of the available methodologies and to hopefully provide some consistency in their definition.

Despite the development and global success of performance measurement standards there are considerable differences in terminology, methodology and attitude to performance measurement throughout the world.

Few books are dedicated to portfolio performance measurement; the aim of this one is to promote the role of performance measurers and to provide some insights into the tools at their disposal.

With its practical examples this book should meet the needs of performance analysts, portfolio managers, senior management within asset management firms, custodians, verifiers and ultimately the clients.

Performance measurement is a key function in an asset management firm, it deserves better than being grouped with the back office. Performance measurers provide real added value, with feedback into the investment decision process and analysis of structural issues. Since their role is to understand in full and communicate the sources of return within portfolios they are often the only independent source equipped to understand the performance of all the portfolios and strategies operating within the asset management firm.

Performance measurers are in effect alternative risk controllers able to protect the firm from rogue managers and the unfortunate impact of failing to meet client expectations.

The chapters of this book are structured in the same order as the performance measurement process itself, namely:

(1) Calculation of portfolio returns.
(2) Comparison against a benchmark.
(3) Proper assessment of the reward received for the risk taken.
(4) Attribution of the sources of return.
(5) Presentation and communicating the results.

First, we must establish what has been the return on assets and to make some assessment of that return compared with a benchmark or the available competition.

In Chapter 2 the "what" of performance measurement is introduced describing the many forms of return calculation, including the relative merits of each method together with calculation examples.

Performance returns in isolation add little value; we must compare these returns against a suitable benchmark. Chapter 3 discusses the merits of good and bad bench-marks and examines the detailed calculation of commercial and customized indexes.

Clients should be aware of the increased risk taken in order to achieve higher rates of return; Chapter 4 discusses the multiple risk measures available to enhance understanding about the quality of return and to facilitate the assessment of the reward achieved for risk taken.

Chapter 5 examines the sources of excess return with the help of a number of performance attribution techniques.

Finally, in Chapter 6 we turn to the presentation of performance and consider the global development of performance presentation standards.

REFERENCE

BAI (1968) *Measuring the Investment Performance of Pension Funds for the purpose of Inter Fund Comparison.* Bank Administration Institute.

The Mathematics of Portfolio Return

Mathematics has given economics rigour, alas also mortis.

Robert Helibroner

SIMPLE RETURN

In measuring the performance of a "portfolio" or collection of investment assets we are concerned with the increase or decrease in the value of those assets over a specific time period – in other words, the change in "wealth".

This change in wealth can be expressed either as a "wealth ratio" or a "rate of return".

The wealth ratio describes the ratio of the end value of the portfolio relative to the start value, mathematically:

$$\frac{V_E}{V_S} \tag{2.1}$$

where: V_E = the end value of the portfolio

V_S = the start value of the portfolio.

A wealth ratio greater than one indicates an increase in value, a ratio less than one a decrease in value.

Starting with a simple example, take a portfolio valued at £100m initially and valued at £112m at the end of the period. The wealth ratio is calculated as follows:

Exhibit 2.1   Wealth ratio

$$\frac{112}{100} = 1.12$$

The value of a portfolio of assets is not always easy to obtain, but should represent a reasonable estimate of the current economic value of the assets. Firms should ensure internal valuation policies are in place and consistently applied over time. A change in valuation policy may generate spurious performance over a specific time period.

Economic value implies that the traded market value, rather than the settlement value of the portfolio should be used. For example, if an individual security has been bought but the trade has not been settled (i.e., paid for) then the portfolio is economically exposed to any change in price of that security. Similarly, any dividend declared and not yet paid or interest accrued on a fixed income asset is an entitlement of the portfolio and should be included in the valuation.

The rate of return, denoted r, describes the gain (or loss) in value of the portfolio relative to the starting value, mathematically:

$$r = \frac{V_E - V_S}{V_S} \tag{2.2}$$

Rewriting Equation (2.2):

$$r = \frac{V_E}{V_S} - \frac{V_S}{V_S} = \frac{V_E}{V_S} - 1 \tag{2.3}$$

Using the previous example the rate of return is:

Exhibit 2.2   Rate of return

$$\frac{112}{100} - 1 = 12\%$$

Equation (2.3) can be conveniently rewritten as:

$$1 + r = \frac{V_E}{V_S} \tag{2.4}$$

Hence, the wealth ratio is actually the rate of return plus one.

Where there are no "external cash flows" it is easy to show that the rate of return for the entire period is the "compounded return" over multiple sub-periods.

Let V_t equal the value of the portfolio after the end of period t then:

$$\frac{V_1}{V_S} \times \frac{V_2}{V_1} \times \frac{V_3}{V_2} \times \cdots \times \frac{V_{n-1}}{V_{n-2}} \times \frac{V_E}{V_{n-1}} = \frac{V_E}{V_S} = 1 + r \tag{2.5}$$

External cash flow is defined as any new money added to or taken from the portfolio, whether in the form of cash or other assets. Dividend and coupon payments, purchases and sales, and corporate transactions funded from within the portfolio are not considered external cash flows.

Substituting Equation (2.4) into Equation (2.5) we establish Equation (2.6):

$$(1 + r_1) \times (1 + r_2) \times (1 + r_3) \times \cdots \times (1 + r_{n-1}) \times (1 + r_n) = (1 + r) \tag{2.6}$$

This process (demonstrated in Exhibit 2.3) of compounding a series of sub-period returns to calculate the entire period return is called "geometric" or "chain" linking.

Exhibit 2.3   Chain linking

		Market value (£m)	Return (%)
Start value	V_S	100	
End of period 1	V_1	112	12.0
End of period 2	V_2	95	−15.18
End of period 3	V_3	99	4.21
End of period 4	V_4	107	8.08
End value	V_E	115	7.48

$$\frac{112}{100} \times \frac{95}{112} \times \frac{99}{95} \times \frac{107}{99} \times \frac{115}{107} = \frac{115}{100} = 1.15 \quad or \quad 15.0\%$$

$$1.12 \times 0.8482 \times 1.0421 \times 1.0808 \times 1.0748 = 1.15 \quad or \quad 15.0\%$$

MONEY-WEIGHTED RETURNS

Unfortunately, in the event of external cash flows we cannot continue to use the ratio of market values to calculate wealth ratios and hence rates of return. The cash flow itself will make a contribution to the valuation. Therefore, we must develop alternative methodologies that adjust for external cash flow.

Internal rate of return (IRR)

To make allowance for external cash flow we can borrow a methodology from economics and accountancy, the "internal rate of return" or IRR.

The internal rate of return has been used for many decades to assess the value of capital investment or other business ventures over the future lifetime of a project. Normally, the initial outlay, estimated costs and expected returns are well known and the internal rate of return of the project can be calculated to determine if the investment is worth undertaking. The IRR is often used to calculate the future rate of return on a bond and called the yield to redemption.

Simple internal rate of return

In the context of the measurement of investment assets for a single period the IRR method in its most simple form requires that a return r be found that satisfies the following equation:

$$V_E = V_S \times (1 + r) + C \times (1 + r)^{0.5} \tag{2.7}$$

where: C = external cash flow.

In this form we are making an assumption that all cash flows are received at the mid-point of the period under analysis. To calculate the simple IRR we need only the start and end market values, and the total external cash flow as shown in Exhibit 2.4:

Exhibit 2.4   Simple IRR

Market start value $74.2m
Market end value $104.4m
External cash flow $37.1m

$$104.4 = 74.2 \times (1 + r) + 37.1 \times (1 + r)^{0.5}$$

We can see $r = -7.41\%$ satisfies the above equation:

$$74.2 \times (0.9259) + 37.1 \times (0.9259)^{0.5} = 104.4$$

Modified internal rate of return

Making the assumption that all cash flows are received midway through the period of analysis is a fairly crude estimate. The midpoint assumption can be modified for all cash flows to adjust for the fraction of the period of measurement that the cash flow is available for investment as follows:

$$V_E = V_S \times (1 + r) + \sum_{t=1}^{t=T} C_t \times (1 + r)^{W_t} \tag{2.8}$$

where: C_t = the external cash flow on day t

W_t = weighting ratio to be applied on day t.

Obviously, there will be no external cash flow for most days:

$$W_t = \frac{TD - D_t}{TD} \tag{2.9}$$

where: TD = total number of days within the period of measurement

D_t = number of days since the beginning of the period including weekends and public holidays.

In addition to the information in Exhibit 2.4 to calculate the modified internal rate of return shown in Exhibit 2.5 we need to know the date of the cash flow and the length of the period of analysis:

Exhibit 2.5   Modified IRR

Market start value   31 December $74.2m
Market end value   31 January $104.4m
External cash flow   14 January $37.1m

Assuming the cash flow at the end of day 14 is:

$$104.4 = 74.2 \times (1+r) + 37.1 \times (1+r)^{17/31}$$

We can see $r = -7.27\%$ satisfies the above equation:

$$74.2 \times (0.9273) + 37.1 \times (0.9273)^{17/31} = 104.4$$

The standard internal rate of return method in Equation (2.8) is often described by performance measurers as the modified internal rate of return method to differentiate it from the simple internal rate of return method described in Equation (2.7) which assumes midpoint cash flows. Students of finance would find the addition of the word "modified" puzzling and unnecessary.

This method assumes a single, constant force of return throughout the period of measurement, an assumption we know not to be true since the returns of investment assets are rarely constant. This assumption also means we cannot disaggregate the IRR into different asset categories since we cannot continue to use the single constant rate.

For project appraisal or calculating the redemption yield of a bond this assumption is not a problem since we are calculating a future return for which we must make some assumptions.

IRR is an example of a money-weighted return methodology: each amount or dollar invested is assumed to achieve the same effective rate of return irrespective of when it was invested. In the US the term "dollar-weighted" rather than "money-weighted" is used.

The weight of money invested at any point of time will ultimately impact the final return calculation. Therefore, if using this methodology it is important to perform well when the amount of money invested is largest.

To calculate the "annual" internal rate of return rather than the "cumulative" rate of return for the entire period we need to solve for r, using the following formula:

$$V_E = V_S \times (1+r)^Y + \sum_{t=1}^{t=T} C_t \times (1+r)^{W_t^y} \tag{2.10}$$

where: Y = length of time period to be measured in years

W_t^y = factor to be applied to external cash flow on day t.

This factor is the time available for investment after the cash flow given by:

$$W_t^y = Y - Y_t \tag{2.11}$$

where: Y_t = number of years since the beginning of the period of measurement.

For example, assume cash flow occurs on the 236th day of the 3rd year for a total measurement period of 5 years. Then:

$$W_t^y = 5 - 2\frac{236}{365} = 2\frac{129}{365}$$

Simple Dietz

Even in its simple form the internal rate of return is not a particularly practical calculation, especially over longer periods with multiple cash flows. Peter Dietz

(1966) suggested as an alternative the following simple adaptation to Equation (2.2) to adjust for external cash flow. Let's call this the simple (or original) Dietz Method:

$$r = \frac{V_E - V_S - C}{V_S + \dfrac{C}{2}}$$

(2.12)

where: C represents external cash flow.

The numerator of Equation (2.12) represents the investment gain in the portfolio. In the denominator replacing the initial market value we now use the average capital invested represented by the initial market value plus half the external cash flow. An assumption has been made that the external cash flow is invested midway through the period of analysis and has been weighted accordingly. The average capital invested is absolutely not the average of the start and end values, which would factor in an element of portfolio performance into the denominator.

This method is also a money (or dollar) weighted return and is in fact the first-order approximation of the internal rate of return method.

To calculate a simple Dietz return, like the simple IRR, only the start market value, end market value and total external cash flow are required.

Exhibit 2.6   Simple Dietz

Using the existing example data:

Market start value $74.2m
Market end value   £104.4m
External cash flow $37.1m

The simple Dietz rate of return is:

$$\frac{104.4 - 74.2 - 37.1}{74.2 + \dfrac{37.1}{2}} = \frac{-6.9}{92.75} = -7.44\%$$

Dietz originally described his method as assuming one-half of the net contributions are made at the beginning of the time interval and one-half at the end of the time interval:

$$r = \frac{V_E - \dfrac{C}{2}}{V_S + \dfrac{C}{2}} - 1$$

(2.13)

which simplifies to the more common description:

$$r = \frac{V_E - \dfrac{C}{2}}{V_S + \dfrac{C}{2}} \quad \frac{V_S + \dfrac{C}{2}}{V_S + \dfrac{C}{2}} = \frac{V_E - V_S - C}{V_S + \dfrac{C}{2}}$$

(2.12)

The Dietz method is easier to calculate and easier to visualize than the IRR method. It can also be disaggregated (i.e., the total return is the sum of the individual parts).

ICAA method

The Investment Counsel Association of America (ICAA, 1971) proposed a straightforward extension of the simple Dietz method as follows:

$$r = \frac{V'_E - V_S - C' + I}{V_S + \dfrac{C'}{2}} \qquad (2.14)$$

where: I = total portfolio income

C' = external cash flow including any reinvested income

V'_E = market end value including any reinvested income.

Extending our previous example in Exhibit 2.7:

Exhibit 2.7   ICAA method

Market start value $74.2m
Market end value $104.2m
External cash flow $37.1m
Total income $0.4m
Income reinvested $0.2m

$$\frac{104.2 - 74.2 - (37.1 + 0.2) + 0.4}{74.2 + \dfrac{(37.1 + 0.2)}{2}} = \frac{-6.9}{92.85} = -7.43\%$$

In this method, income (equity dividends, interest or coupon payments) is not automatically assumed to be available for reinvestment. The gain in the numerator is appropriately adjusted for any reinvested income included in the final value by including reinvested income in the definition of external cash flow.

Interestingly, although the average capital is increased for any reinvested income in the denominator there is no negative adjustment for any income not reinvested. This is perhaps not unreasonable from the perspective of the client if the income is retained and not paid until the end of period.

However, from the asset manager's viewpoint, if this income is not available for reinvestment it should be treated as a negative cash flow as follows:

$$r = \frac{V_E - V_S - C + I}{V_S + \dfrac{(C - I)}{2}} \qquad (2.15)$$

Extending our previous example again in Exhibit 2.8:

Exhibit 2.8   Income unavailable

Market start value	$74.2m
Market end value	$104.0m
External cash flow	$37.1m
Total income	$0.4m

$$\frac{104.0 - 74.2 - 37.1 + 0.4}{74.2 + \dfrac{(37.1 - 0.4)}{2}} = \frac{-6.9}{92.55} = -7.46\%$$

In Equation (2.15) any income received by the portfolio is assumed to be unavailable for investment by the portfolio manager and transferred to a separate income account for later payment or alternatively paid directly to the client.

Obviously, income paid or transferred is no longer included in the final value V_E of the portfolio. In effect, in this methodology income is treated as negative cash flow. Since income is normally always positive, this method has the effect of reducing the average capital employed, decreasing the size of the denominator and thus leveraging (or gearing) the final rate of return.

Consequently, this method should only be used if portfolio income is genuinely unavailable to the portfolio manager for further investment. Typically, this method is used to calculate the return of an asset category (sector or component) within a portfolio.

Modified Dietz

Making the assumption that all cash flows are received midway through the period of analysis is a fairly crude estimate. The simple Dietz method can be further modified by day weighting each cash flow by the following formula to establish a more accurate average capital employed:

$$r = \frac{V_E - V_S - C}{V_S + \Sigma C_t \times W_t} \tag{2.16}$$

where: C = total external cash flow within period

C_t = external cash flow on day t

W_t = weighting ratio to be applied to external cash flow on day t.

Recall from Equation (2.9):

$$W_t = \frac{TD - D_t}{TD}$$

where: TD = total number of days within the period of measurement

D_t = number of days since the beginning of the period including weekends and public holidays.

In determining D_t the performance analyst must establish if the cash flow is received at the beginning or end of the day. If the cash flow is received at the start of the day then it is reasonable to assume that the portfolio manager is aware of the cash flow and able to respond to it; therefore, it is reasonable to include this day in the weighting calculation. On the other hand if the cash flow is received at the end of the day the portfolio manager is unable to take any action at that point and, therefore, it is unreasonable to include the current day in the weighting calculation.

For example, take a cash flow received on the 14th day of a 31-day month. If the cash flow is at the start of the day, then there are 18 full days including the 14th day available for investment and the weighting factor for this cash flow should be $(31 - 13)/31$. Alternatively, if the cash flow is at the end of the day then there are 17 full days remaining and the weighting factors should be $(31 - 14)/31$.

Performance analysts should determine a company policy to apply consistently to all cash flows.

Extending our standard example in Exhibit 2.9:

Exhibit 2.9   Modified Dietz

Market start value   31 December $74.2m
Market end value   31 January $104.4m
External cash flow   14 January $37.1m

Assuming the cashflow is at the end of day 14:

$$\frac{104.4 - 74.2 - 37.1}{74.2 + \dfrac{(31 - 14)}{31} \times 37.1} = \frac{-6.9}{94.55} = -7.30\%$$

Assuming the cashflow is at the beginning of day 14 with 18 full days in the month left:

$$\frac{104.4 - 74.2 - 37.1}{74.2 + \dfrac{(31 - 13)}{31} \times 37.1} = \frac{-6.9}{95.74} = -7.21\%$$

TIME-WEIGHTED RETURNS

True time-weighted

Time-weighted rates of return provide a popular alternative to money-weighted returns in which each time period is given equal weight regardless of the amount invested, hence the name "time-weighted".

In the "true or classical time-weighted" methodology, performance is calculated for each sub-period between cash flows using simple wealth ratios. The sub-period returns are then chain-linked as follows:

$$\frac{V_1 - C_1}{V_S} \times \frac{V_2 - C_2}{V_1} \times \frac{V_3 - C_3}{V_2} \times \cdots \times \frac{V_{n-1} - C_{n-1}}{V_{n-2}} \times \frac{V_E - C_n}{V_{n-1}} = 1 + r \qquad (2.17)$$

where: $V_t =$ is the valuation immediately after the cash flow C_t at the end of period t.

Since $\dfrac{V_t - C_t}{V_{t-1}} = 1 + t_t$ is the wealth ratio immediately prior to receiving the external cash flow, Equation (2.17) simplifies to the familiar Equation (2.6) from before:

$$(1 + r_1) \times (1 + r_2) \times (1 + r_3) \times \cdots \times (1 + r_{n-1}) \times (1 + r_n) = (1 + r)$$

In Equation (2.17) we have made the assumption that any cash flow is only available for the portfolio manager to invest at the end of the day. If we make the assumption that the cash flow is available from the beginning of the day we must change Equation (2.17) to:

$$\frac{V_1}{V_S + C_1} \times \frac{V_2}{V_1 + C_2} \times \frac{V_3}{V_2 + C_3} \times \cdots \times \frac{V_{n-1}}{V_{n-2} + C_{n-1}} \times \frac{V_E}{V_{n-1} + C_n} = 1 + r \qquad (2.18)$$

Alternatively, we may wish to make the assumption that the cash flow is available for investment midday and use a half-weight assumption as follows:

$$\frac{V_1 - \dfrac{C_1}{2}}{V_S + \dfrac{C_1}{2}} \times \frac{V_2 - \dfrac{C_2}{2}}{V_1 + \dfrac{C_2}{2}} \times \cdots \times \frac{V_E - \dfrac{C_n}{2}}{V_{n-1} + \dfrac{C_n}{2}} = 1 + r \qquad (2.19)$$

Note from equation (2.12):

$$r_t = \frac{V_t - V_{t-1} - C_t}{V_{t-1} + \dfrac{C_t}{2}} = \frac{V_t - \dfrac{C_t}{2}}{V_{t-1} + \dfrac{C_t}{2}} - 1$$

Equation (2.19) is really a hybrid methodology combining both time weighting and a money-weighted return for each individual day and, therefore, ceases to be a true time-weighted rate of return.

Using our standard example data we now need to know the value of the portfolio immediately after the cash flow as shown in Exhibits 2.10, 2.11 and 2.12:

Exhibit 2.10   True time-weighted end of day cash flow

End of day cash flow assumption:

Market start value	31 December	$74.2m
Market end value	31 January	$104.4m
External cash flow	14 January	$37.1m
Market value end of	14 January	$103.1m

$$\frac{103.1 - 37.1}{74.2} \times \frac{104.4}{103.1} - 1 = 0.8895 \times 1.0126 - 1 = -9.93\%$$

Exhibit 2.11   True time-weighted start of day cash flow

Start of day cash flow assumption:

Market start value   31 December $74.2m
Market end value   31 January $104.4m
External cash flow   14 January $37.1m
Market value start of   14 January $67.0m

$$\frac{67.0}{74.2} \times \frac{104.4}{67.0 + 37.1} - 1 = 0.9030 \times 1.0029 - 1 = -9.44\%$$

Exhibit 2.12   Time-weighted midday cash flow

Midday cash flow assumption:

Market start value   31 December $74.2m
Market end value   31 January $104.4m
External cash flow   14 January $37.1m
Market value start of   14 January $67.0m
Market value end of   14 January $103.1m

$$\frac{67.0}{74.2} \times \frac{103.1 - \dfrac{37.1}{2}}{67.0 + \dfrac{37.1}{2}} \times \frac{104.4}{103.1} - 1 = 0.9030 \times 0.9883 \times 1.0126 - 1 = -9.63\%$$

Unit price method

The "unit price" or "unitized" method is a useful variant of the true time-weighted methodology. Rather than use the ratio of market values between cash flows, a standardized unit price or "net asset value" price is calculated immediately before each external cash flow by dividing the market value by the number of units previously allocated. Units are then added or subtracted (bought or sold) in the portfolio at the unit price corresponding to the time of the cash flow – the unit price is in effect a normalized market value.

The starting value of the portfolio is also allocated to units, often using a notional, starting unit price of say 1 or 100.

The main advantage of the unit price method is that the ratio between end of period unit price and the start of period unit price always provides the rate of return irrespective of the change of value in the portfolio due to cash flow. Therefore, to calculate the rate of return between any two points the only information you need to know is the start and end unit prices.

Let NAV_i equal the net asset value unit price of the portfolio at the end of period i. Then:

$$\frac{NAV_1}{NAV_S} \times \frac{NAV_2}{NAV_1} \times \frac{NAV_3}{NAV_2} \times \cdots \times \frac{NAV_{n-1}}{NAV_{n-2}} \times \frac{NAV_E}{NAV_{n-1}} = \frac{NAV_E}{NAV_S} = 1 + r \qquad (2.20)$$

The unitized method is so convenient for quickly calculating performance that returns calculated using other methodologies are often converted to unit prices for ease of use, particularly over longer time periods.

The unitized method is a variant of the true or classical time-weighted return and will always give the same answer, as can be seen in Exhibit 2.13:

Exhibit 2.13   Unit price method

Market value of portfolio at start of period	31 December	$74.2m
Market value of portfolio at end of period	31 January	$104.4m
Cash flow at end of day 14	14 January	$37.1m
Market value of portfolio immediately prior to cash flow	14 January	$66.0m

Emerging market index return in January	−7.92%
Index return 31 December to 14 January	−10.68%
Index return 14 January to 31 January	+3.09%

	Valuation	Unit price	Units allocated	Total units
Start value	74.2	1.0000	74.20	74.2
Valuation (14 January)	66.0	0.8895		74.2
Cash flow (14 January)	37.1	0.8895	41.71	115.9
End value	104.4	0.9007		115.9

$$\frac{90.07}{100.00} - 1 = -9.93\%$$

TIME-WEIGHTED VERSUS MONEY-WEIGHTED RATES OF RETURN

Time-weighted returns measure the returns of the assets irrespective of the amount invested. This can generate counter-intuitive results as shown in Exhibit 2.14:

Exhibit 2.14   Time-weighted returns versus money-weighted returns

Start period 1	Market value	£100
End period 1	Market value	£200

Cash flow   £1,000
Start period 2   Market value   £1,200
End period 2   Market value   £700

Time-weighted return:

$$\frac{1,200 - 1,000}{100} \times \frac{700}{1,200} - 1 = 16.67\%$$

Money-weighted return:

$$\frac{700 - 100 - 1,000}{100 + \dfrac{1,000}{2}} = -33.3\%$$

In Exhibit 2.14 the client has lost £400 over the entire period, yet the time-weighted return is calculated as a positive 16.67%. The money-weighted return reflects this loss, −33.3% of the average capital employed. It is important to perform well in period 2 when the majority of client money is invested.

If the client had invested all the money at the beginning of the period of measurement then a 16.67% return would have been achieved. The difference in return calculated is due to the timing of cash flow. Over a single period of measurement the money-weighted rate of return will always reflect the cash gain and loss over the period.

The time-weighted rate of return adjusts for cash flow and weights each time period equally, measuring the performance that would have been achieved had there been no cash flows. Clearly, this return is most appropriate for comparing the performance of different portfolio managers with different patterns of cash flows and with benchmark indexes which, for the most part, are calculated using a time-weighted approach.

In effect the time-weighted rate of return measures the portfolio manager's performance adjusting for cash flows, and the money-weighted rate of return measures the performance of the client's invested assets including the impact of cashflows.

With such large potential differences between methodologies, which method should be used and in what circumstances?

Most performance analysts would prefer time-weighted returns. By definition, time-weighted returns weight each time period equally, irrespective of the amount invested; therefore, the timing of external cash flows does not affect the calculation of return. In the majority of cases portfolio managers do not determine the timing of external cash flows; therefore, it is desirable to use a methodology that is not impacted by the timing of cash flow.

A major drawback of true time-weighted returns is that accurate valuations are required at the date of each cash flow. This is an onerous and expensive requirement for some asset managers. The manager must make an assessment of the benefits of increased accuracy against the costs of frequent valuations for each external cash flow and the potential for error. Asset management firms must have a daily valuation mindset to succeed with daily performance calculations. Exhibit 2.15 demonstrates the impact of a valuation error on the return calculation:

Exhibit 2.15   Valuation error

Market start value	31 December	$74.2m
Market end value	31 January	$104.4m
External cash flow	14 January	$37.1m
Erroneous market value	14 January	$101.1m

$$\frac{101.1 - 37.1}{74.2} \times \frac{104.4}{101.1} - 1 = 0.8625 \times 1.0326 - 1 = -10.94\%$$

A significant and permanent difference from the accurate time-weighted return of −9.93% calculated in Exhibit 2.12.

Not unreasonably, institutional clients such as large pension funds paying significant fees might expect that the asset manager has sufficient quality information on a daily basis to manage their portfolio accurately. Most managers of large funds will also have mutual or other pooled funds in their stable, which in most cases will already require daily valuations (not just at the date of each external cash flow). The industry, driven by performance presentation standards and the demand for more accurate analysis, is gradually moving to daily calculations as standard.

In terms of statistical analysis, daily calculation adds more noise than information; however, in terms of return analysis, daily calculation (or at the least valuation at each external cash flow which practically amounts to the same thing) is essential to ensure the accuracy of long-term returns.

I do not believe in the daily analysis of performance, which is far too short-term for long-term investment portfolios, but I do believe in accurate returns, which require daily calculation. It is also useful for the portfolio manager or performance measurer to analyse performance between any two dates other than standard calendar period ends.

APPROXIMATIONS TO THE TIME-WEIGHTED RETURN

Asset managers without the capability or unwilling to pay the cost of achieving accurate valuations on the date of each cash flow may still wish to use a time-weighted methodology and can use methodologies that approximate to the "true" time-weighted return by estimating portfolio values on the date of cash flow, such as the methodologies outlined in the next three subsections.

Index substitution

Assuming an accurate valuation is not available, an index return may be used to estimate the valuation on the date of the cash flow, thus approximating the "true" time-weighted return, as demonstrated in Exhibit 2.16:

Exhibit 2.16   Index substitution

Given an assigned benchmark performance of −10.68% up to the point of cash flow and using the data from Exhibit 2.10, the estimated valuation at the date of the cash flow is:

$$74.2 \times (1 - 10.68\%) = 66.28$$

Therefore the approximate time-weighted return is:

$$\frac{66.28}{74.2} \times \frac{104.4}{66.28 + 37.1} - 1 = 0.8932 \times 1.0099 - 1 = -9.80\%$$

In Exhibit 2.16 the index is a good estimate of the portfolio value and, therefore, the resultant return is a good estimate of the true time-weighted rate of return. However, if the index is a poor estimate of the portfolio value, see Exhibit 2.17, then the resultant return may be inaccurate despite being in this case a better estimate of underlying return than, say, the modified Dietz or IRR.

Exhibit 2.17   Index substitution

Using an index return of −7.90% to estimate the portfolio value at the point of cash flow:

$$74.2 \times (1 - 7.9\%) = 68.34$$

Therefore the approximate time-weighted return is:

$$\frac{68.34}{74.2} \times \frac{104.4}{68.34 + 37.1} - 1 = 0.9210 \times 0.9901 - 1 = -8.81\%$$

Regression method (or β method)

The regression method is an extension of the index substitution method. A theoretically more accurate estimation of portfolio value can be calculated adjusting for the systematic risk (as represented by the portfolio's *beta*) normally taken by the portfolio manager.

Exhibit 2.18   Regression method

Again using the data from Exhibit 2.16 but assuming a portfolio beta of 1.05 in comparison with the benchmark, the revised estimated valuation at the time of cash flow is:

$$74.2 \times (1 - 10.68\%) \times 1.05 = 69.59$$

Therefore, the approximate time-weighted return is:

$$\frac{69.59}{74.2} \times \frac{104.4}{69.59 + 37.1} - 1 = 0.9379 \times 0.9785 - 1 = -9.18\%$$

The index substitution method is only as good as the resultant estimate of portfolio value; making further assumptions about portfolio beta need not improve accuracy.

Analyst's test

A further more accurate approximation was proposed by a working group of the UK's Society of Investment Analysts (SIA, 1972). They demonstrated that the ratio between the money-weighted return of the portfolio and the money-weighted return of the notional fund (portfolio market values and cash flows invested in the benchmark) approximates the ratio between the time-weighted return of the portfolio and the time-weighted return of the notional fund, mathematically:

$$\frac{(1 + MWA)}{(1 + MWN)} = \frac{V_A - (C_T - C_W)}{V_N - (C_T - C_W)} \simeq \frac{(1 + TWA)}{(1 + TWN)} \qquad (2.21)$$

where: MWA = money-weighted return of actual portfolio

MWN = money-weighted return of notional fund

V_A = value of portfolio at end of period

V_N = value of notional fund at end of period

C_T = total external cash flow in period

C_W = weighted external cash flow in period

TWA = time-weighted return of actual portfolio

TWN = time-weighted return of notional fund.

Rearranging Equation (2.21):

$$TWA \cong \frac{(1 + MWA)}{(1 + MWN)} \times (1 + TWN) - 1 \qquad (2.22)$$

or

$$TWA \cong \frac{V_A - (C_T - C_W)}{V_N - (C_T - C_W)} \times (1 + TWN) - 1 \qquad (2.23)$$

In other words, the time-weighted return of the portfolio can be approximated by the ratio of the money-weighted return of the portfolio divided by the money-weighted return of the notional fund and then multiplied by the notional fund time-weighted rate of return. Since all commercial indexes are time-weighted (they don't suffer cash flows and are therefore useful for comparative purposes) we can use an index return for the time-weighted notional fund.

Again, using the standard example in Exhibit 2.19:

Exhibit 2.19   Analyst's test

Market start value	31 December	$74.2m
Market end value	31 January	$104.4m
External cash flow	14 January	$37.1m

Index return in January	−7.92%
Index return (31 December to 14 January)	−10.68%
Index return (14 January to 31 January)	+3.09%

Final value of notional fund:

$$V_N = (74.2 \times (1 - 0.1068) + 37.1) \times 1.0309 = 106.57$$

$$C_T = 37.1$$

$$C_W = 37.1 \times \left(\frac{31 - 18}{31}\right) = 15.56$$

$$TWA = \frac{104.4 - (37.1 - 15.56)}{106.57 - (37.1 - 15.56)} \times (1 - 0.0792) - 1$$

$$TWA = \frac{82.86}{85.03} \times 0.9288 - 1 = -9.49\%$$

The advantage of these three approximate methods is that a time-weighted return may be estimated even without sufficient data to calculate an accurate valuation and hence an accurate time-weighted return. The disadvantages are clear: if the index, regression and notional fund assumptions, respectively, are incorrect or inappropriate the resultant return calculated will also be incorrect. Additionally, the actual portfolio return appears to change if a different index is applied which is counter-intuitive (surely, the portfolio return ought to be unique) and is very difficult to explain to the lay trustee.

HYBRID METHODOLOGIES

In practice, many managers neither use true time-weighted nor money-weighted calculations exclusively but rather a hybrid combination of both.

If the standard period of measurement is monthly, it is far easier and quicker to calculate the modified (or even simple) Dietz return for the month and then chain-link the resulting monthly returns. This approach treats each monthly return with equal weight and is therefore a version of time-weighting. All of the methods mentioned previously can be calculated for a specific time period and then chain-linked to create a time-weighted type of return for that time period.

Linked modified Dietz

Currently, the standard approach for institutional asset managers is to chain-link monthly modified Dietz returns. Often described as a time-weighted methodology, in fact it is a hybrid chain-linked combination of monthly money-weighted returns. Each monthly time period is given equal weight and is therefore time-weighted, but within the month the return is money-weighted.

BAI method

The US Bank Administration Institute (BAI, 1968) proposed an alternative hybrid approach that essentially links simple internal rates of return rather than linking modified Dietz returns.

Because of the difficulties in calculating internal rates of return this is not a popular method and is virtually unknown outside the US.

For clarification both the BAI method and the linked modified Dietz methods can be described as a type of time-weighted methodology because each standard period (normally monthly) is given equal weight. True time-weighting requires the calculation of performance between each cash flow.

The index substitution, regression and analyst test methods are approximations of the true time-weighted rate of return. The simple Dietz, modified Dietz and ICAA methods are approximations of the internal rate of return and are therefore money-weighted.

WHICH METHOD TO USE?

Determining which methodology to use will ultimately depend on the requirements of the client, the degree of accuracy required, the type and liquidity of assets, and cost and convenience factors.

Time-weighted returns neutralize the impact of cash flow. If the purpose of the return calculation is to measure and compare the portfolio manager's performance against other managers and commercially published indexes then time-weighting is the most appropriate. On the other hand, if there is no requirement for comparison and only the performance of the client's assets are to be analysed then money-weighting may be more appropriate.

As demonstrated in Exhibit 2.14, a time-weighted return that does not depend on the amount of money invested may lead to a positive rate of return over the period in which the client may have lost money. This may be difficult to present to the ultimate client although in truth the absolute loss of money in this example is due to the client giving the portfolio manager more money to manage prior to a period of poor performance in the markets. If there had been no cash flows the client would have made money.

Confidence in the accuracy of asset valuation is key in determining which method to use. If accurate valuations are available only on a monthly basis then a linked monthly modified Dietz methodology may well be the most appropriate. The liquidity of assets is also a key determinant of methodology. If securities are illiquid it may be difficult to establish an accurate valuation at the point of cash flow, in which case any perceived accuracy in the true time-weighted return could be quite spurious.

Internal rates of return are traditionally used for venture capital and private equity for a number of reasons:

(i) The initial investment appraisal for non-quoted investments often uses an IRR approach.
(ii) Assets are difficult to value accurately and are illiquid.
(iii) The venture capital manager often controls the timing of cash flow.

Money-weighted rates of return are often used for private clients to avoid the difficulty of explaining why a loss could possibly lead to a positive time-weighted rate of return.

Mutual funds suffer a particular performance problem caused by backdating unit prices, as illustrated in Exhibit 2.20:

Exhibit 2.20   Late trading

Start portfolio value	$5,000,000
Units in issue	10,000,000
Start unit price	0.50
End portfolio value	$5,250,000
Units in issue	10,000,000
End period unit price	0.525

Assume because of administrative error that $500,000 should have been allocated at the start of period. The administrator determines the client should not suffer and allocates the $500,000 in 1,000,000 units at 0.50:

The final price is now	$5,750,000
Units in issue	11,000,000
Erroneous unit price	0.5227

In effect, existing unit holders have been diluted by 0.44%. Units should only be issued at the current price, 1,000,000 at 0.525 = $525,000. The administrator should inject $25,000 to correct the error.

This is in effect what happened in the "late trading and market timing" scandal in US mutual funds revealed in 2003. Privileged investors were allowed to buy or sell units in international funds at slightly out-of-date prices with the knowledge that overseas markets had risen or fallen significantly already, resulting in small but persistent dilution of performance for existing unit holders.

SELF-SELECTION

With the choice of so many different, acceptable calculation methodologies, managers should establish an internal policy to avoid both intentional and unintentional abuse. Table 2.1 illustrates the range of different returns calculated for our standard example in just the one period.

The fundamental reason for the difference in all of the returns in Table 2.1 is the assumptions relating to external cash flow. Without cash flow all these

Table 2.1 Return variations due to methodology.

Method	Return (%)
Simple Dietz	−7.44
Modified Dietz (end of day)	−7.30
Modified Dietz (beginning of day)	−7.21
Simple IRR	−7.41
Modified IRR	−7.27
True time-weighted (end of day)	−9.93
True time-weighted (beginning of day)	−9.63
Time-weighted midday cash flow	−9.40
Index substitution	−9.80
Regression	−9.18
Analyst's test	−9.49

methods – money-weighted, time-weighted and approximations to time-weighted – will all give the same rate of return.

The reason for the difference effectively lies in the denominator (or average capital invested) of the return calculation. Each of these methods makes different assumptions about the impact of external cash flow on the denominator: the greater the cash flow the greater the impact.

The differences in the simple Dietz and the modified Dietz returns in Table 2.1 are so significant in this example because the cash flow is large relative to the starting value. If the cash flow is not large then the assumptions used to weight the cash flow will not have a measurable effect.

Because this effect is often not significant it is not always worth revaluing the portfolio for each cash flow. Many institutional asset managers employ a standard modified Dietz method and only revalue for a large external cash flow above a set percentage limit (10% is common). Asset management firms should set a limit and apply it rigorously. The limit may be defined to apply to a single cash flow during the period or the total cash flow during the period.

If multiple returns are routinely calculated for each methodology and the best return chosen for each period, even poor performing portfolios could appear to be performing quite well. Clearly, it is unethical to calculate performance using multiple methods and then choose the best return.

Intentional self-selection of the best methodology is easy to avoid, but unintentional abuse can occur. Portfolio managers are well aware that cash flow can impact performance and often they have a good feel for the performance of their own portfolios. If they have underperformed their expectations by say 0.2% they may require the performance measurer to investigate the return. The measurer identifying that a cash flow has occurred (but less than the normal limit) may conclude that the return has been adversely impacted by the cash flow. It would be entirely inappropriate for the performance measurer to adjust the return (even though it is theoretically more accurate) because the portfolio manager is unlikely to require the same analysis if the return is 0.2% above expectations, resulting in only positive adjustments taking place.

Table 2.2 lists the advantages and disadvantages of each return methodology available to the performance measurer together with my personal preference from the asset manager's perspective.

ANNUALIZED RETURNS

When comparing returns over long periods it is easier to think in terms of standardized periods – annual returns being the most convenient. The average annual return over a number of years can be calculated arithmetically or geometrically as follows:

$$\text{Arithmetic average or average return} \quad r_A = \frac{f}{n} \times \sum_{i=1}^{i=n} r_i \tag{2.24}$$

$$\text{Geometric average or annualized return} \quad r_G = \left(\prod_{i=1}^{n} (1 + r_i) \right)^{f/n} - 1 \tag{2.25}$$

where: n = the number of periods under analysis

f = the number of periods within the year (monthly $f = 12$, quarterly $f = 4$).

Average and annualized returns are calculated in Exhibit 2.21:

Exhibit 2.21   Average and annualized returns

Annual returns:

2003	10.5%
2002	−5.6%
2001	23.4%
2000	−15.7%
1999	8.6%

Arithmetic average:

$$\frac{10.5\% - 5.6\% + 23.4\% - 15.7\% + 8.6\%}{5} = 4.24\%$$

Geometric average or annualized return:

$$(1.105 \times 0.944 \times 1.234 \times 0.843 \times 1.086)^{1/5} - 1 = 3.3\%$$

It is poor performance measurement practice to annualize returns for periods less than 1 year. It is inappropriate to assume the rate of return achieved in the year to date will continue for the remainder of the year.

The terms "arithmetic" and "geometric" are common in the field of performance measurement: arithmetic reflects additive relationships and geometric reflects multiplicative or compounding relationships.

Table 2.2 Calculation methodologies

Method	Advantages	Disadvantages	Authors ranking
Simple Dietz	(i) Simple to calculate (ii) Not sensitive to valuation errors (iii) Can be disaggregated	(i) Crude estimate for timing of cash flows (ii) Not suitable for comparison against other funds or published indexes	**4**
Modified Dietz	(i) Simple to calculate (ii) Not sensitive to valuation errors (iii) Can be disaggregated	(i) Not suitable for comparison against other funds or published indexes	**8**
ICCA	(i) Simple to calculate (ii) Not sensitive to valuation errors (iii) Can be disaggregated	(i) Not suitable for comparison against other funds or published indexes (ii) Potential gearing effect because of treatment of income	**7**
Simple IRR	(i) Reflects the value added from the client's perspective (ii) Not sensitive to valuation errors	(i) Crude estimate for timing of cash flows (ii) Cannot be disaggregated (ii) Not suitable for comparison against other funds or published indexes	**3**
Internal rate of return	(i) Reflects the value added from the client's perspective. (ii) Not sensitive to valuation errors (iii) Common measure in finance. Frequently used in private equity/venture capital	(i) Relatively difficult to calculate (ii) Cannot be disaggregated (iii) Not suitable for comparison against other funds or published indexes	**5**

Method	Advantages	Disadvantages	
BAI	(i) Hybrid time-weighted, money-weighted return (ii) Not sensitive to valuation errors	(i) Relatively difficult to calculate (ii) Cannot be disaggregated	6
Linked modified Dietz	(i) Hybrid time-weighted, money-weighted return (ii) Easier to calculate than BAI method (iii) Can be disaggregated within single periods (iv) Well established and in common usage	(i) Can be impacted by large cash flows	9
True time-weighted	(i) Measures the true performance of the portfolio manager adjusting for cash flows (ii) Suitable for comparison with other asset managers and benchmarks	(i) Sensitive to incorrect valuations	10
Analyst's test	(i) Good estimate of true time-weighted rate of return (ii) Does not require accurate daily valuations	(i) Change in benchmark appears to change portfolio return	2
Index substitution	(i) Time-weighted methodology (ii) Does not require accurate daily valuations	(i) Approximation only as good as index assumption. Less accurate than Analyst's test (ii) Change in benchmark appears to change portfolio return	1
Regression	(i) Time-weighted methodology (ii) Does not require accurate daily valuations (iii) Use of systematic risk may provide a more accurate valuation approximation than index substitution method	(i) Approximation only as good as index and systematic risk assumption (ii) Change in benchmark or systematic risk calculation appears to change portfolio return	0

Investment returns compound. When assessing historic performance it is essential to use the constant rate of return that will compound to the same value as the historic series of returns, as shown in Exhibit 2.22:

Exhibit 2.22   Positive bias

Assume the rate of return is +20% in period 1 and −20% in period 2. Assume also a start value of £100:

Value at the end of period 1   £120
Value at the end of period 2   £96

The arithmetic average is $\dfrac{20.0\% - 20.0\%}{2} = 0\%$

The annualized return is $(1.2 \times 0.8)^{1/2} - 1 = -2.02\%$

−2.02% compounded over the two periods will generate the accurate end value of £96.

Arithmetic averages are positively biased; if returns are not constant the annualized return will always be less than the arithmetic average. The annualized return provides a better indicator of wealth at the end of the period than the arithmetic average. Performance analysts should use annualized rather than average returns.

CONTINUOUSLY COMPOUNDED RETURNS

While simple returns are positively biased, continuously compounded returns are not.

We observe from the operation of our bank accounts that interest paid into our accounts compounds over time: in other words, we receive interest on our interest payments. The more frequent the payments the higher the compounded return at the end of the year.

For example, to achieve an equivalent rate of 12% in one year we need only obtain a rate of return in each half-year period of 5.83% ($1.0583 \times 1.0583 = 1.12$). The nominal rate of return in each half-period required to achieve an effective rate of return of 12% is therefore 5.83% × 2 = 11.66%.

For n periods in the year we can calculate the effective return $\tilde{r}$ as follows:

$$\tilde{r} = \left(1 + \frac{r}{n}\right)^n - 1 \qquad (2.26)$$

The nominal rate of return in each monthly period required to achieve an effective rate of return of 12% is 11.39%.

If we continue to break down the periods into smaller and smaller periods, eventually we find the continuously compounded return or in effect the "force of return":

$$1 + \tilde{r} = \lim_{n \to \infty} \left(1 + \frac{r}{n}\right)^n = e^r \qquad (2.27)$$

$$\tilde{r} = \ln(1 + r) \qquad (2.28)$$

The continuously compounded return required to achieve an effective return of 12% is therefore $\ln(1.12) = 11.33\%$.

The main advantage of continuously compounded returns are that they are additive. The total return can be calculated as follows:

$$\ln(1 + r) = \ln(1 + r_1) + \ln(1 + r_2) + \cdots + \ln(1 + r_n) \qquad (2.29)$$

Continuously compounded returns should be used in statistical analysis because, unlike simple returns, they are not positively biased.

GROSS- AND NET-OF-FEE CALCULATIONS

A key component in long-term investment performance is the fee charged by the asset manager. Fees are charged in many different ways by several different parties. In evaluating and comparing the performance of a portfolio manager it is essential that the impact of fees be appropriately assessed.

There are three basic types of fees or costs incurred in the management of an investment portfolio:

(i) Transaction fees – the costs directly related to buying and selling assets including broker's commission, bid/offer spread, transaction-related regulatory charges and taxes (stamp duty, etc.), but excluding transaction-related custody charges.
(ii) Portfolio management fee – the fees charged by the asset manager for the management of the account.
(iii) Custody and other administrative fees including audit fees, performance measurement fees, legal fees and any other fee.

Portfolio managers should be evaluated against those factors that are under their control. Clearly, the portfolio manager has a choice whether or not to buy or sell securities; therefore, performance should always be calculated after (or net of) transaction costs. This is naturally reflected in the valuations used in the methods described previously and no more action need be taken.

Portfolio management fees are traditionally taken direct from the account, but need not be; the portfolio manager may invoice the client directly, thereby receiving payment from another source.

If payments were not taken directly from the portfolio then any return calculated would be before or "gross" of fees.

The gross-of-fee effect can replicated if the fee is deducted from the account by treating the management fee as an external cash flow. If the fee is not treated as an external cash flow, then the return calculated is after or "net" of fees.

The gross return is the investment return achieved by the portfolio manager and normally the most appropriate return to use for comparison purposes since institutional clients are normally able to negotiate fees.

Custody and other administration fees are not normally in the control of the portfolio manager and hence should not be reflected in the calculation of performance return for evaluation purposes. It should be noted, however, that the "client return" after administration fees is the real return delivered to the client.

Portfolio managers may bundle all their services together and charge a "bundled fee". If the bundled fee includes transaction costs that cannot be separated, then the entire fee must be subtracted to obtain the investment return.

In most countries local regulators will require mutual funds to report and advertise their performance net of all fees.

Estimating gross- and net-of-fee returns

The most accurate way to calculate the gross and net series of returns for a portfolio would be to calculate each set of returns separately, treating the fee as an external cashflow for the gross return but making no adjustment for the net return.

Alternatively, if only one series is calculated (either gross or net) the other can be estimated using the fee rate as follows:

(i) "Grossing up" net returns:

$$r_g = (1 + r_n) \times (1 + f) - 1 \tag{2.30}$$

(ii) "Netting down" gross returns:

$$r_n = \frac{(1 + r_g)}{(1 + f)} - 1 \tag{2.31}$$

where: r_g = return gross of portfolio management fee

r_n = return net of portfolio management fee

f = nominal period portfolio management fee rate.

In Table 2.3 actual and estimated grossed-up returns are shown over a period of 6 months. Note the underlying growth in the portfolio has appeared to exaggerate the arithmetic difference between gross and net returns $35.8\% - 35.0\% = 0.8\%$. The expected fee difference for a 1.2% per annum fee over 6 months would be 0.6%. In fact, the geometric difference $1.358/1.35 = 0.6\%$ between gross and net returns will provide a better representation of the fees charged. In this example the estimated gross return is a good estimate of the actual gross return. Timing of fee cash flows, payment in advance or in arrears and the frequency of calculation (i.e., monthly or quarterly) will all have minor impacts on the gross return calculation.

Performance fees

Performance fees by their very nature are variable and paid on an infrequent basis. Performance fee entitlements can build up over a period of 3 or even 5 years. Because

Table 2.3 Gross- and net-of-fee calculations, based on fees at 1.2% per annum calculated monthly in arrears (assume paid at the midpoint of next month)

	Market value (£m)	Fee (£m)	Net-of-fee return (%)	Gross-of-fee return (%)	Estimated gross-of-fee return (%)
Start value	100	0.1			
End of month 1	112	0.112	$\dfrac{112}{100} - 1 = 12.0$	$\dfrac{112 - 100 + 0.1}{100 - \frac{0.1}{2}} = 12.106$	$1.12 \times 1.001 - 1 = 12.112$
End of month 2	95	0.095	$\dfrac{95}{112} - 1 = -15.178$	$\dfrac{95 - 112 + 0.112}{112 - \frac{0.112}{2}} = -15.086$	$0.8482 \times 1.001 - 1 = -15.095$
End of month 3	99	0.099	$\dfrac{99}{95} - 1 = 4.211$	$\dfrac{99 - 95 + 0.095}{95 - \frac{0.095}{2}} = 4.313$	$1.04211 \times 1.001 - 1 = 4.315$
End of month 4	107	0.107	$\dfrac{107}{99} - 1 = 8.081$	$\dfrac{107 - 99 + 0.099}{99 - \frac{0.099}{2}} = 8.185$	$1.08081 \times 1.001 - 1 = 8.189$
End of month 5	115	0.115	$\dfrac{115}{107} - 1 = 7.477$	$\dfrac{115 - 107 + 0.107}{107 - \frac{0.107}{2}} = 7.580$	$1.07477 \times 1.001 - 1 = 7.584$
End of month 6	135		$\dfrac{135}{115} - 1 = 17.391$	$\dfrac{135 - 115 + 0.115}{115 - \frac{0.115}{2}} = 17.500$	$1.17391 \times 1.001 - 1 = 17.508$

Six-month return net of fees $135/100 = 35.0\%$.

Actual gross-of-fee return $1.121\,06 \times 0.849\,14 \times 1.043\,13 \times 1.081\,85 \times 1.0758 \times 1.175 - 1 = 35.794\%$.

Estimated gross-of-fee return $1.121\,12 \times 0.849\,05 \times 1.043\,15 \times 1.081\,89 \times 1.075\,84 \times 1.175\,08 - 1 = 35.810\%$.

base fees are inevitably lower due to the existence of the performance fee it would be inappropriate not to accrue for any performance fee element earned in a net-of-fee calculation.

Clients should think through the implications before establishing a performance fee structure for their asset managers. Theoretically, the existence of a performance fee should not alter the actual performance enjoyed. The asset manager cannot favour performance fee clients over and above other clients without a performance fee. They have a fiduciary duty to treat all clients equally.

Why pay a performance fee for performance you might expect to receive anyway? The only possible reason to enter a performance fee arrangement is because the desired and demonstrably better asset manager will only accept a performance fee arrangement to manage the client's assets.

Obviously, the client chooses the asset manager. Is it not rather perverse that the client is then rewarded by a lower fee (i.e., no performance fee) for choosing an under-performing asset manager and penalized (by paying a performance fee) for choosing an outperforming asset manager?

The flawed logic often applied by the owners of capital is that since there is more money available to pay fees then the asset manager should share in this success. This absurdity is taken to extremes with hedge fund managers who charge high base fees and very high performance fees (potentially 20% or more of any gain). These managers are incentivized to take risks with their client's capital, which they borrow from them at an effective negative rate of interest.

Asset managers certainly view performance fees as a way of increasing average revenue expectations – this can only result in clients paying higher fees for ultimately the same level of performance.

Most performance fee arrangements are also badly written. Often the original authors have long since left their respective roles and the original rationale for the performance fee is lost or forgotten. At a time when both clients and asset managers should be celebrating good performance there is frequently unpleasant disputes about the calculation of the performance fee.

The existence of a performance fee may adversely affect the asset manager's decision processes, increasing the risk profile inappropriately to increase the chance of gaining performance fees or, alternatively, locking in outperformance by inappropriately decreasing risk after a period of good performance. If performance fee structures are to be used at all the most appropriate measures should be risk-adjusted.

PORTFOLIO COMPONENT RETURNS

Calculating the performance of the total portfolio is only part of the analytical process. If we are to understand all the sources of return in a portfolio we must calculate the returns of subsets (sectors or components) of assets that contribute to the total return of a portfolio.

The calculation methodologies for component returns are the same as for the total portfolio; however, cash flows between components or sectors should be treated as external cash flows. Dividend and coupon payments should be treated as cash flow out of the relevant sector into an appropriate cash sector – that is, if these sectors are defined separately.

Provided return calculation methodologies are consistent the sum of component returns should equal the total portfolio return. This is a key requirement for performance return attribution analysis. Because internal rates of return assume a constant rate of return for all assets within the portfolio it is not appropriate to use internal rates of return to calculate component returns.

Component weight

Both simple and modified Dietz total returns can be broken down or disaggregated into component returns. If r_i is the return of the portfolio in the ith component, sector or asset category, then using modified Dietz:

$$r_i = \frac{{}^i V_E - {}^i V_S - {}^i C}{{}^i V_S + \sum {}^i C_t \times {}^i W_t} \tag{2.32}$$

where: ${}^i V_E$ = end value of sector i

${}^i V_S$ = start value of sector i

${}^i C$ = total cash flow in sector i

${}^i C_t$ = cash flow in sector i on day t

${}^i W_t$ = weighting ratio in sector i on day t.

Then the total portfolio return:

$$r = \sum_{i=1}^{i=n} w_i \times r_i \tag{2.33}$$

where: w_i = weight of the portfolio in the ith asset class.

Now:

$$w_i = \frac{{}^i V_S + \sum {}^i C_t \times {}^i W_t}{V_S + \sum C_t \times W_t} \tag{2.34}$$

Note that:

$$\sum_{i=1}^{i=n} w_i = 1$$

since

$$\sum_{i=1}^{i=n} {}^i V_S = V_S \quad \text{and} \quad \sum_{i=1}^{i=n} \sum {}^i C_t \times {}^i W_t = \sum C_t \times W_t$$

Time-weighted returns can be disaggregated as well. The weight allocated to transactions within the time-weighted period must be the same as that used for the overall portfolio (i.e., beginning of day, middle of day or end of day). Because cash flows will exist between categories within a portfolio it is no longer sufficient to revalue only at the date of an external cash flow. To calculate the time-weighted return for a component or sector, valuations are required for internal cash flows, which in effect requires daily valuations.

In rare circumstances, due to transaction activity, the effective weight in a sector may total zero but still contribute a gain or loss to the overall portfolio. The most common instance of this is a buy transaction in a sector with no current holding but using the end of day cash flow assumption. In these circumstances it is acceptable to use the size of cash flow as the weight for that sector, ensuring there is a cancelling cash flow in the cash sector.

Carve-outs

Sub-sector returns of larger portfolios are often calculated and presented separately by asset managers to demonstrate competence in managing assets of that type, particularly if the manager does not manage that type of asset in stand-alone portfolios. These sub-sector returns are often called "carve-outs".

Cash equivalents in a portfolio should be measured using the same methodology as any other asset within the portfolio. Because the cash sector naturally suffers large and frequent cash flows, calculation assumptions with regard to cash flow may result in a return which on face value is most unlike a cash return: crucially, the combination of average weight and return will replicate the contribution of the cash component to total return.

Multi-period component returns

Portfolio managers will make asset allocation decisions between different portfolio components over time. The timing of these decisions will impact the overall return of the portfolio. It is entirely possible that the overall portfolio return is less or more than all of the component returns (see Exhibit 2.23):

Period	Equity weight (%)	Fixed income weight (%)	Equity return (%)	Fixed income return (%)	Total return (%)
Q1	20	80	10.4	2.3	3.9
Q2	60	40	3.5	1.3	2.6
Q3	90	10	−15.7	1.4	−14.0
Q4	30	70	12.7	8.7	9.9
Year	50	50	8.6	14.2	0.8

Exhibit 2.23 Multi-period component returns

In Exhibit 2.23 both the equity and fixed income returns exceed the total return for the full year by a considerable margin. The total return is so low because of the high weight in equities in quarter 3. The timing of asset allocation decisions can make a significant difference.

BASE CURRENCY AND LOCAL RETURNS

Clearly, international portfolios will include assets denominated in foreign currencies. The methods of calculation previously described are still appropriate to calculate returns provided the securities denominated in foreign currencies are converted at appropriate exchange rates.

The impact of currency on a single asset portfolio is shown in Exhibit 2.24:

Exhibit 2.24   Currency returns

	Portfolio value ($)	Exchange rate ($: €)	Portfolio value (€)
Start value	100*	1 : 0	$100 × 1.0 = €100
End value	110**	1 : 1	$110 × 1.1 = €121

* 100 units of stock priced at $1.0
** 100 units of stock priced at $1.1

Note the dollar buys €1.1 at the end of the period compared with €1.0 at the start; the dollar has increased in value.

The return of the portfolios in dollars is:

$$\frac{110}{100} = 1.1 \qquad \text{or a return of 10\%}$$

The currency return is:

$$\frac{1.1}{1.0} = 1.1 \qquad \text{or a return of 10\%}$$

The return of the portfolio in euros:

$$\frac{110 \times 1.1}{100 \times 1.0} = \frac{121}{100} = 1.21 \qquad \text{or a return of 21\%}$$

Note the portfolio return in Exhibit 2.24 is not the addition of the local return and currency return but the compound of returns:

$$(1 + r_L) \times (1 + r_C) = (1 + r) \qquad (2.35)$$

where: r_L = return in local currency

r_C = currency return.

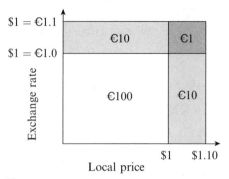

Figure 2.1 Components of base currency return.

r is the return of the portfolio in the base currency, the currency denomination or reference currency of the portfolio. Figure 2.1 illustrates the currency impact on portfolio valuation. The shaded top right-hand quadrant (€1) represents the combined impact of market returns with currency return.

The base currency returns of the portfolio can be readily converted to any other currency return for presentation purposes as follows:

$$(1 + r) \times (1 + c) - 1 = r_C \tag{2.36}$$

where: c = currency return relative to the base currency

r_C = portfolio return expressed in currency c.

Local currency returns are calculated ignoring the impact of changes in the currency exchange rate. Although in reality the local currency return of a portfolio consisting of assets in multiple currencies does not exist, it is useful to make an intermediate calculation. The local return of a multi-currency portfolio is defined as the weighted average local return for assets in each currency as follows:

$$r_L = \sum_{j=1}^{j=n} w_i \times r_{Li} \tag{2.37}$$

where: w_i = weight of sector i

r_{Li} = local return of sector i.

The ratio between the base currency return and the local return of the portfolio will calculate the implicit return due to currency in the portfolio.

REFERENCES

BAI (1968) *Measuring the Investment Performance of Pension Funds for the Purpose of Inter Fund Comparison*. Bank Administration Institute.

Dietz, P.O. (1966) *Pension Funds: Measuring Investment Performance*. Free Press.

ICAA (1971) *The Standards of Measurement and Use for Investment Performance Data.* Investment Counsel Association of America.

SIA (1972) *The Measurement of Portfolio Performance for Pension Funds* (Working group report). Society of Investment Analysts.

3
Benchmarks

> *Business is a good game – lots of competition and a minimum of rules. You keep score with money.*
>
> Atari founder Nolan Bushnell

BENCHMARKS

Measuring the return of a portfolio in isolation provides only part of the story; we need to know if the return is good or bad. In other words, we need to evaluate performance return and risk against an appropriate benchmark.

Benchmark attributes

Good benchmarks should be:

(i) *Appropriate*. The chosen benchmark must be relevant to the appropriate investment strategy. It is essential that the benchmark matches the client's requirements.
(ii) *Investable*. The portfolio manager should be able to invest in all the securities included in the benchmark. If not, there will always be an element of relative performance for which the portfolio manager has no control.
(iii) *Accessible*. To allow the portfolio manager to construct the portfolio against the benchmark it is essential that there is access not only to the returns of the benchmark but the constituent elements and their weights at the start of the period of measurement.
(iv) *Independent*. An independent third party should calculate all benchmark returns to ensure fair comparison.
(v) *Unambiguous*. The chosen benchmark should be clear and unambiguous. It is bad performance measurement practice to measure performance against more than one benchmark and to change benchmarks retrospectively.

There are two main forms of benchmark used in the evaluation of portfolio performance, "indexes" and "peer groups". Students of Latin may disagree but according to the *Oxford English Dictionary* both indexes and indices are acceptable plurals of index, I prefer to use indexes.

Commercial indexes

Commercial indexes and averages have been available for over 100 years and continue to multiply to the present day. Index providers create indexes for a variety of reasons, to promote investment in certain markets (e.g., emerging markets), to provide added services for trading clients, to provide a broad indicator of market movements, to promote the use of derivative instruments and to generate revenue in their own right.

Index providers create "intellectual property" in the construction of indexes in terms of the selection of securities to be included, calculation formulae, weighting schemes and construction rules. The relevance of the index to the asset manager or ultimate client will depend very much on the investment strategy and the original purpose of the index.

Calculation methodologies

For effective portfolio construction, managers should be cognizant of the calculation methodologies and the rules for including and excluding various securities.

Indexes may be calculated excluding income (price index) or including income (total return). Performance measurers should always use total return indexes.

The weight of each security in an index is normally determined by its market capitalization; however, this may be adjusted by a free float factor if an index provider determines that not all the market capitalization of a security is available to the general investing public. In international indexes the total weight of respective countries is determined by the sum of securities in that country qualified for entry into the index. In some indexes entire country weights might be adjusted to better reflect the economic strength of that country by reweighting in proportion to the GDP of countries.

Some would argue equal weighted indexes in which each security is given equal weight represent a fair index for portfolio managers because they have an equal opportunity to buy each stock arguing that capitalization weights are arbitrary.

Ultimately, the key determinant will be the client's requirements. Clients will be concerned about the coverage and concentration of indexes. Coverage is the percentage by market capitalization of securities included in the index compared with the total market capitalization of all securities in that market. Concentration measures the percentage weight of the top few securities in the index. A highly concentrated index may well introduce significant specific risk for the client.

Index turnover

Securities are constantly added and deleted from commercial indexes caused by take-over, business failure or simply major changes in market capitalization. Most indexes suffer no transaction costs to effect these changes; however, portfolio managers will suffer costs:

$$\text{Index turnover} = \frac{\text{Market cap (additions + deletions)}}{\text{Average total market} \times 2} \tag{3.1}$$

Turnover will be greatest in mid-cap indexes due to traffic in both directions, including securities promoted into the large-cap index and previously large-cap securities falling into the mid-cap index.

All other things being equal an index with high turnover will be more difficult for a portfolio manager to outperform because of potentially higher transaction costs. Portfolio managers start with a small structural disadvantage when compared with index providers.

Hedged indexes

Many index providers calculate index returns in a specific base currency, in local currency terms and hedged back to the base currency.

Hedged calculation methods differ, one approach being to sell notional 1-month forward contracts at the start of the period of measurement and calculating a return based on the gain or loss on those contracts in conjunction with the gain or loss in the underlying assets. This method does not hedge dynamically. Currency positions caused by the market gains of the underlying assets during the month are therefore not hedged leading to a residual currency element in the hedged return.

Alternatively, the local currency return can be compounded with the interest-rate differential (between the base currency and the currency of the underlying assets) as in Equation (3.2):

$$b_{Hi} = (1 + b_{Li}) \times (1 + d_i) - 1 \tag{3.2}$$

where: b_{Li} = local benchmark return for category i

b_{Hi} = benchmark return for category i hedged back to the base currency

d_i = interest-rate differential.

Since there is no currency exposure in a hedged return the only contributing factor to the difference between the local and hedged returns is the interest-rate differential.

The hedged return will be greater than the local return if interest rates are lower in the underlying currency than the base return, if d_i is positive.

Alternatively, the hedged return can be derived from the base return as follows:

$$b_{Hi} = \frac{(1 + b_i)}{(1 + f_i)} - 1 \tag{3.3}$$

where: f_i = return on forward currency contract.

Customized (or composite) indexes

Generic indexes are irrelevant to clients who have specific requirements based on their liabilities. Increasingly, clients require benchmarks that are customized to their own requirements.

Benchmarks derived or customized from multiple indexes are often called composite indexes (not to be confused with indexes allocated to a composite of portfolio manager returns).

Index providers in the past may have been more relaxed about the reuse of their data in customized form but are increasingly seeking to leverage their intellectual capital and will often charge for the extended use of their data. Asset managers should ensure that they are licensed to use the index data in the form they want to use it.

Table 3.1 Sample index data

	Weight	Base currency return	Local return	Hedged return
	(%)	(£)	(%)	(%)
UK	20	15.00	15.00	15.00
Norway	4	−4.21	−7.00	−7.19
Sweden	3	−3.10	−5.00	−5.10
France	15	−10.75	−15.00	−14.75
US	35	6.70	10.00	10.55
Japan	20	26.50	15.00	15.81
Australia	3	20.75	5.00	4.48
Total	*100*	*9.39*	*6.97*	*7.34*

Index information is normally provided in a specified base currency with local and possibly hedged returns. Given base local and hedged returns it is relatively simple to convert these returns into any alternative base currency.

The sample index in Table 3.1 is customized to exclude Australia in Exhibit 3.1:

Exhibit 3.1 Customized index

Contribution to total return excluding Australia:

$$20\% \times 15.0\% + 4\% \times -4.21\% + 3\% \times -3.1\% + 15\% \times -10.75\% \times 35\%$$
$$\times 6.7\% + 20\% \times 26.5\% = 9.04\%$$

Customized index excluding Australia:

$$\frac{8.77}{1 - 3\%} = 9.04\%$$

From Table 3.1 currency returns and hedge differentials can be calculated for each currency as shown in Table 3.2. Exhibit 3.2 demonstrates how to convert the base currency of an index:

Exhibit 3.2 Benchmark currency conversions

Converting the sterling-based customized index in Exhibit 3.1 to an Australian dollar return:

$$\frac{1.0904}{1.15} - 1 = -5.18\%$$

Fixed weight and dynamized benchmarks

Customized indexes are often defined using fixed weights for certain asset categories. The performance of asset categories will diverge over time, thus impacting the original

Table 3.2 Index currency returns

	Currency return $\dfrac{b_i}{b_{Li}} - 1$	Interest differential $\dfrac{b_{Hi}}{b_{Li}} - 1$
Norwegian krona	$\dfrac{0.9579}{0.93} - 1 = 3.0\%$	$\dfrac{0.9281}{0.93} - 1 = -0.2\%$
Swedish krone	$\dfrac{0.929}{0.95} - 1 = 2.0\%$	$\dfrac{0.949}{0.95} - 1 = -0.1\%$
Euro	$\dfrac{0.8925}{0.85} - 1 = 5.0\%$	$\dfrac{0.8525}{0.85} - 1 = 0.3\%$
US dollar	$\dfrac{1.067}{1.1} - 1 = -3.0\%$	$\dfrac{1.1055}{1.1} - 1 = 0.5\%$
Yen	$\dfrac{1.265}{1.15} - 1 = 10.0\%$	$\dfrac{1.1581}{1.15} - 1 = 0.7\%$
Australian dollar	$\dfrac{1.2075}{1.05} - 1 = 15.0\%$	$\dfrac{1.0448}{1.05} - 1 = -0.5\%$

strategic asset allocation. It is essential that the frequency of fixed weight rebalancing is established within the benchmark definition. If the initial fixed weight is allowed to float with the performance of individual categories, the impact compared with that of a genuine fixed weight can be significant, as demonstrated in Table 3.3.

Exhibit 3.3 illustrates how the floating weights are calculated for each quarter. The quarterly balanced fixed weight index outperforms the floating weight index. This outperformance is for the most part generated in the third quarter; the fixed weight index is required to reduce the exposure to equities at the beginning of the period immediately before a big fall in the market. Note, to replicate the annual return resulting from

Table 3.3 Fixed weight and dynamized benchmarks

	1st quarter		2nd quarter		3rd quarter		4th quarter		*Year*
	Weight (%)	Return	Weight (%)	Return	Weight (%)	Return	Weight (%)	Return	*Return*
Fixed weights									
Equities	50	10.4	50	3.5	50	−15.7	50	12.7	*8.56*
Bonds	50	2.3	50	1.3	50	1.4	50	8.7	*14.22*
Total		6.35		2.4		−7.15		10.70	*11.94*
Floating weights									
Equities	50	10.4	51.90	3.5	52.44	−15.7	47.83	12.7	*8.56*
Bonds	50	2.3	48.10	1.3	47.56	1.4	52.17	8.7	*14.22*
Total		6.35		2.44		−7.57		10.61	*11.39*

applying the 50% : 50% fixed weight to the category annual returns, floating weights must be used each quarter.

Exhibit 3.3   Dynamized benchmark

Applying the 50% : 50% weight to the annual returns, the total benchmark return is:

$$50\% \times 8.56 + 50\% \times 14.22 = 11.39$$

To achieve this return using quarterly data we need to reweight each quarter to reflect underlying market movements.

2nd quarter weights:

$$50\% \times 10.4\% = 55.2\% \quad 50\% \times 2.3\% = 51.15\% \quad \text{Total } 106.35\%$$

Revised weights $\dfrac{55.2\%}{106.35\%} = 51.9\% \quad \dfrac{51.15\%}{106.35\%} = 48.1\%$

3rd quarter weights:

$$51.9\% \times 3.5\% = 53.72\% \quad 48.1\% \times 1.3\% = 48.72\% \quad \text{Total } 102.44\%$$

Revised weights $\dfrac{53.72\%}{102.44\%} = 52.44\% \quad \dfrac{48.72\%}{102.44\%} = 47.56\%$

4th quarter weights:

$$52.44\% \times -15.7\% = 44.21\% \quad 47.56\% \times 1.4\% = 48.23\% \quad \text{Total } 92.43\%$$

Revised weights $\dfrac{44.21\%}{92.43\%} = 47.83\% \quad \dfrac{48.72\%}{92.43\%} = 51.17\%$

With the revised weights the quarterly benchmark returns compound to 11.39%, using fixed weights the benchmark return compounds to 11.94% – a significant difference.

Capped indexes

Due to regulatory requirements or the specific requirements of the clients, customized indexes often include maximum limits for securities, countries, industrial sectors, etc. These limits should be reflected by fixed weights in the customized index, either at the maximum limit or to allow the portfolio manager an overweight allocation at a fixed level lower than the limit.

Blended (or spliced) indexes

It is possible to change the index associated with the measurement of a specific portfolio over time, a good example being after a change in investment strategy. It is bad performance measurement practice to change the associated index retrospectively; therefore, a blended or spliced index should be calculated in order to maintain the long-term return series of the associated benchmark. This can be achieved by chain-linking the respective indexes.

PEER GROUPS AND UNIVERSES

Peer groups are collections of competitor portfolios of similar strategies grouped together to provide both an average and range of competitor returns.

Some would argue that peer groups offer a more appropriate comparison than indexes for a portfolio manager because they offer a genuine alternative to the client and, as a result of consisting of real portfolios, they suffer transaction costs.

There are a number of disadvantages associated with peer groups; first, you are reliant on the independent peer group compiler to control the quality of the peer group. Comparisons are only relevant between similar strategies if the peer group compiler adopts loose entry criteria; the peer group may be larger but may consist of widely divergent strategies.

Peer groups generate different challenges for portfolio managers: not only are they required to make good investment decisions but they must have a good understanding of what their competitors are doing. For example, if a portfolio manager likes IBM, against the index it is easy to ensure the position is overweight. But, in the peer group there is an element of guesswork involved: the portfolio manager must guess the average weight in the competitor portfolios and then determine the weight of IBM required. A peer group benchmark requires an additional competency from the portfolio manager.

Peer groups suffer "survivorship bias", in which poor performing portfolios are either closed or removed from the universe because the asset manager is unwilling to keep a poor performing portfolio in the survey. The result is increasing, good, long-term performance of the peer group as poor performing portfolios cease to belong to the long-term track record.

Percentile rank

One way of describing the relative performance of a portfolio or fund in a peer group is to provide the rank (or position) of the portfolio compared with the total number of portfolios in the universe.

Raw ranks however are very hard to compare against peer groups of different size. To allow comparison we can convert the raw rank to an equivalent rank based on a total peer group size of one hundred using the following formula:

$$\text{Percentile rank} \quad \frac{n-1}{N-1} \tag{3.4}$$

where: $n =$ the raw rank of the portfolio in its peer group universe

$N =$ the total number of portfolios in the peer group universe.

The percentile rank's function is to rank portfolios between 0% and 100%, 0% being the top-ranked portfolio and 100% being the bottom-ranked portfolio. There are other methodologies for calculating percentile rank but this method at least ensures that the middle ranked portfolio, the median, has a percentile rank of 50%. For example, the

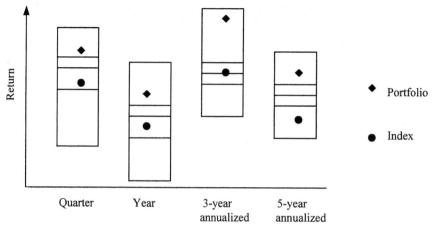

Figure 3.1   Football field chart.

percentile rank of the portfolio ranked 8 out of a peer group size of 15 (the median portfolio) is calculated as follows:

$$\frac{8-1}{15-1} = \frac{7}{14} = 50\%$$

Percentile ranks are often banded as follows:

0%–25%   1st quartile

25%–50%   2nd quartile

50%–75%   3rd quartile

75%–100%   4th quartile

Quintiles (20% bands) and deciles (10% bands) are also common.

An extremely useful way of showing peer group information is in the form of a football field chart (American football) as shown in Figure 3.1.

The bars (or football fields) represent the range of returns of the peer group, which are banded by quartiles. Note the bandwidth for the 2nd and 3rd quartiles is much narrower than the 1st and 4th quartiles, indicating a normal distribution of returns. For convenience many peer group managers ignore the top and bottom 5% of returns to ensure the distribution can fit onto the page.

In this example it is easy to see that the portfolio has performed well within the 1st quartile for all periods as well as outperforming the index.

NOTIONAL FUNDS

Notional funds are specific benchmark calculations used to replicate or simulate the impact of unique effects or calculation conditions within real portfolios. The analyst Test method in Equation (2.24) utilizes notional funds. In this method the benchmark return is recalculated with the cash flow experience of the real portfolio, thus replicating the error in the money-weighted return calculation.

Notional funds can be used as alternative benchmarks that include the cost of transactions resulting from external cash flow.

The main disadvantage of notional funds is that the adjusted return is clearly different from the published index return and unique to the cash flow or transaction experience of that portfolio. It makes the comparison of portfolio to notional fund performance more accurate but does not aid the comparison of performance of multiple different portfolios.

Normal portfolio

Commercial indexes may not adequately reflect the investment options open to individual portfolio managers. Normal portfolios provide an alternative benchmark consisting of specific securities available for investment (e.g., the recommended list of securities from the in-house research team).

Although a useful comparison against the real alternatives of the portfolio manager, they lack the stamp of independence required in the definition of a good benchmark.

Growth and value

Growth investors look for companies that are likely to have strong earnings growth. Strong earnings growth will lead to higher dividends encouraging other investors to buy, leading to higher prices. Growth investors are less concerned about the current value and more concerned by future prospects.

On the other hand, value investors look for companies whose value is not reflected in the current price. Value investors will use valuation tools like discounted cash flow to calculate a current fair price. If the market price is less than the calculated fair price the value investor is likely to buy, assuming other investors will eventually realize the company is undervalued.

In the technology boom growth investors fared best because they bought loss-making companies on the expectation of future profits with valuations often based on multiples of revenue (real or manipulated), not profits. Value investors are unlikely to buy new loss-making companies.

Portfolios managed with a growth or value strategy should be measured against growth or value indexes. The index should be appropriate to the portfolio manager's style.

EXCESS RETURN

Given portfolio and benchmark returns it is only natural to make a comparison and calculate the difference in performance or "excess return".

There are two common measures of excess return: "arithmetic" and "geometric".

Arithmetic excess return

Arithmetic excess return is the profit in excess of a notional or benchmark fund expressed as a percentage of the initial amount invested:

$$a = r - b \tag{3.5}$$

where: a = arithmetic excess return

b = benchmark return.

Geometric excess return

Geometric excess return is the profit in excess of a notional or benchmark fund expressed as a percentage of the final value of the notional or benchmark fund:

$$g = \frac{1 + r}{1 + b} - 1 \tag{3.6}$$

where: g = geometric excess return.

In both these definitions the added value (or profit) is identical. Both definitions attempt to explain the same added value in cash terms. The arithmetic excess return explains the added value relative to the initial amount invested and the geometric excess return explains the same added value but relative to the notional fund or the amount expected if the client had invested in the benchmark.

This simple difference is crucial, as demonstrated in Exhibit 3.4:

Exhibit 3.4   Arithmetic and geometric excess returns

Portfolio start value $1,000,000
Portfolio end value $1,070,000

$$\frac{1,070,000 - 1,000,000}{1,000,000} = 7\%$$

Notional fund start value = $1,000,000 (i.e., same as the portfolio start value). For benchmark performance assume a 5% return. Therefore, notional fund end value = $1,050,000. The portfolio's added value above the benchmark or notional fund is:

$$\$70,000 - \$50,000 = \$20,000$$

The arithmetic excess return:

$$\frac{\$20,000}{\$1,000,000} = 2\%$$

or, alternatively:

$$7\% - 5\% = 2\%$$

> The geometric excess return or the increase in value of the portfolio compared with what would have been achieved if invested in the benchmark is:
>
> $$\frac{\$1,070,000 - \$1,050,000}{\$1,050,000} = 1.9\%$$
>
> or
>
> $$\$20,000/\$1,050,000 \quad \text{or} \quad \frac{1.07}{1.05} - 1 = 1.9\%$$
>
> In other words, the portfolio is 1.9% larger than it would have been had it been invested in the benchmark.

Both versions of excess return are used worldwide with neither dominating globally. I strongly prefer the geometric version and fully expect this to be standard in the long term. The three main arguments for using geometric excess returns are quite persuasive:

(i)   Proportionality.
(ii) Convertibility.
(iii) Compoundability.

Most arguments in favour of using arithmetic excess returns centre on its ease of use, simplicity and intuitive feel. It is clearly easier to subtract two numbers, rather than to calculate a wealth ratio. Even proponents of the use of geometric excess returns will occasionally resort to arithmetic excess returns when reporting to clients. They argue that its simply not worth valuable time discussing why the ratio of returns is favoured over a more simple subtraction, the message of the report is more important.

To some extent I would agree, but the arithmetic or geometric debate is not a continuous discussion. Once understood, you need not have the same debate with the client again.

In fact, the geometric excess return is *more*, not less intuitive to the layperson.

The pension fund client is most concerned about the value of the portfolio at the end of period (not the start) and quite rightly should ask how much larger the portfolio is now, than it would have been had the portfolio invested in the benchmark. This is the natural question of pension fund trustees, particularly before calculating rates of return confuses the issue.

Rearranging Equation (3.6) we see that there is a relationship between the arithmetic and geometric excess return:

$$\frac{1+r}{1+b} - 1 = \frac{1+r}{1+b} - \frac{1+b}{1+b} = \frac{r-b}{1+b} \tag{3.7}$$

This relationship is important, it demonstrates that in rising markets the arithmetic excess return is always greater than the geometric excess return and in falling markets the reverse is true. If I were a cynic I would suggest that asset managers prefer arithmetic excess returns because they look better in most market conditions.

The geometric excess return represents a better measure of the relative added value of the asset manager's performance – it is proportionate, as demonstrated in Exhibit 3.5:

Exhibit 3.5   Proportionality

Portfolio start value	$1,000,000
Portfolio end value	$500,000
Portfolio return	−50%
Notional fund start value	$1,000,000
Notional fund end value	$250,000
Notional or benchmark return	−75%

$$\text{Arithmetic excess return} = -50\% - (-75\%) = +25\%$$

$$\text{Geometric excess return} = \frac{0.5}{0.25} - 1 = +100\%$$

The geometric excess return correctly demonstrates that the portfolio is double the size that would have been achieved by investing in the benchmark.

The most convincing argument for using geometric excess returns is their convertibility across different currencies. Exhibit 3.6 illustrates the impact of reporting excess returns in different currencies:

Exhibit 3.6   Convertibility

In an extension of Exhibit 3.4 let's look at the same portfolio from the perspective of a client whose base currency is euros (€). Assume a beginning of period exchange rate of $1 = €1 and an end of period exchange rate of $1 = €1.1.

Portfolio start value	€1,000,000
Portfolio end value	1,070,000 × 1.1 = €1,177,000
Portfolio return in euros	17.7%
Notional start value	€1,000,000
Notional end value	1,050,000 × 1.1 = €1,155,000

The portfolio's added value above the notional fund is:

$$€177,000 - €155,000 = €22,000$$

The arithmetic excess return:

$$\frac{€22,000}{€1,000,000} = 2.2\%$$

alternatively

$$17.7\% - 15.5\% = 2.2\%$$

The geometric excess return or increase in value of the portfolio compared with what would have been achieved if invested in the benchmark is:

$$\frac{€1,177,000 - €1,155,000}{€1,155,000} = 1.9\%$$

or

$$\text{€}22{,}000/\text{€}1{,}155{,}000 \quad \text{or} \quad \frac{1.177}{1.155} - 1.9\%$$

In Exhibit 3.6 we can see that simply by expressing the same performance in a different currency the arithmetic excess return appears to have increased from 2.0% in Exhibit 3.4 to 2.2%.

We cannot add more value simply by presenting returns in a different currency; the underlying increase in the benchmark, compounded with the currency return, has increased the added value relative to the initial amount invested. Crucially, because the portfolio and notional fund have been compounded by the same currency return, the added value relative to the final value of the notional fund remains the same regardless of the currency in which the report is denominated. The geometric excess return is always the same regardless of the currency used to calculate performance. This explains why geometric excess returns are more popular in the UK and Europe than, say, in the US and Australia. In Europe, particularly in the UK the asset management community has been more international in nature for some time. The problem of presenting the same portfolio or composite returns in many currencies was addressed many years ago.

This relationship holds since the currency return c is identical for both the portfolio and the benchmark.

Let r_L = the portfolio return in local currency and b_L = the benchmark return in local currency. Then the portfolio return in currency:

$$c = (1 + r_L) \times (1 + c) - 1 = r_c \tag{3.8}$$

and the benchmark return in currency:

$$c = (1 + b_L) \times (1 + c) - 1 = b_c \tag{3.9}$$

It follows that:

$$\frac{(1 + r_c)}{(1 + b_c)} = \frac{(1 + r_L) \times (1 + c)}{(1 + b_L) \times (1 + c)} = \frac{(1 + r_L)}{(1 + b_L)} \tag{3.10}$$

Geometric excess returns are also compoundable over time. This is an extremely useful property in the measurement of portfolio performance.

In Chapter 2 we established by definition that time-weighted rates of return are calculated by "chain-linking" each finite performance period within the overall period as follows:

$$(1 + r_1) \times (1 + r_2) \times (1 + r_3) \times \cdots \times (1 + r_{n-1}) \times (1 + r_n) = (1 + r) \tag{2.6}$$

Similarly, the total benchmark return b can be derived in a similar calculation:

$$(1 + b) = (1 + b_1) \times (1 + b_2) \times \cdots \times (1 + b_{n-1}) \times (1 + b_n) \tag{3.11}$$

It can be seen that the geometric excess return for the total period g can be calculated by chain-linking the geometric excess returns of the sub-periods g_i as follows:

$$(1 + g) = \frac{(1 + r)}{(1 + b)} = \frac{(1 + r_1)}{(1 + b_1)} \times \frac{(1 + r_2)}{(1 + b_2)} \times \cdots \times \frac{(1 + r_n)}{(1 + b_n)} \tag{3.12}$$

or

$$(1+g) = (1+g_1) \times (1+g_2) \times \cdots \times (1+g_n) \qquad (3.13)$$

Compoundability is demonstrated in Exhibit 3.7:

Exhibit 3.7   Compoundability

Assume that the same returns in Exhibit 3.4 are repeated over four quarters. The portfolio return is:

$$(1.07) \times (1.07) \times (1.07) \times (1.07) - 1 = 31.1\%$$

The benchmark return is:

$$(1.05) \times (1.05) \times (1.05) \times (1.05) - 1 = 21.6\%$$

The arithmetic excess return over the entire period is:

$$31.1\% - 21.6\% = 9.5\%$$

There is no apparent straightforward link between the individual arithmetic excess returns for each quarter and the total arithmetic excess return:

$$2\% + 2\% + 2\% + 2\% \neq 9.5\%$$

$$(1.02) \times (1.02) \times (1.02) \times (1.02) - 1 \neq 9.5\%$$

The geometric excess return over the entire period is:

$$\frac{1.311}{1.216} - 1 = 7.8\%$$

The geometric excess return for each finite period can be compounded to calculate the geometric excess return for the entire period:

$$(1.019) \times (1.019) \times (1.019) \times (1.019) - 1 = 7.8\%$$

4
Risk

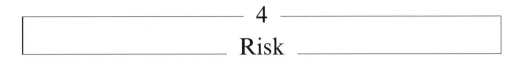

> *Money is like muck, not good except it be spread.*
>
> Francis Bacon, 1561–1626

DEFINITION OF RISK

Risk is defined as the uncertainty of expected outcomes.

Within asset management firms there are many types of risk that should concern portfolio managers and senior management; for convenience I've chosen to classify risk into four main categories:

- Compliance risk.
- Operational risk.
- Counterparty or credit risk.
- Portfolio risk.

Although a major concern of all asset managers, reputational risk does not warrant a separate category; a risk failure in any category can cause significant damage to a firm's reputation.

Compliance or regulatory risk is the risk of breaching a regulatory, client or internally imposed limit. I draw no distinction between internal or external limits; the breach of an internal limit indicates a control failure, which could just have easily been a regulatory or client-mandated limit.

Operational risk, often defined as a residual catch-all category to include risks not defined elsewhere, actually includes the risk of human error, fraud, system failure, poor controls, management failure and failed trades. Risks of this type are more common but often less severe. Nevertheless, it is important to continuously monitor errors of all types, even those that don't result in financial loss. An increase in the frequency of errors regardless of size or sign may indicate a more serious problem that requires further investigation and corrective action.

Counterparty risk occurs when counterparties are unwilling or unable to fulfil their contractual obligations. This could include profits on a derivatives contract, unsettled transactions and even, with the comfort of appropriate collateral, the failure to return stock that has been used for stock lending.

In performance measurement we are most concerned with portfolio risk, which I define as the uncertainty of meeting client expectations.

Risk management versus risk control

There is a clear distinction between risk management and risk control. Portfolio managers are risk managers, they are paid to take risk and they need to take risk to achieve higher returns.

Risk controllers on the other hand are paid to monitor risk (or often from their perspective to reduce risk). The risk controller's objective is to reduce the probability or eliminate entirely a major loss event on their watch. Risk managers' and risk controllers' objectives are in conflict. To resolve this conflict we need measures that assess the quality of return and answer the question: "Are we achieving sufficient return for the risk taken?"

Risk aversion

It is helpful to assume that investors are risk-averse (i.e., that given portfolios with equal rates of return they will prefer the portfolio with the lowest risk).

Investors will only accept additional risk if they are compensated by higher returns.

RISK MEASURES

Ex post and *ex ante* risk

Risk is calculated in two fundamentally different ways: *ex post* and *ex ante*. *Ex post* or historical risk is the analysis of risk after the event; it answers the question: "How risky has the portfolio been in the past?"

On the other hand, *ex ante* risk or prospective risk is forward-looking, based on a snapshot of the current assets within the portfolio; it is an estimate or forecast of the future risk of the portfolio.

Ex post and *ex ante* risk calculations are substantially different and therefore can lead to completely different results and conclusions. Differences between *ex post* and *ex ante* risk calculations provide significant additional information, although as performance measurers we are more concerned about analysing past performance and are therefore more concerned with *ex post* risk.

Variability

In considering risk we are concerned with the variability (or dispersion) of returns from the average or mean return. Mean absolute deviation, variance and standard deviation are three related measures used to calculate variability.

Mean absolute deviation

Clearly, if added together, the positive and negative differences of each return from the average return would cancel; however, using the absolute difference (i.e., ignore the sign) we are able to calculate the mean or average absolute deviation as follows:

$$\text{Mean absolute deviation} = \frac{\sum_{i=1}^{i=n} |r_i - \bar{r}|}{n} \tag{4.1}$$

where: n = number of observations

r_i = return in month i

$\bar{r}$ = mean return.

Variance

The variance of returns is the average squared deviation of returns from the mean return calculated as:

$$\text{Variance } \sigma^2 = \frac{\sum_{i=1}^{i=n}(r_i - \bar{r})^2}{n} \tag{4.2}$$

Deviations from the mean $(r_i - \bar{r})$ are squared; this avoids the problem of negative deviations cancelling with positive deviations.

Standard deviation

For analysis it is more convenient to use our original non-squared units of return; therefore, we take the square root of the variance to obtain the standard deviation:

$$\text{Standard deviation } \sigma = \sqrt{\frac{\sum_{i=1}^{i=n}(r_i - \bar{r})^2}{n}} \tag{4.3}$$

A higher standard deviation would indicate greater uncertainty, variability or risk. In this version of standard deviation n not $n-1$ is used in the denominator. The use of $n-1$ would calculate the sample standard deviation. For large n it will make little difference whether n or $n-1$ is used. Since the majority of performance analysts tend to use n, for the sake of consistency and comparability I prefer to use n.

Equation (4.3) calculates standard deviation based on the periodicity of the data used, daily, monthly, quarterly, etc. For comparison, standard deviation is normally annualized for presentation purposes.

To annualize standard deviation we need to multiply by the square root of the number of observations in the year:

$$\text{Annualized standard deviation } \sigma^A = \sqrt{t} \times \sigma \tag{4.4}$$

where: t = number of observations in year (quarterly = 4, monthly = 12, etc.).

For example, to annualize a monthly standard deviation multiply by $\sqrt{12}$ and for a quarterly standard deviation multiply by $\sqrt{4}$ or 2.

Basic risk calculations are actually very straightforward and relatively simple to compute as shown in Tables 4.1 and 4.2. It is perhaps unfortunate that risk is considered a complex subject that requires an understanding of advanced mathematics. It is the role of both the performance analyst and risk controller to ensure the broadest understanding of the statistics presented.

Table 4.1 Portfolio variability

Portfolio monthly return r_i (%)	Deviation from average $(r_i - \bar{r})$ (%)	Absolute deviation $\lvert r_i - \bar{r}\rvert$ (%)	Deviation squared $(r_i - \bar{r})^2$ (%)
0.3	−0.6	0.6	0.36
2.6	1.7	1.7	2.89
1.1	0.2	0.2	0.04
−1.0	−1.9	1.9	3.61
1.5	0.6	0.6	0.36
2.5	1.6	1.6	2.56
1.6	0.7	0.7	0.49
6.7	5.8	5.8	33.64
−1.4	−2.3	2.3	5.29
4.0	3.1	3.1	9.61
−0.5	−1.4	1.4	1.96
8.1	7.2	7.2	51.84
4.0	3.1	3.1	9.63
−3.7	−4.6	4.6	21.16
−6.1	−7.0	7.0	49.0
1.7	0.8	0.8	0.64
−4.9	−5.8	5.8	33.64
−2.2	−3.1	3.1	9.61
7.0	6.1	6.1	37.21
5.8	4.9	4.9	24.01
−6.5	−7.4	7.4	54.76
2.4	1.5	1.5	2.25
−0.5	−1.4	1.4	1.96
−0.8	−1.7	1.7	2.89

Average monthly return $\bar{r} = 0.9\%$		*Total* $\displaystyle\sum_{i=1}^{i=n} \lvert r_i - \bar{r}\rvert = 74.5\%$	*Total* $\displaystyle\sum_{i=1}^{i=n} (r_i - \bar{r})^2 = 359.41\%$
	Mean absolute difference	$\dfrac{74.5\%}{24} = 3.1\%$	
	Monthly standard deviation		$\sigma_P = \sqrt{\dfrac{359.41}{24}} = 3.87\%$
	Annualized standard deviation		$\sigma_p^A = 3.87\% \times \sqrt{12} = 13.4\%$

Sharpe ratio (reward to variability)

Investors are risk-averse; given the same return they would prefer the portfolio with less risk or less variability. Therefore, how do we evaluate portfolios with different returns and different levels of risk?

With two variables it is natural to resort to a graphical representation with return represented by the vertical axis and risk represented by the horizontal axis, as shown in Figure 4.1 which uses data from Table 4.3.

Table 4.2   Benchmark variability

Benchmark monthly return b_i (%)	Deviation from average $(b_i - \bar{b})$ (%)	Absolute deviation $|b_i - \bar{b}|$ (%)	Deviation squared $(b_i - \bar{b})^2$ (%)
0.2	−0.8	0.8	0.64
2.5	1.5	1.5	2.25
1.8	0.8	0.8	0.64
−1.1	−2.1	2.1	4.41
1.4	0.4	0.4	0.16
1.8	0.8	0.8	0.64
1.4	0.4	0.4	0.16
6.5	5.5	5.5	30.25
−1.5	−2.5	2.5	6.25
4.2	3.2	3.2	10.24
−0.6	−1.6	1.6	2.56
8.3	7.3	7.3	53.29
3.9	2.9	2.9	8.41
−3.8	−4.8	4.8	23.04
−6.2	−7.2	7.2	51.84
1.5	0.5	0.5	0.25
−4.8	−5.8	5.8	33.64
2.1	1.1	1.1	1.21
6.0	5.0	5.0	25.0
5.6	4.6	4.6	21.16
−6.7	−7.7	7.7	59.29
1.9	0.9	0.9	0.81
−0.3	−1.3	1.3	1.69
0.0	−1.0	1.0	1.0

Average monthly return $\bar{b} = 1.0\%$		*Total* $\sum_{i=1}^{i=n} |b_i - \bar{b}| = 69.7\%$	*Total = 338.83%* $\sum_{i=1}^{i=n} (b_i - \bar{b})^2 = 338.83\%$
	Mean absolute difference	$\dfrac{69.7\%}{24} = 2.9\%$	
		Monthly standard deviation	$\sigma_M = \sqrt{\dfrac{338.83}{24}} = 3.76\%$
		Annualized deviation	$\sigma_M^A = 3.76\% \times \sqrt{12} = 13.0\%$

A straight line is drawn from a fixed point on the vertical axis to points A and B representing the annualized returns and annualized variability (risk) of portfolios A and B, respectively.

The fixed point represents the natural starting point for all investors: the risk-free rate, the return I should expect on a riskless asset (e.g., the interest return on cash or Treasury bills). An investor can achieve this return without any variability or risk. It is important to ensure the same risk-free rate is used for all portfolios for comparison purposes.

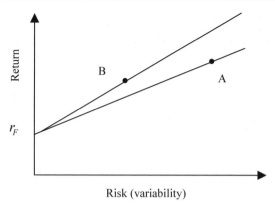

Figure 4.1 Sharpe ratio.

Clearly, the investor will prefer to be in the top left-hand quadrant of this graph representing high return and low risk. The gradient of the line determines how far toward the left-hand quadrant each portfolio is represented: the steeper the gradient, the further into the top left-hand side the investor goes. This gradient is called the Sharpe ratio which is calculated as follows:

$$SR = \frac{r_P - r_F}{\sigma_P} \tag{4.5}$$

where: r_P = portfolio return

r_F = risk-free rate

σ_P = portfolio risk (variability, standard deviation of return) normally annualized.

The higher the Sharpe ratio, the better the combined performance of risk and return. The Sharpe ratio can be described as the return (or reward) per unit of variability (or risk).

Both graphically in Figure 4.1 and in the Sharpe ratios calculated in Table 4.3 we can see that portfolio B has a better risk-adjusted performance than either portfolio A or the benchmark.

Negative returns will generate negative Sharpe ratios, which despite the views of some commentators still retain meaning. Perversely for negative returns, it is better to be more variable not less! For those that think higher variability is always less desirable, negative Sharpe ratios are difficult statistics to interpret.

Risk-adjusted return: M^2

The Sharpe ratio is sometimes erroneously described as a risk-adjusted return; actually, it's a ratio. We can rank portfolios in order of preference with the Sharpe ratio but it is difficult to judge the size of relative performance. We need a risk-adjusted return measure to gain a better feel of risk-adjusted outperformance.

In Figure 4.2 a straight line is drawn vertically through the risk of the benchmark σ_M.

Table 4.3   Sharpe ratio

	Portfolio A	Portfolio B	Benchmark
Annualized return	7.9%	6.9%	7.5%
Annualized risk	5.5%	3.2%	4.5%
Sharpe ratio (risk-free rate = 2%)			
$SR = \dfrac{r_P - r_F}{\sigma_P}$	$\dfrac{7.9\% - 2.0\%}{5.5\%} = 1.07$	$\dfrac{6.9\% - 2.0\%}{3.2\%} = 1.53$	$\dfrac{7.5\% - 2.0\%}{4.5\%} = 1.22$

Table 4.4 M^2

	Portfolio A	Portfolio B
Annualized return	7.9%	6.9%
Annualized risk	5.5%	3.2%
Sharpe ratio	1.07	1.53
$M^2 = r_P + SR \times (\sigma_M - \sigma_P)$	$7.9\% + 1.07 \times (4.5\% - 5.5\%)$ $= 6.83\%$	$6.9\% + 1.53$ $\times (4.5\% - 3.2\%) = 8.74\%$

The intercept with the Sharpe ratio line of portfolio B would give the return of the portfolio with the same Sharpe ratio of portfolio B but at the risk of the benchmark. This return is called M^2, a genuinely risk-adjusted return extremely useful for comparing portfolios with different levels of risk:

$$M^2 = r_P + SR \times (\sigma_M - \sigma_P) \qquad (4.6)$$

where: σ_M = market risk (variability, standard deviation of benchmark return).

The statistic is called M^2 not because any element of the calculation is squared but because it was first proposed by the partnership of Leah Modigliani (1997) and her grandfather Professor Franco Modigliani.

Alternatively, you might see the equation for M^2 expressed as:

$$M^2 = (r_P - r_F) \times \frac{\sigma_M}{\sigma_P} + r_F \qquad (4.7)$$

Using the data from Table 4.3 M^2 is calculated in Table 4.4.

M^2 excess return

Exactly the same arguments apply to geometric or arithmetic M^2 excess returns as they do to normal excess returns. Simple geometry from Figure 4.2 might suggest arithmetic excess return would be more appropriate; however, it is easy to argue that continuously compounded returns should be used. For consistency I prefer the geometric definition:

$$M^2 \text{ excess return} = \frac{(1 + M^2)}{(1 + b)} - 1 \qquad (4.8)$$

or, arithmetically:

$$M^2 \text{ excess return} = M^2 - b \qquad (4.9)$$

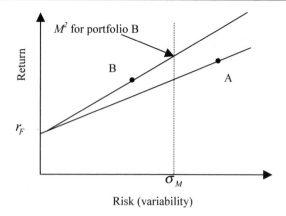

Figure 4.2 M^2.

Differential return

Differential return (Figure 4.3) is similar in concept to M^2 excess return except that the benchmark return is adjusted to the risk of the portfolio. The differential return is the difference between the portfolio return and the adjusted benchmark return. For the same portfolio the M^2 excess return and the differential return will differ because the Sharpe ratio lines of the portfolio and benchmark will diverge over time.

The adjusted benchmark return b' is calculated as follows:

$$b' = r_F + \left(\frac{b - r_F}{\sigma_M} \right) \times \sigma_P \tag{4.10}$$

Therefore, subtracting the adjusted benchmark return from the portfolio return we derive the differential return:

$$DR = r_P - r_F - \left(\frac{b - r_F}{\sigma_M} \right) \times \sigma_P \tag{4.11}$$

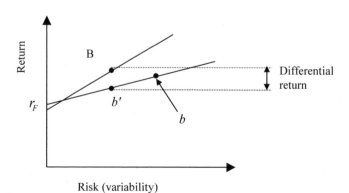

Figure 4.3 Differential return.

Table 4.5   Differential return

	Portfolio A	Portfolio B
Annualized return	7.9%	6.9%
Annualized risk	5.5%	3.2%
M^2	6.83%	8.74%
M^2 excess return (arithmetic) $= M^2 - b$	$6.8\% - 7.5\% = -0.7\%$	$8.7\% - 7.5\% = +1.2\%$
Differential return $r_P - r_F - \left(\dfrac{b - r_F}{\sigma_M}\right) \times \sigma_P$	$7.9\% - 2.0\% - \dfrac{7.5\% - 2.0\%}{4.5} \times 5.5\% = -0.8\%$	$6.9\% - 2.0\% - \dfrac{7.5\% - 2.0\%}{4.5\%} \times 3.2\% = +1.0\%$

Differential returns are calculated in Table 4.5 based on the data from Table 4.3.

Differential return is less useful for comparing multiple portfolios because multiple risk-adjusted benchmark returns need to be calculated, whereas for M^2 the benchmark returns are consistent for all portfolios. M^2 is a demonstrably better measure than either Sharpe ratio from which it is derived or differential return. It is possible to calculate differential return geometrically.

REGRESSION ANALYSIS

We can gain further information from a portfolio by plotting the portfolio returns against the corresponding benchmark returns in a scatter diagram (see Figure 4.4).

We might expect portfolio returns to move in line with benchmark returns; if so, we can fit a line of best fit through these points, the aim of which is to minimize the vertical distance of any one point from this line.

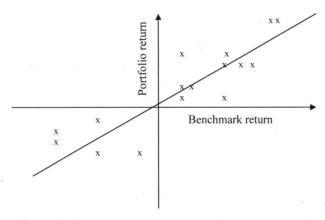

Figure 4.4   Regression analysis.

Regression equation

The formula of any straight line is given by the slope or gradient of the line plus the intercept with the vertical access. Thus the return of the portfolio might be described as:

$$r_p = \alpha_R + \beta_R \times b + \varepsilon_R \qquad (4.12)$$

This equation is called the regression equation.

Regression alpha (α_R)

The regression alpha is the intercept of the regression equation with the vertical axis.

Regression beta (β_R)

The regression beta is the slope or gradient of the regression equation. The slope of the regression equation is given by:

$$\beta_R = \frac{\displaystyle\sum_{i=1}^{i=n}[(r_i - \bar{r}) \times (b_i - \bar{b})]}{\displaystyle\sum_{i=1}^{i=n}(b_i - \bar{b})^2} \qquad (4.13)$$

where: b_i = benchmark return in month i

$\bar{b}$ = mean benchmark return.

Regression epsilon (ε_R)

The regression epsilon is an error term measuring the vertical distance between the return predicted by the equation and the real result.

Capital Asset Pricing Model (CAPM)

In the CAPM model we can factor in the risk-free rate and use the following revised regression equation to calculate a new beta and alpha (Jensen's alpha):

$$r_p - r_F = \alpha + \beta \times (b - r_F) + \varepsilon \qquad (4.14)$$

Beta (β) (systematic risk or volatility)

I prefer the term volatility, not the more commonly used term systematic risk, to describe beta. Unfortunately, although originally used in the context of volatility it is now almost universally used to describe standard deviation and used interchangeably with variability. Needless to say I prefer the term variability when used in the context of standard deviation:

$$\beta = \frac{\sum_{i=1}^{i=n}[(r_i - r_{Fi} - \bar{r} - \bar{r}_F) \times (b_i - r_{Fi} - \bar{b} - \bar{r}_F)]}{\sum_{i=1}^{i=n}(b_i - r_{Fi} - \bar{b} - \bar{r}_F)^2} \qquad (4.15)$$

where: $\bar{r}_F$ = mean risk-free rate

r_{Fi} = risk-free rate in month i

$\bar{b}$ = mean benchmark return.

Jensen's alpha (or Jensen's measure or Jensen's differential return)

Jensen's alpha is the intercept of the regression equation in the Capital Asset Pricing Model and is in effect the excess return adjusted for systematic risk.

Ignoring the error term for *ex post* calculations and using Equation (4.15):

$$\alpha = r_P - r_F - \beta_P \times (b - r_F) \qquad (4.16)$$

Note the similarities to the related formula for differential return (Equation 4.11), hence the alternative name, Jensen's differential return.

Portfolio managers often talk in terms of alpha to describe their added value, rarely are they referring to either the regression or even Jensen's alpha; in all probability they are referring to their excess return above the benchmark. Confusingly, academics also frequently refer to excess return as the return above the risk-free rate.

Bull beta (β^+)

We need not restrict ourselves to fitting lines of best fit to all market returns, positive and negative. If we calculate a regression equation for only positive market returns we gain information on the behaviour of the portfolio in positive or "bull" markets.

Bear beta (β^-)

The beta for negative market returns is described as the "bear" beta.

Beta timing ratio

Ideally, we would prefer a portfolio manager with a beta greater than 1 in rising markets and less than 1 in falling markets. In all likelihood such a manager would be a good timer of asset allocation decisions:

$$\text{Beta timing ratio} = \frac{\beta^+}{\beta^-} \qquad (4.17)$$

Covariance

Covariance measures the tendency of the portfolio and benchmark returns to move together:

$$\text{Covariance} = \frac{\sum_{i=1}^{i=n}(r_{Pi} - \bar{r}_P) \times (b_i - \bar{b})}{n} \qquad (4.18)$$

Equation (4.18) multiplies the period portfolio return over the average portfolio return with the same period benchmark return over the average benchmark return. If both are positive or negative this will make a positive contribution; if they are of different signs it will make a negative contribution.

Therefore, a total positive covariance indicates the returns are associated, they move together. A total negative covariance indicates the returns move in opposite directions. A low or near-zero covariance would indicate no relationship between portfolio and benchmark returns.

Correlation (ρ)

In isolation covariance is a difficult statistic to interpret. We can standardize the covariance to a value between 1 and -1 by dividing by the product of the portfolio standard deviation using the benchmark standard deviation as follows:

$$\text{Correlation} \quad \rho_{P,M} = \frac{\text{Covariance}}{\sigma_P \times \sigma_M} \qquad (4.19)$$

Note correlation is also:

$$\rho_{P,M} = \frac{\text{Systematic risk}}{\text{Total risk}} \qquad (4.20)$$

or

$$\rho_{P,M} = \frac{\beta_P \times \sigma_M}{\sigma_P}$$

Therefore, beta and correlation are linked by the formula:

$$\beta_p = \rho_{P,M} \times \frac{\sigma_P}{\sigma_M} \qquad (4.21)$$

Correlation measures the variability in the portfolio that is systematic compared with the total variability.

Covariance, correlation and regression beta are calculated for our standard set of example data in Table 4.6. A CAPM beta would require monthly risk-free rates; however, if the risk-free rate is constant the regression beta is the same as the CAPM beta.

Portfolio monthly return r_i (%)	Deviation from average $(r_i - \bar{r})$ (%)	Benchmark monthly return b_i (%)	Deviation from average $(b_i - \bar{b})$ (%)	Portfolio deviation × benchmark deviation $(r_i - \bar{r}) \times (b_i - \bar{b})$	Benchmark deviation squared $(b_i - \bar{b})^2$
0.3	−0.6	0.2	−0.8	0.48	0.64
2.6	1.7	2.5	1.5	2.55	2.25
1.1	0.2	1.8	0.8	0.16	0.64
−1.0	−1.9	−1.1	−2.1	3.99	4.41
1.5	0.6	1.4	0.4	0.24	0.16
2.5	1.6	1.8	0.8	1.28	0.64
1.6	0.7	1.4	0.4	0.28	0.16
6.7	5.8	6.5	5.5	31.90	30.25
−1.4	−2.3	−1.5	−2.5	5.75	6.25
4.0	3.1	4.2	3.2	9.92	10.24
−0.5	−1.4	−0.6	−1.6	2.24	2.56
8.1	7.2	8.3	7.3	52.56	53.29
4.0	3.1	3.9	2.9	9.00	8.41
−3.7	−4.6	−3.8	−4.8	22.08	23.04
−6.1	−7.0	−6.2	−7.2	50.40	51.84
1.7	0.8	1.5	0.5	0.40	0.25
−4.9	−5.8	−4.8	−5.8	33.64	33.64
−2.2	−3.1	2.1	1.1	−3.41	1.21
7.0	6.1	6.0	5.0	30.50	25.00
5.8	4.9	5.6	4.6	22.54	21.16
−6.5	−7.4	−6.7	−7.7	56.98	59.29
2.4	1.5	1.9	0.9	1.35	0.81
−0.5	−1.4	−0.3	−1.3	1.82	1.69
−0.8	−1.7	0.0	−1.0	1.70	1.00
				Total = 338.35	*Total = 338.83*

Covariance $\dfrac{338.35\%}{24} = 14.1$

Correlation $\dfrac{14.1}{3.87 \times 3.76} = 0.97$

Regression beta $\dfrac{338.35}{338.83} = 1.0$

Regression alpha $0.9 - 1.0 \times 1.0 = -0.1$

R^2 (or coefficient of determination)

R^2 is the proportion of variance in fund returns that is related to the variance of benchmark returns; it is a measure of portfolio diversification. Note variance is the square of standard deviation or variability.

The closer R^2 is to 1 the more portfolio variance is explained by benchmark variance. A low R^2 would indicate returns are more scattered and would indicate a less reliable line of best fit leading to unstable alphas and betas. Therefore, if a portfolio has a low R^2 (say, much less than 0.8) then any alphas and betas and their derivative statistics should probably be ignored:

$$R^2 = \frac{\text{Systematic variance}}{\text{Total variance}} = \text{Correlation}^2 \tag{4.22}$$

Systematic risk

Michael Jensen (1969) described beta as systematic risk. If we multiply beta by market risk we obtain a measure of systematic risk calculated in the same units as variability. In my view this is a better definition of systematic risk:

$$\text{Systematic risk} \quad \sigma_S = \beta \times \sigma_M \tag{4.23}$$

Specific or residual risk

Residual or specific risk is not attributed to general market movements but is unique to the particular portfolio under consideration. It is represented by the standard deviation of the error term in the regression equation σ_ε.

Since specific risk and systematic risk are by definition independent we can calculate total risk by using Pythagoras's theorem:

$$\text{Total risk}^2 = \text{systematic risk}^2 + \text{specific risk}^2 \tag{4.24}$$

Table 4.7 demonstrates that Equation (4.24) holds for our standard example.

Treynor ratio (reward to volatility)

Treynor ratio (Figure 4.5) is similar to Sharpe ratio, the numerator (or vertical axis graphically speaking) is identical but in the denominator (horizontal axis) instead of total risk we have systematic risk as calculated by beta:

$$TR = \frac{r_P - r_F}{\beta_P} \tag{4.25}$$

Presumably, because it is included in most MBA studies, the Treynor ratio is extremely well known but perhaps less frequently used because it ignores specific risk. If a portfolio is fully diversified with no specific risk the Treynor and Sharpe ratios will give the same ranking. Sharpe actually favoured the Treynor ratio because he felt any value gained from being not fully diversified was transitory. Unfortunately, the performance analyst does not have the luxury of ignoring specific risk when assessing historic returns.

Table 4.7   Specific risk

Portfolio monthly return r_i (%)	Regression residual or error term $(r_i - b_i \times \beta - \alpha)$ (%)
0.3	0.20
2.6	0.20
1.1	−0.60
−1.0	0.20
1.5	0.20
2.5	0.80
1.6	0.30
6.7	0.31
−1.4	0.20
4.0	−0.10
−0.5	0.20
8.1	−0.09
4.0	0.20
−3.7	0.19
−6.1	0.19
1.7	0.30
−4.9	−0.01
−2.2	−4.20
7.0	1.11
5.8	0.31
−6.5	0.29
2.4	0.60
−0.5	−0.10
−0.8	−0.70
Specific risk (annualized standard deviation of error term σ_ε)	3.28
Systematic risk ($\beta \times \sigma_M$)	$1.0 \times 13.0 = 13.0\%$

$$Total\ risk^2 = systematic\ risk^2 + specific\ risk^2$$
$$Total\ risk^2 = 13.0\%^2 + 3.28\%^2 = 13.4\%^2$$

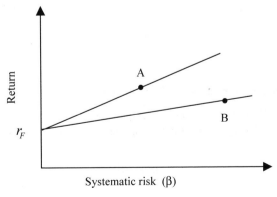

Figure 4.5   Treynor ratio.

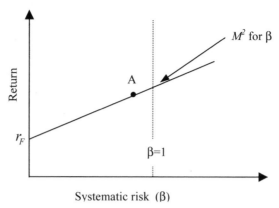

Figure 4.6 M^2 for β.

Modified Treynor ratio

A logical alternative form of the Treynor ratio might use systematic risk σ_S in the denominator, which is more consistent with the Sharpe ratio, for convenience called the modified Treynor ratio:

$$MTR = \frac{r_P - r_F}{\sigma_M} \qquad (4.26)$$

M^2 for beta

M^2 can be calculated for systematic risk in the same way as it is calculated for total risk. In Figure 4.6 a straight line is drawn vertically through the risk of the benchmark $\beta = 1$. The intercept with the Treynor ratio line of portfolio A would give the return of the portfolio with the same Treynor ratio of portfolio A but at the systematic risk of the benchmark:

$$M^2 = r_P + TR \times (1 - \beta_P)$$

$$= r_P + TR - (r_P + r_F) \times \frac{\beta_P}{\beta_P}$$

$$= r_F + TR \qquad (4.27)$$

Appraisal ratio (Sharpe ratio adjusted for systematic risk)

The appraisal ratio is similar in concept to the Sharpe ratio; but, using Jensen's alpha, excess return adjusted for systematic risk in the numerator is divided by specific risk, not total risk:

$$\text{Appraisal ratio} = \frac{\alpha}{\sigma_\varepsilon} \qquad (4.28)$$

This measures the systematic risk-adjusted reward for each unit of specific risk taken.

Modified Jensen

Smith and Tito (1969) suggested the use of modified Jensen to rank portfolio performance. Similar to the appraisal ratio, Jensen's alpha is divided by systematic risk rather than specific risk:

$$\text{Modified Jensen} = \frac{\alpha}{\beta} \qquad (4.29)$$

This measures the systematic risk-adjusted return per unit of systematic risk. Although not suggested in their paper a logical alternative might be:

$$\text{Alternative modified Jensen} = \frac{\alpha}{\sigma_S} \qquad (4.30)$$

Fama decomposition

Fama (1972) extended the concept of Treynor's ratio in his paper "Components of investment performance" to further break down the return of a portfolio.

The excess return above risk-free rate can be expressed as selectivity (or Jensen's alpha) plus the return due to systematic risk as follows:

$$\underbrace{r_P - r_F}_{\text{Excess return}} = \underbrace{r_P - \beta_P(b - r_F)}_{\text{Selectivity}} + \underbrace{(\beta_P(b - r_F) - r_F}_{\text{Systematic risk}} - r_F \qquad (4.31)$$

If a portfolio is completely diversified there is no specific risk and the total portfolio risk will equal the systematic risk. Portfolio managers will give up diversification seeking additional return. Selectivity can be broken down into net selectivity and the return required to justify the diversification given up.

Selectivity

Isolating selectivity in Equation (4.31), we notice that it is equivalent to Jensen's alpha:

$$\alpha = r_P - r_F - \beta_P \times (b - r_F) \qquad (4.32)$$

Diversification

Diversification is always positive and is the measure of return required to justify the loss of diversification for the specific risk taken by the portfolio manager.

To calculate the loss of diversification we have to calculate the effective beta required so that the systematic risk is equivalent to the total portfolio risk. We call this the Fama beta, calculated as follows:

$$\beta_F = \frac{\sigma_P}{\sigma_M} \qquad (4.33)$$

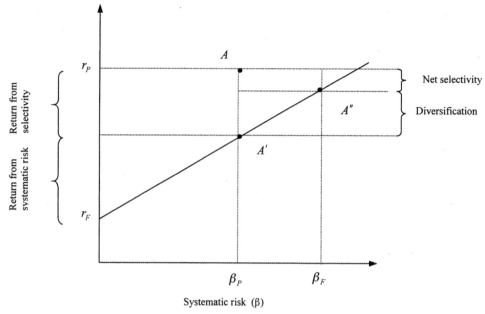

Figure 4.7   Fama decomposition.

Therefore, the return required to justify not being fully diversified is calculated as follows:

$$d = (\beta_F - \beta_P) \times (b - r_F) \tag{4.34}$$

Net selectivity

Net selectivity is the remaining selectivity after deducting the amount of return required to justify not being fully diversified:

$$\text{Net selectivity} \quad S_{Net} = \alpha - d \tag{4.35}$$

Obviously, if net selectivity is negative the portfolio manager has not justified the loss of diversification.

Fama decomposition is a useful analysis if we only have access to total fund returns and are unable to perform more detailed analysis on the components of return (e.g., mutual funds).

Figure 4.7 illustrates Fama's decomposition for portfolio A. A' represents the return from systematic risk plus the risk-free rate, and A'' represents the return from the Fama equivalent systematic risk plus risk-free rate.

RELATIVE RISK

The risk measures we have discussed so far are examples of absolute rather than relative risk measures: that is to say, the returns and risks of the portfolio and benchmark are calculated separately and then used for comparison.

Relative risk measures on the other hand focus on the excess return of portfolio against benchmark. The variability of excess return calculated using standard deviation is called tracking error, tracking risk, relative risk or active risk.

Tracking error

Tracking error is often forecast and, since the calculation methods and meaning are quite different, it is essential to clearly label whether you are using an *ex post* or *ex ante* tracking error:

$$\text{Tracking error} = \sqrt{\frac{\sum_{i=1}^{i=n}(a_i - \bar{a})^2}{n}} \tag{4.36}$$

where: a_i = arithmetic excess return in month i

$\bar{a}$ = mean arithmetic excess return.

Or, if you prefer geometric excess returns:

$$\text{Tracking error} = \sqrt{\frac{\sum_{i=1}^{i=n}(g_i - \bar{g})^2}{n}} \tag{4.37}$$

where: g_i = geometric excess return in month i

$\bar{g}$ = mean geometric excess return.

Tracking error is a function of the portfolio standard deviation and the correlation between portfolio and benchmark returns and can also be calculated by:

$$\text{Tracking error} = \sigma_P \times \sqrt{(1 - \rho_{P,M})^2} \tag{4.38}$$

Information ratio (or modified Sharpe ratio)

In exactly the same way we compared absolute return and absolute risk in the Sharpe ratio you can compare excess return and tracking error (the standard deviation of excess return) graphically (see Figure 4.8).

The information ratio is extremely similar to the Sharpe ratio except that, instead of absolute return, on the vertical axis we have excess return and, instead of absolute risk, on the horizontal axis we have tracking error or relative risk (the standard deviation of excess return), hence the alternative name modified Sharpe ratio.

We have no need for a risk-free rate since we are dealing with excess returns; information ratio lines always originate from the origin. The gradient of the line is simply the ratio of excess return and tracking error as follows:

$$IR = \frac{\text{Annualized excess return}}{\text{Annualized tracking error}} \tag{4.39}$$

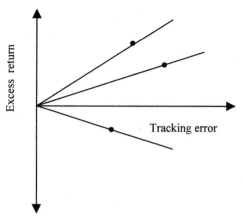

Figure 4.8   Information ratio.

Normally, information ratios are calculated using annualized excess returns and annualized tracking errors. To aid comparison it is absolutely essential to disclose the method of calculation (i.e., frequency of data, overall time period, arithmetic or geometric excess returns, arithmetic or geometric means, n or $n - 1$, *ex post* or *ex ante*).

The method of calculation can certainly generate different results and, therefore, it is essential to ensure information ratios are calculated in the same way if comparisons are to be made.

If *ex ante* tracking errors are used in the denominator please remember it is only a forecast based on a current snapshot of the portfolio. The portfolio manager will be able to "window-dress" the portfolio by reducing any "bets" at the point of measurement, thus reducing the forecast tracking error and therefore apparently improving the information ratio.

Information ratio is a key statistic, used extensively by institutional asset managers, it's often described as the measure of a portfolio manager's skill.

Views vary on what constitutes a good information ratio. In his research commentary Thomas Goodwin (1998) quotes Grinold and Kahn stating that an information ratio of 0.5 is good, 0.75 is very good and 1.0 is exceptional. These numbers certainly accord with my personal experience if sustained over a substantial period (3 to 5 years). Clearly, a positive information ratio indicates outperformance and a negative information ratio indicates underperformance. Unlike the Sharpe ratio, there is more consensus that, if you are going to underperform, consistent underperformance (as indicated by low tracking error) is worse than inconsistent underperformance (high tracking error)

It is quite easy to obtain a good information ratio for a single period; like all statistics the development of the information ratio should be viewed over time. Goodwin suggests that sustaining a high information ratio above 0.5 is more difficult than Grinold and Kahn suggest in their article.

Tracking error and information ratios are calculated for our standard example data in Table 4.8.

Table 4.8 Information ratio

Portfolio monthly return r_i (%)	Benchmark monthly return b_i (%)	Arithmetic excess return $a_i = r_i - b_i$ (%)	Deviation from average $(a_i - \bar{a})$	Deviation squared $(a_i - \bar{a})^2$
0.3	0.2	0.1	0.2	0.04
2.6	2.5	0.1	0.2	0.04
1.1	1.8	-0.7	0.6	0.36
-1.0	-1.1	0.1	0.2	0.04
1.5	1.4	0.1	0.2	0.04
2.5	1.8	0.7	0.8	0.64
1.6	1.4	0.2	0.3	0.09
6.7	6.5	0.2	0.3	0.09
-1.4	-1.5	0.1	0.2	0.04
4.0	4.2	-0.2	0.1	0.01
-0.5	-0.6	0.1	0.2	0.04
8.1	8.3	-0.2	0.1	0.01
4.0	3.9	0.1	0.2	0.04
-3.7	-3.8	0.1	0.2	0.04
6.1	6.2	0.1	0.2	0.04
1.7	1.5	0.2	0.3	0.09
-4.9	-4.8	-0.1	0.0	0.00
-2.2	2.1	-4.3	4.2	17.64
7.0	6.0	1.0	1.1	1.21
5.8	5.6	0.2	0.3	0.09
-6.5	-6.7	0.2	0.3	0.09
2.4	1.9	0.5	0.6	0.36
-0.5	-0.3	-0.2	0.1	0.01
-0.8	0.0	-0.8	0.7	0.49

| Annualized portfolio return 10.42% | Annualized benchmark return 11.80% | | | *Total* = 21.54 |

Tracking error $\quad \sqrt{\dfrac{21.54}{24}} = 0.95$

Annualized tracking error (close to specific risk in this example because β is close to 1) $\quad 0.95 \times \sqrt{12} = 3.282$

Or annualized tracking error $= \sigma_P \times \sqrt{(1 - \rho_{P,M})^2} \quad 13.4 \times \sqrt{(1 - 0.97)^2} = 3.282$

Information ratio $\quad \dfrac{(10.42\% - 11.80\%)}{3.282} = -0.42\%$

RETURN DISTRIBUTIONS

Normal distribution

A distribution is said to be normal if there is a high probability that an observation will be close to the average and a low probability that an observation is far away from the average. A normal distribution curve peaks at the average value.

A normal distribution has special properties that are useful if we can assume returns or excess returns are normally distributed. If returns are normally distributed we can use the average return and variability or standard deviation of returns to describe the distribution of returns, such that:

- Approximately 68% of returns will be within a range of one standard deviation above and below the average return.
- Approximately 95% of returns will be within a range of 2 standard deviations above and below the average return.

This property is obviously very useful for calculating the probability of an event occurring outside a specified range of returns. Normal distributions are popular because of these statistical properties and because many random events can be approximated by a normal distribution.

Skewness

Not all distributions are normal-distributed: if there are more returns extending to the right tail of a distribution it is said to be positively skewed and if there are more returns extending to the left it is said to be negatively skewed. We can measure the degree of skewness in the following formula:

$$\text{Skewness} = \sum \left(\frac{r_i - \bar{r}}{\sigma_P} \right)^3 \times \frac{1}{n} \tag{4.40}$$

A normal distribution will have a skewness of 0.

We can use skewness in making a judgement about the possibility of large negative or positive outliers when comparing portfolio returns. Skewness provides more information about the shape of return distribution.

Kurtosis

Kurtosis provides additional information about the shape of return distributions; it measures the flatness of the distribution:

$$\text{Kurtosis} = \sum \left(\frac{r_i - \bar{r}}{\sigma_p} \right)^4 \times \frac{1}{n} \tag{4.41}$$

The kurtosis of a normal distribution is 3; less than 3 would indicate a flat distribution with thin tails and greater than 3 would indicate a more peaked distribution with fat tails. Again a better understanding of the shape of the distribution of returns will aid in assessing the relative qualities of portfolios. Whether we prefer higher or lower kurtosis (or for that matter positive or negative skewness) will depend on the type of return series we want to see.

Equity markets tend to have fat tails: when markets fall portfolio managers tend to sell and when they rise portfolio managers tend to buy. There is a higher probability of extreme events than the normal distribution would suggest. Therefore, tracking error and Value at Risk (VaR) statistics calculated using normal assumptions might underestimate risk.

d ratio

The *d* ratio measures the ratio of the total value of downside returns (less than 0) compared with the total value of upside returns (greater than 0):

$$d \ ratio = \frac{-n_d \times \sum_{i=1}^{i=n} \min(r_i, 0)}{n_u \times \sum \max(r_i, 0)} \tag{4.42}$$

where: n_d = number of returns less than 0

n_u = number of returns greater than 0.

The *d* ratio will have values between 0 and ∞ and can be used to rank the performance of portfolios. The lower the *d* ratio the better the performance, a value of 0 indicating there are no returns less than 0 and a value of infinity indicating there are no returns greater than 0. Portfolio managers with positively skewed returns will have lower *d* ratios.

DOWNSIDE RISK

Some would argue that investors should not be concerned by outperformance and should focus on the variability of underperformance.

Semi-standard deviation measures the variability of underperformance below a minimum target rate. The minimum target rate could be the risk-free rate, the benchmark or any other fixed threshold required by the client. All positive returns are included as zero in the calculation of semi-standard deviation or downside risk as follows:

$$\text{Downside risk} \quad \sigma_D = \sqrt{\sum_{i=1}^{n} \frac{\min[(r_i - r_T), 0]^2}{n}} \tag{4.43}$$

where: r_T = Minimum target return.

Clearly, since positive returns are excluded there are potentially fewer or in some cases no observations less than the target return. Therefore, great care must be taken to ensure there are sufficient returns to ensure the calculation is meaningful.

Alternatively, a distribution curve can be fitted to the data points and integral calculus used to model the probability of returns below the minimum target return (Sortino and Satchell, 2001).

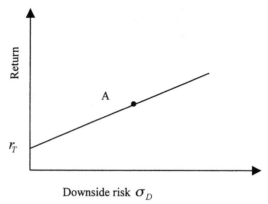

Figure 4.9 Sortino ratio.

Sortino ratio

The Sortino ratio (Figure 4.9) is similar to the Sharpe or Treynor ratios; it can be calculated to measure the reward per unit of downside risk:

$$\text{Sortino ratio} = \frac{(r_P - r_T)}{\sigma_D} \qquad (4.44)$$

It's a moot point as to whether the rational starting point should remain the risk-free rate or the minimum target rate. Certainly, if the risk-free rate is greater than the minimum target rate I believe it should be used in the calculation of Sortino ratio. In most cases however the minimum target rate will exceed the risk-free rate.

M^2 for Sortino

M^2 can be calculated for downside risk in the same way as it is calculated for total risk or systematic risk. In Figure 4.10 a straight line is drawn vertically through the downside risk of the benchmark; the intercept with the Sortino ratio line of portfolio A

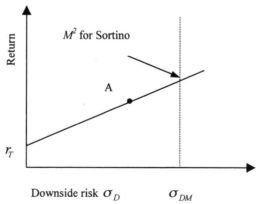

Figure 4.10 M^2 for Sortino.

would give the return of the portfolio with the same Sortino ratio of portfolio A but at the same downside risk of the benchmark:

$$M_S^2 = r_P + \text{Sortino ratio} \times (\sigma_{DM} - \sigma_D) \qquad (4.45)$$

Upside potential ratio

The upside potential ratio can also be used to rank portfolio performance and combines upside potential with downside risk as follows:

$$UPR = \frac{\sum_{i=1}^{i=n} \max(r_i - r_T, 0)\Big/ n}{\sigma_D} \qquad (4.46)$$

Portfolio downside risk, Sortino ratio and upside potential ratio are calculated in Table 4.9. Benchmark downside risk and M_S^2 are calculated in Table 4.10.

Omega excess return

Another form of downside risk-adjusted return is *omega* excess return (Sortino et al., 1997). Similar to differential return the downside risk-adjusted benchmark return is calculated by multiplying the downside variance of the style benchmark by 3 times the style beta. The 3 is arbitrary and assumes the investor requires 3 units of return for 1 unit of variance ($3 \times \sigma_{MD}^2$ effectively take the place of the benchmark excess return above the risk-free rate in the differential return calculation). The style beta adjusts for the downside risk taken by the portfolio manager by taking the ratio of the downside risk of the portfolio divided by the downside risk of the style benchmark:

$$\text{Downside risk-adjusted style benchmark} \quad 3 \times \beta_S \times \sigma_{MD}^2 \qquad (4.47)$$

$$\text{Omega excess return} \quad \omega = r_p - 3 \times \beta_S \times \sigma_{MD}^2 \qquad (4.48)$$

where:

$$\text{style beta } \beta_S = \frac{\sigma_D}{\sigma_{MD}} \qquad (4.49)$$

$$\sigma_{MD}^2 = \text{style benchmark variance}$$

For much the same reasons as I prefer M^2 excess return above differential return I prefer M^2 for Sortino to omega excess return.

Volatility skewness

A similar measure to the d ratio, the volatility skewness measures the ratio of the upside variance compared with the downside variance. Values greater than 1 would indicate positive skewness and values less than 1 would indicate negative skewness:

$$\text{Volatility skewness} = \frac{\sigma_U^2}{\sigma_D^2} \qquad (4.50)$$

where: $\sigma_U^2 = $ upside variance.

Table 4.9 Portfolio downside risk when monthly minimum target return $= 0.5\%$ and annual minimum target return $= 6.17\%$

Portfolio monthly return r_i (%)	Deviation against target (downside only) $(r_i - r_T)$ (%)	Squared deviation $(r_i - r_T)^2$	Upside only $(r_i - r_T)$ (%)
0.3	−0.2	0.04	
2.6			2.1
1.1			0.6
−1.0	−1.5	2.25	
1.5			1.0
2.5			2.0
1.6			1.1
6.7			6.2
−1.4	−1.9	3.61	
4.0			3.5
−0.5	−1.0	1.00	
8.1			7.6
4.0			3.5
−3.7	−4.2	17.64	
−6.1	−6.6	43.56	
1.7			1.2
−4.9	−5.4	29.16	
−2.2	−2.7	7.29	
7.0			6.5
5.8			5.3
−6.5	−7.0	49.00	
2.4			1.9
−0.5	−1.0	1.00	
−0.8	−1.3	1.69	

Annualized portfolio return 10.42%

Total = 156.24   *Total = 42.5%*

$$\text{Monthly downside risk} \quad \sqrt{\frac{156.24}{24}} = 2.55\%$$

$$\text{Annualized downside risk} \quad 2.55\% \times \sqrt{12} = 8.84\%$$

$$\text{Sortino ratio} \quad \frac{10.42\% - 6.17\%}{8.84\%} = 0.48$$

$$\text{Upside potential} \quad \frac{42.5\%}{24} = 1.77\%$$

$$\text{Upside potential ratio} \quad \frac{1.77\%}{8.84\%} = 0.20$$

Value at Risk (VaR)

VaR measures the worst expected loss over a given time interval under normal market conditions at a given confidence level. For example, an annual value at risk of £5m at a 95% confidence level for a portfolio would suggest that only once in 20 years would the

Table 4.10 Benchmark downside risk when monthly minimum target return $= 0.5\%$ and annual minimum target return $= 6.17\%$

Benchmark monthly return b_i (%)	Deviation against target (downside only) $(b_i - r_T)$ (%)	Squared deviation $(b_i - r_T)^2$
0.2	−0.3	0.09
2.5		
1.8		
−1.1	−1.6	2.56
1.4		
1.8		
1.4		
6.5		
−1.5	−2.0	4.00
4.2		
−0.6	−1.1	1.21
8.3		
3.9		
−3.8	−4.3	18.49
−6.2	−6.7	44.89
1.5		
−4.8	−5.3	28.09
2.1		
6.0		
5.6		
−6.7	−7.2	51.84
1.9		
−0.3	−0.8	0.64
0.0	−0.5	0.25

Total = 152.06

Monthly downside risk	$\sqrt{\dfrac{152.06}{24}} = 2.52\%$
Annualized downside risk	$2.52\% \times \sqrt{12} = 8.72\%$
$M_S^2 = r_P + \text{Sortino ratio} \times (\sigma_{DM} - \sigma_D)$	$10.42\% + 0.48 \times (8.72\% - 8.84\%) = 10.36\%$

annual loss exceed £5m. Therefore, it is far from the maximum possible loss. Value at Risk measures the downside, upside potential measures the best-expected gain over the given time interval under normal market conditions at a given confidence level. Confidence levels of 99% are also used.

VaR like tracking error can be calculated *ex post* or *ex ante*. Typically, VaR is calculated *ex ante* although like tracking error it is useful to calculate *ex post* as well to monitor risk efficiency.

VaR can be calculated in conjunction with tracking error, since tracking error is a 1 standard deviation measure covering approximately 68% of returns; within 1 standard deviation of the average it is entirely possible that a change in strategy may reduce tracking error while increasing VaR in the tails of the distribution. Client preferences will determine which of these measures is the most relevant.

VaR ratio

VaR ratio is the ratio of value at risk divided by the total size of the portfolio, essentially the percentage of the portfolio at risk:

$$\frac{\text{VaR}}{\text{Assets}} \qquad (4.51)$$

Hurst index

The Hurst index* is a useful statistic for detecting whether a portfolio manager's returns are mean-reverting (anti-persistent), totally random or persistent. It is calculated as follows:

$$H = \frac{\log(m)}{\log(n)} \qquad (4.52)$$

where:

$$m = \frac{[\max(r_i) - \min(r_i)]}{\sigma_p} \qquad (4.53)$$

n = number of observations.

A Hurst index between 0 and 0.5 would suggest a portfolio manager's series of returns are mean-reverting (anti-persistent). A Hurst index of 0.5 would suggest the series of returns was totally random. A Hurst index between 0.5 and 1 would suggest the series of returns are persistent (i.e., there is memory in the return series).

FIXED INCOME RISK

Duration

In many ways fixed income securities or bonds are easier to measure than equities; they consist (for the most part) of predictable future cash flows in the form of coupon payments and a final redemption value.

Duration is defined as the average life of the present values of all future cash flows from a fixed income security. In calculating the present value of the future cash flows, a discount rate equal to the redemption yield is used. This measures fixed income securities' sensitivities to changes in interest rates.

---

* H.E. Hurst originally developed the Hurst index to help in the difficult task of establishing optimal water storage along the Nile. Nile floods are extremely persistent as evidenced by a Hurst index of 0.9. Equity markets have a Hurst index of around 0.7.

Macaulay duration

Macaulay duration is defined as the weighted maturity of each bond payment, where the weights are proportional to the present value of cash flows:

$$D = \frac{\sum_{i=1}^{n} F_i \times t_i \times d^{t_i}}{\sum_{i=1}^{n} F_i \times d^{t_i}} \tag{4.54}$$

where: n = number of future coupon and capital repayments

F_i = ith future coupon or capital repayment

t_i = time in years to the ith coupon or capital repayment

d = discount factor.

Note that:

$$d = \frac{1}{(1+y)} \tag{4.55}$$

where: y = interest rate.

However, the denominator in Equation (4.54) is equal to the present value of future coupon and capital repayments of the securities or, in other words, the price P:

$$P = \sum_{i=1}^{n} F_i \times d^{t_i} \tag{4.56}$$

Substituting Equation (4.56) into Equation (4.54) we have the formula for Macaulay duration:

$$D = \frac{\sum_{i=1}^{n} F_i \times t_i \times d^{t_i}}{P} \tag{4.57}$$

Modified duration

Modified duration measures the price sensitivity of bonds to changes in yield:

$$MD = d \times \frac{\sum_{i=1}^{n} F_i \times t_i \times d^{t_i}}{P} \tag{4.58}$$

Effective duration

Modified duration does not calculate the effective duration of the bond if there is any optionality in future payments. To calculate the effective duration the estimate price must be calculated for both a positive and negative change in interest rates:

$$ED = \frac{P_- - P_+}{2 \times P \times \Delta y} \tag{4.59}$$

where: Δy = change in interest rates

P_- = estimated price if interest rate is decreased by Δy

P_+ = estimated price if interest rate is increased by Δy.

Convexity

Duration is only the first-order approximation in the change of the fixed income securities' price. The approximation is due to the fact that a curved line represents the relationship between bond prices and interest rates. Duration assumes there is a linear relationship. This approximation can be improved by using a second approximation, convexity:

$$C = \sum_{i=1}^{n} F_i \times t_i \times (t_i + 1) \times d^{t_i} \tag{4.60}$$

Modified convexity

$$MC = d^2 \times \frac{\sum_{i=1}^{n} F_i \times t_i \times (t_i + 1) \times d^{t_i}}{P} \tag{4.61}$$

Effective convexity

Again modified convexity does not calculate the effective convexity of the bond if there is any optionality in future payments. Using estimated prices to calculate effective convexity:

$$EC = \frac{P_- + P_+ - 2 \times P}{P \times (\Delta y)^2} \tag{4.62}$$

Duration beta

The ratio of the portfolio's sensitivity to yield changes with that of the benchmark provides a systematic risk measure equivalent to beta:

$$D_\beta = \frac{D_P}{D_M} \tag{4.63}$$

WHICH RISK MEASURES TO USE?

Risk like beauty is very much in the eye of the beholder. Determining which risk measure to use is determined by the objectives and preferences of the investor. Although most risk measures are easy to calculate they are not all easy to interpret and are often contradictory.

My advice is to calculate only a few risk measures which are consistent with the investment objectives and easily understood by all parties.

Whichever risk measure you decide to focus on it is important to monitor the change in that measure over time. Too much time and energy, in particular for *ex ante* risk measures, is expended determining whether the measure is accurate. Risk controllers can never assume the measure is accurate; far better to analyse the change over time and investigate any sudden changes.

The measure may be incorrect but any sudden change from one reference point to the next provides additional information. The change may result from data errors, system or model errors, change in model assumptions, or an intentional or unintentional change in portfolio risk. Whatever the reason for the change it should be discussed and fully understood with the portfolio manager.

Ex post risk measures will not change dramatically; but, for effective risk control it is essential to compare the predictive risk calculated by internal systems with the actual realized risk of portfolios.

Risk efficiency ratio

It is important to monitor changes over time in both the *ex ante* and *ex post* tracking errors; it is also important to compare the forecast tracking error with the realized tracking error to gauge how close the forecast is to reality.

The risk efficiency ratio compares realized risk with forecast risk – ideally, we would like the ratio to be 1, indicating that our forecasting tools were efficient. If the ratio is much greater than 1 then we are aware that our forecasting tool is underestimating relative risk:

$$\frac{Ex\ post\ \text{tracking error}}{Ex\ ante\ \text{tracking error}} \quad \text{or} \quad \frac{\text{Realized risk}}{\text{Forecast risk}} \tag{4.64}$$

Or alternatively:

$$\frac{Ex\ post\ \text{VaR}}{Ex\ ante\ \text{VaR}} \tag{4.65}$$

RISK CONTROL STRUCTURE

Performance measurers have a key role to play in the risk control environment of asset managers. In the ideal asset management organization I would have performance measurement, risk control, the legal department and the internal audit function reporting to the head of middle office. Performance measurers should never report to the front office or the marketing department (Figure 4.11).

For effective risk management in an asset management firm the following should be in place:

(i) *Written risk policy*. To provide a framework for the risk control environment every asset management firm should have a risk policy that clearly articulates the firm's attitude to risk.

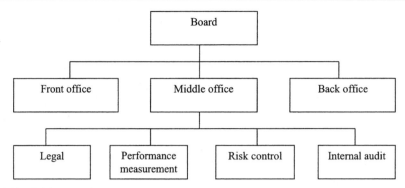

Figure 4.11   Risk control structure.

(ii) *Independence*. For effective risk control it is essential there are appropriate checks and balances within the firm with a clear front-, middle- and back-office structure with clear areas of responsibility and reporting lines.

(iii) *Risk awareness*. Risk awareness should be embedded within the firm. All employees will own some aspect of risk, it is essential they understand the risks they own and are constantly self-assessing their own risks. Once identified there are four possible responses to risk:

   (a) Ignore the identified risk. A risk although identified maybe ignored if the cost (including opportunity cost) of controlling is greater than the potential cost of risk failure.

   (b) Mitigate. Arranging appropriate insurance cover may mitigate the cost of risk failure.

   (c) Control. Risk may be controlled by establishing risk limits and establishing monitoring procedures.

   (d) Eliminate. It may be appropriate to eliminate an identified risk by ceasing that type of activity.

(iv) *Clear risk limits*. Risk limits should be clear and unambiguous and agreed by the client and asset manager in the investment management agreement.

(v) *Risk and performance attribution*. The sources of risk and return should be identified and monitored independently using performance return attribution and other techniques. Accurate return and risk attribution can be used to identify the consistency of added value across the firm and consistency with the agreed investment objectives.

(vi) *Appropriate risk-adjusted measures*. Risk and reward should be combined in risk-adjusted performance measures appropriate to the investment management strategy.

(vii) *Review process for new products, instruments and strategies*. All new products, instruments and strategies should be rigorously reviewed. For example, a new derivative instrument may meet the needs of the portfolio manager but could generate significant operational and counterparty risks that must be assessed and approved.

An appropriate risk control infrastructure for an asset management firm would include:

(i) *Risk Management Committee.* Reporting to the board, probably chaired by the head of risk control. Co-ordinating all risk control activity including senior representatives from front, middle and back office. Responsible for portfolio risk, counterparty risk, compliance risk, review of insurance arrangements, disaster recovery and systems change control.

(ii) *Portfolio Risk Committee.* Reporting to the Risk Management Committee, probably chaired by the head of front office. Review that portfolios are managed within client expectations and mandate restrictions. Approve new products, strategies and instruments.

(iii) *Credit Risk Committee.* Reporting to the Risk Management Committee. Approve counterparties and limits and monitor firm exposures.

(iv) *Operational Risk Committee.* Reporting to the Risk Management Committee. Responsible for error monitoring and information quality

REFERENCES

Clarkson, R. (2001) FARM: A financial actuarial risk model. In: F. Sortino and S. Satchell (eds), *Managing Downside Risk in Financial Markets*. Butterworth-Heinemann.

Fama, E. (1972) Components of investment performance. *Journal of Finance*, **27**(3), June.

Goodwin, T. (1998) *The Information Ratio: More than You Ever Wanted to Know about One Performance Measure* (Research commentary). Russell.

Jensen, M. (1969) Risk, the pricing of capital assets, and the evaluation of investment portfolios. *Journal of Business*, April.

Modigliani, L. (1997) *Risk-adjusted Performance, Part 1: The Time for Risk Measurement Is Now* (Investment perspectives). Morgan Stanley.

Smith, K. and Tito, D. (1969) Risk return of ex-post portfolio performance. *Journal of Financial and Quantitative Analysis*, **4**(14), December.

Sortino, F. and Satchell, S. (2001) *Managing Downside Risk in Financial Markets*. Butterworth-Heinemann.

Sortino, F., Miller, G. and Messina, J. (1997) Short term risk-adjusted performance: A style based analysis. *Journal of Investing*, Summer.

5
Performance Attribution

Never try to walk across a river just because it has an average depth of four feet.

Martin Friedman

Definition   *Performance attribution is a technique used to quantify the excess return of a portfolio against its benchmark into the active decisions of the investment decision process.*

Performance return attribution is a key management tool for several key stakeholders in the asset management process.

Above all it is the key tool for performance analysts; it allows them to participate in the investment decision process and demonstrably add value, thus justifying their salary. Performance return attribution, together with risk analysis, is the key tool that allows the analyst to understand the sources of return in a portfolio and to communicate that understanding to portfolio managers, senior management and clients.

Effective attribution requires that the analyst thoroughly understands the investment decision process. The task of the analyst is to quantify the decisions taken by the portfolio manager. If the analyst can demonstrate an understanding of the decision process and accurately quantify the decisions taken, then the confidence of the portfolio manager will soon be gained. There is little value in analysing factors that are not part of the decision process.

Portfolio managers are obviously major users of attribution analysis. Clearly, they will have a good qualitative understanding of the portfolio but not necessarily a good quantitative understanding. It is all too easy to overestimate the impact of good-performing securities and underestimate failures. It is even harder, sometimes, to consider the impact of stocks not held in the portfolio. Stocks represented in the index but not in the portfolio are often large "bets" and may have a significant impact on relative performance, positive or negative.

Attribution analysis provides a good starting point for a dialogue with clients entering a discussion on the positive and negative aspects of recent performance. It is possible to use attribution analysis extremely aggressively, identifying underperformance early and visiting clients with a thorough explanation of underperformance. It is crucial to gain the confidence of the client by demonstrating a good understanding of the drivers of performance.

Senior management take an active interest in attribution analysis to provide them with a tool to monitor their portfolio managers. They will be keen to identify performance outliers – good or bad – and to ensure that value is added consistently across the firm.

ARITHMETIC ATTRIBUTION

The foundations of performance attribution were established in two articles published by Brinson et al. (1986) and Brinson and Fachler (1985), now collectively known as the Brinson model. These articles build on the assumption that the total portfolio returns and benchmark returns are the sum of their parts; in other words, both portfolio and benchmark returns can be disaggregated as follows:

$$\text{Portfolio return} \quad r = \sum_{i=1}^{i=n} w_i \times r_i \qquad (5.1)$$

where: w_i = weight of the portfolio in the ith asset class $\left(\text{note} \sum_{i=1}^{i=n} w_i = 1\right)$

r_i = return of the portfolio assets in the ith asset class.

$$\text{Benchmark return} \quad b = \sum_{i=1}^{i=n} W_i \times b_i \qquad (5.2)$$

where: W_i = weight of the benchmark in the ith asset class $\left(\text{note also} \sum_{i=1}^{i=n} W_i = 1\right)$

b_i = return of the benchmark in the ith asset class.

The challenge for single-period attribution is to quantify each of the portfolio manager's active decisions that contribute to the difference between the portfolio return r and the benchmark return b.

Brinson, Hood and Beebower

Brinson, Hood and Beebower suggested a model to break down the arithmetic excess return $(r - b)$ assuming a standard investment decision process in which the portfolio manager seeks to add value through both *asset allocation* and *security selection*.

In asset allocation the portfolio manager (or asset allocator) will seek to add value by taking different asset category (or sector) weights in the portfolio in comparison to category benchmark weights. A category weight in the portfolio greater than the equivalent benchmark category weight would be described as *overweight* and a lesser weight would be described as *underweight*.

Clearly, the asset allocator will aim to overweight good-performing categories and underweight poor-performing categories. In their original article Brinson, Hood and Beebower called this impact timing; asset or market allocation is now a more common and appropriate description.

In security selection the portfolio manager (or stock selector) will seek to add value by selecting individual securities within the asset category.

Again the stock selector will aim to be overweight in good-performing securities and underweight in poor-performing securities.

Asset allocation

To identify the added value from asset allocation we must calculate the return of an intermediate fund called the "allocation or semi-notional fund", which is one step away from the benchmark portfolio, one step toward the actual portfolio.

In the semi-notional fund the asset allocation weights of the actual fund are applied to index returns within each category. By definition the return on this notional fund reflects the portfolio manager's asset allocation "bets", but since index returns are used within the asset category it includes no stock selection:

$$\text{Allocation or semi-notional fund}\quad b_S = \sum_{i=1}^{i=n} w_i \times b_i \tag{5.3}$$

The contribution from asset allocation is therefore the difference between the semi-notional fund and the benchmark fund or:

$$b_S - b = \sum_{i=1}^{i=n} w_i \times b_i - \sum_{i=1}^{i=n} W_i \times b_i = \sum_{i=1}^{i=n} (w_i - W_i) \times b_i \tag{5.4}$$

The contribution to asset allocation in the ith category is:

$$A_i = (w_i - W_i) \times b_i \tag{5.5}$$

Note that:

$$\sum_{i=1}^{i=n} A_i = b_S - b \tag{5.6}$$

Security (or stock) selection

Similarly, to identify the added value from security selection we must calculate the return of a different intermediate fund called the "selection notional fund", which is also by definition one step away from the benchmark return. In the selection notional fund the asset allocation weights of the benchmark are kept static and applied to the category returns within the actual portfolio. By definition the return on this notional fund reflects the portfolio manager's stock selection since real returns are applied to index weights, but excludes any contribution from asset allocation:

$$\text{Selection notional fund}\quad r_S = \sum_{i=1}^{i=n} W_i \times r_i \tag{5.7}$$

The contribution from stock selection is therefore the difference between the selection notional fund and the benchmark fund or:

$$r_S - b = \sum_{i=1}^{i=n} W_i \times r_i - \sum_{i=1}^{i=n} W_i \times b_i = \sum_{i=1}^{i=n} W_i \times (r_i - b_i) \tag{5.8}$$

The contribution to stock selection in category i is:

$$S_i = W_i \times (r_i - b_i) \tag{5.9}$$

Note that:

$$\sum_{i=1}^{i=n} S_i = r_S - b \qquad (5.10)$$

Interaction

In this, the "classical" definition of attribution, stock selection and asset allocation do not explain the arithmetic difference completely – a third term is required:

$$\text{Stock selection} + \text{Asset allocation} = r_S - b + b_S - b$$

or

$$= r_S + b_S - 2 \times b \qquad (5.11)$$

To achieve $r - b$ we must add a third term called interaction:

$$\underbrace{r_S - b}_{\text{Stock selection}} + \underbrace{b_S - b}_{\text{Asset allocation}} + \underbrace{r - r_S - b_S + b = r - b}_{\text{Interaction}} \qquad (5.12)$$

In their article Brinson, Hood and Beebower described this term as *other*; interaction is perhaps a better description and is in common usage today:

$$r - r_S - b_S + b = \sum_{i=1}^{i=n} w_i \times r_i - \sum_{i=1}^{i=n} W_i \times r_i - \sum_{i=1}^{i=n} W_i \times b_i + \sum_{i=1}^{i=n} W_i \times b_i \qquad (5.13)$$

which simplifies to:

$$\sum_{i=1}^{i=n} (w_i - W_i) \times (r_i - b_i) \qquad (5.14)$$

It can be seen from Equation (5.14) that interaction is the combination of asset allocation and stock selection effects.

The contribution to interaction in category i is:

$$I_i = (w_i - W_i) \times (r_i - b_i) \qquad (5.15)$$

Note that:

$$\sum_{i=1}^{i=n} I_i = r - r_S - b_S + b \qquad (5.16)$$

Figure 5.1 illustrates the Brinson framework for return attribution.

Figure 5.2 graphically illustrates the attribution factors for each category i. The contribution to total portfolio return from category i is the area $r_i \times w_i$, the contribution from the benchmark is area $b_i \times W_i$.

The contribution to excess return in category i is the sum of the areas representing selection $W_i \times (r_i - b_i)$, allocation $(w_i - W_i) \times b_i$ and interaction $(w_i - W_i) \times (r_i - b_i)$.

Table 5.1 provides the data for a simple numerical example of a three-category portfolio consisting of UK, Japanese and US equities.

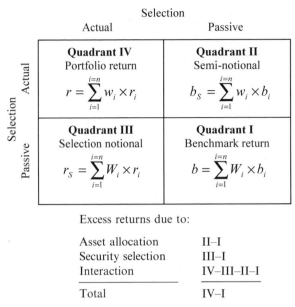

Excess returns due to:

Asset allocation	II–I
Security selection	III–I
Interaction	IV–III–II–I
Total	IV–I

Figure 5.1   Brinson framework for return attribution.

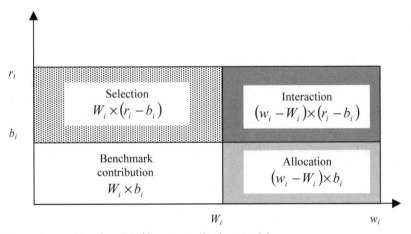

Figure 5.2   Brinson, Hood and Beebower attribution model.

Table 5.1   Three-category portfolio.

	Portfolio weight (%)	Benchmark weight (%)	Portfolio return (%)	Benchmark return (%)
UK equities	40	40	20	10
Japanese equities	30	20	−5	−4
US equities	30	40	6	8
Total	*100*	*100*	*8.3*	*6.4*

Total portfolio, benchmark and notional funds are calculated in Exhibit 5.1:

Exhibit 5.1   Return calculations

Using the data from Table 5.1 the portfolio return $r = \sum_{i=1}^{i=n} w_i \times r_i$ is:

$$r = 40\% \times 20\% + 30\% \times -5\% + 30\% \times 6\% = 8.3\%$$

The benchmark return $b = \sum_{i=1}^{i=n} W_i \times b_i$ is:

$$b = 40\% \times 10\% + 20\% \times -4\% + 40\% \times 8\% = 6.4\%$$

The allocation notional return $b_S = \sum_{i=1}^{i=n} w_i \times b_i$ is:

$$b_S = 40\% \times 10\% + 30\% \times -4\% + 30\% \times 8\% = 5.2\%$$

The selection notional return $r_S = \sum_{i=1}^{i=n} W_i \times r_i$ is:

$$r_S = 40\% \times 20\% + 20\% \times -5\% + 40\% \times 6\% = 9.4\%$$

The challenge of attribution analysis is to break down and quantify the decisions made by the portfolio manager contributing to the arithmetic excess return of 1.9%.

Using Equation (5.5) we can derive the asset allocation effects shown in Exhibit 5.2 for the data in Table 5.1:

Exhibit 5.2   Asset allocation

Total asset (or country) allocation:

$$b_S - b = 5.2\% - 6.4\% = -1.2\%$$

Individual country asset allocation effects are:

UK equities $(40\% - 40\%) \times 10\% = 0.0\%$

Japanese equities $(30\% - 20\%) \times -4.0\% = -0.4\%$

US equities $(30\% - 40\%) \times 8\% = -0.8\%$

Total $0.0\% - 0.4\% - 0.8\% = -1.2\%$

In Exhibit 5.2 the portfolio weight in UK equities is exactly in line with the benchmark weight; therefore, there is no contribution to asset allocation in this category. There is, however, an overweight position of 10% in Japanese equities which when applied to the negative market return in Japanese equities of −4.0% results in a negative contribution of −0.4%.

If there is an overweight position in a portfolio it follows there must be at least one underweight position. In Table 5.1 there is a 10% underweight position in US equities resulting in a negative contribution of -0.8% when applied to the positive market return in the US market of 8.0%.

Total contribution to arithmetic excess return from asset allocation is -1.2%.

Using Equation (5.9) stock selection effects are calculated in Exhibit (5.3):

Exhibit 5.3   Stock selection

Total stock selection:

$$r_S - b = 9.4\% - 6.4\% = 3.0\%$$

Individual country stock selection effects are:

UK equities $40\% \times (20\% - 10\%) = 4.0\%$

Japanese equities $20\% \times (-5.0\% - 4.0\%) = -0.2\%$

US equities $40\% \times (6.0\% - 8.0\%) = -0.8\%$

Total $4.0\% - 0.2\% - 0.8\% = 3.0\%$

UK equity performance is very strong, outperforming the benchmark by 10%; the benchmark suggests that 40% of the portfolio should be invested in this category resulting in a 4.0% contribution to arithmetic excess return.

Japanese equities underperformed by 1%; the benchmark suggested a 20% weighting, therefore resulting in a negative contribution of -0.2% from Japanese stock selection.

US equity performance is also poor, underperforming by 2%; the benchmark suggests a 40% weighting, therefore generating a negative contribution of -0.8% from US stock selection.

Total contribution to arithmetic excess return from stock selection is $+3.0\%$. Combining asset allocation of -1.2% and stock selection of $+3.0\%$, 1.8% of added value is explained. The remaining term is interaction; this is calculated by Equation (5.15) as demonstrated in Exhibit 5.4:

Exhibit 5.4   Interaction

Total interaction in Table 5.1 is:

$$r - r_S - b_S + b = 8.3\% - 9.4\% - 5.2\% + 6.4\% = 0.1\%$$

Individual interaction effects are:

UK equities $(40\% - 40\%) \times (20\% - 10\%) = 0.0\%$

Japanese equities $(30\% - 20\%) \times (-5.0\% - 4.0\%) = -0.1\%$

US equities $(30\% - 40\%) \times (6.0\% - 8.0\%) = 0.2\%$

Total $0.0\% - 0.1\% - 0.2\% = 0.1\%$

Table 5.2   Brinson, Hood and Beebower attribution

	Portfolio weight w_i (%)	Benchmark weight W_i (%)	Portfolio return r_i (%)	Benchmark return b_i (%)	Asset allocation $(w_i - W_i) \times b_i$ (%)	Stock selection $w_i \times (r_i - b_i)$ (%)	Interaction $(w_i - W_i) \times (r_i - b_i)$ (%)
UK equities	40	40	20	10	0.0	4.0	0.0
Japanese equities	30	20	−5	−4	−0.4	−0.2	−0.1
US equities	30	40	6	8	−0.8	−0.8	0.2
Total	*100*	*100*	*8.3*	*6.4*	*−1.2*	*3.0*	*0.1*

The overall contribution from interaction is small. For UK equities the portfolio weight is in line with the benchmark weight and therefore there is no contribution to interaction.

For Japanese equities there is an asset allocation bet of 10%; we have 10% more of this underperforming asset category than suggested by the benchmark, therefore causing a further negative impact of −0.1%.

In US equities there is an underweight bet of 10% in this underperforming category. There is less of this underperforming category than the benchmark suggests; therefore, the combined effect of an underweight position in an underperforming category is an added value of +0.2%. Total contribution from interaction is +0.1%

· The attribution results are summarized in Table 5.2. Clearly, Brinson, Hood and Beebower's attribution model successfully breaks down the sources of arithmetic excess return. But does it reflect the investment decision process of the portfolio manager?

For the most part asset allocation decisions are taken in the context of an overall benchmark return; the asset allocator is not seeking to be overweight in positive markets but rather to be overweight in markets that outperform the overall benchmark. The asset allocator will have lost value by being overweight in a market with a positive return that nevertheless returns less than the overall benchmark. We therefore need an attribution model that follows this decision process.

BRINSON AND FACHLER

In the Brinson, Hood and Beebower* model all overweight positions in positive markets will generate positive attribution factors irrespective of the overall benchmark return, while all overweight positions in negative markets will generate negative attribution factors.

Clearly, if the asset allocator is overweight in a negative market that has outperformed the overall benchmark, then there should be a positive effect.

---

* In fact, the original Brinson, Hood and Beebower article does not attempt to attribute returns to individual categories. In all likelihood I do not believe the authors intended their top-level formulae to be applied to individual categories as shown; however, over the years many practitioners have done just that.

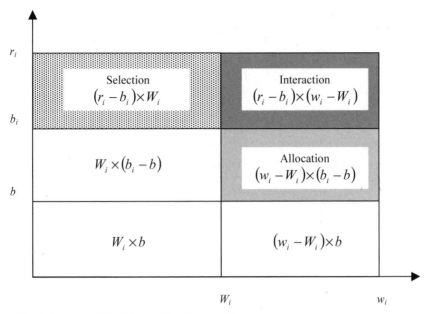

Figure 5.3   Brinson and Fachler attribution model.

The Brinson and Fachler model solves this problem by modifying the asset allocation factor to compare returns against the overall benchmark as follows:

$$b_S - b = \sum_{i=1}^{i=n}(w_i - W_i) \times b_i = \sum_{i=1}^{i=n}(w_i - W_i) \times (b_i - b) \tag{5.17}$$

Since $\sum_{i=1}^{i=n} w_i = \sum_{i=1}^{i=n} W_i = 1$ the contribution to asset allocation in the ith category is now:

$$A_i = (w_i - W_i) \times (b_i - b) \tag{5.18}$$

Graphically extending Figure 5.2 to include the benchmark return in Figure 5.3 we observe no change to the areas representing selection and interaction, but allocation is now described by the area $(w_i - W_i) \times (b_i - b)$.

Equation (5.17) demonstrates that the sum of allocation areas in Figure 5.3 for all categories is equal to the sum of allocation areas in Figure 5.2.

Since $\sum_{i=1}^{n=1} W_i = 1$ the benchmark return is derived by the sum of areas $W_i \times b$ for all categories:

$$\sum_{i=1}^{i=n} W_i \times b = b \tag{5.19}$$

and since both $\sum_{i=1}^{n=1} W_i = 1$ and $\sum_{i=1}^{n=1} w_i = 1$ the sum of areas $(w_i - W_i) \times b$ reduces to 0:

$$\sum_{i=1}^{n=1}(w_i - W_i) \times b = 0 \tag{5.20}$$

Revised Brinson and Fachler asset allocation effects are calculated in Exhibit 5.5:

Exhibit 5.5 Brinson and Fachler asset allocation

$$b_S - b = 5.2\% - 6.4\% = -1.2\%$$

Individual country asset allocation effects are:

UK equities $(40\% - 40\%) \times (10.0\% - 6.4\%) = 0.0\%$

Japanese equities $(30\% - 20\%) \times (-4.0\% - 6.4\%) = -1.04\%$

US equities $(30\% - 40\%) \times (8.0\% - 6.4\%) = -0.16\%$

Total $0.0\% - 1.04\% - 0.16\% = -1.2\%$

The impact in Japanese equities is much greater. In addition to being overweight in a negative market which cost -0.4%, we are also rightly penalized the opportunity cost of not being invested in the overall market return of 6.4%, generating a further cost of $10\% \times -6.4\% = -0.64\%$ resulting in a total impact of -1.04%.

The impact in US equities is much smaller. Although being underweight in a positive market cost -0.8% we must have back the opportunity cost of being invested in the overall market return of 6.4%, generating a contribution of $-10\% \times -6.4\% = 0.64\%$ resulting in a total impact of -0.16%.

The revised attribution effects are summarized in Table 5.3.

Table 5.3 Brinson and Fachler attribution

	Portfolio weight w_i	Benchmark weight W_i	Portfolio return r_i	Benchmark return b_i	Asset allocation $(w_i - W_i) \times (b_i - b)$	Stock selection $w_i \times (r_i - b_i)$	Interaction $(w_i - W_i) \times (r_i - b_i)$
	(%)	(%)	(%)	(%)	(%)	(%)	(%)
UK equities	40	40	20	10	0.0	4.0	0.0
Japanese equities	30	20	−5	−4	−1.04	−0.2	−0.1
US equities	30	40	6	8	−0.16	−0.8	0.2
Total	*100*	*100*	*8.3*	*6.4*	*−1.2*	*3.0*	*0.1*

INTERACTION

A flaw of both Brinson models is the inclusion of the interaction or other term. Interaction is not part of the investment decision process; you are unlikely to identify in any asset management firm individuals responsible for adding value through interaction.

While it is true that interaction reflects the combined effect of asset allocation bets with stock selection decisions, portfolio managers simply do not seek to add value through interaction. For most investment decision processes the asset allocation decision comes first and stock selection decisions are taken after the cash has been allocated.

For genuine bottom-up stock pickers, asset allocation decisions are not made; therefore, the attribution model should reflect this process and measure the contribution of each stock decision to the overall performance, ignoring asset allocation.

Because interaction is not well understood, presumably because it is not intuitively part of the investment decision process, it is often abused. It may be ignored and not shown, randomly allocated to other factors, split proportionally or simply split 50:50 between stock selection and asset allocation and therefore potentially misleading the user.

Assuming the asset allocation decision comes first, then the contribution from stock selection must be:

$$r - b_s = \sum_{i=1}^{i=n} w_i \times r_i - \sum_{i=1}^{i=n} w_i \times b_i = \sum_{i=1}^{i=n} w_i \times (r_i - b_i) \tag{5.21}$$

The contribution to stock selection in the ith category is now:

$$S_i = w_i \times (r_i - b_i) \tag{5.22}$$

Figure 5.4 graphically demonstrates the revised impact on individual categories.

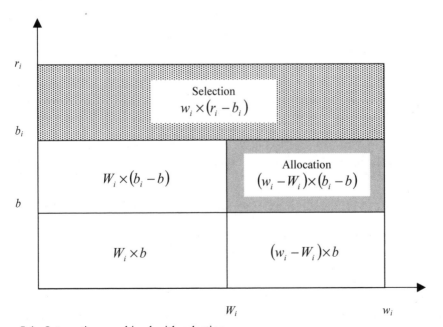

Figure 5.4 Interaction combined with selection.

Revised stock selection effects including interaction are calculated in Exhibit 5.6:

Exhibit 5.6   Stock selection including interaction

Total stock selection including interaction using the data from Table 5.1 is:

$$r - b_S = 8.3\% - 5.2\% = 3.1\%$$

Individual country stock selection effects are:

$$\text{UK equities}\quad 40\% \times (20\% - 10\%) = 4.0\%$$

$$\text{Japanese equities}\quad 30\% \times (-5.0\% - 4.0\%) = -0.3\%$$

$$\text{US equities}\quad 30\% \times (6.0\% - 8.0\%) = -0.6\%$$

$$Total\quad 4.0\% - 0.3\% - 0.6\% = 3.1\%$$

Table 5.4   Brinson and Fachler (stock selection and interaction combined)

	Portfolio weight w_i (%)	Benchmark weight W_i (%)	Portfolio return r_i (%)	Benchmark return b_i (%)	Asset allocation $(w_i - W_i) \times (b_i - b)$ (%)	Stock selection $w_i \times (r_i - b_i)$ (%)
UK equities	40	40	20	10	0.0	4.0
Japanese equities	30	20	−5	−4	−1.04	−0.3
US equities	30	40	6	8	−0.16	−0.6
Total	*100*	*100*	*8.3*	*6.4*	*−1.2*	*3.1*

Actual portfolio weights are now used to calculate stock selection effects. Stock pickers rightly point out that their contribution to stock selection is impacted by the weight of assets chosen by the asset allocator. This is true for either portfolio or benchmark weight; there is no particular advantage in calculating the stock selection impact had the portfolio been at the benchmark weight. Individual stock pickers should be judged by the performance within the asset category not their contribution to overall performance. The revised results are summarized in Table 5.4.

Rather than the Brinson quadrants of Figure 5.1, I prefer to think in terms of the steps of the investment decision process illustrated in Figure 5.5.

GEOMETRIC EXCESS RETURN ATTRIBUTION

The Brinson models described so far quantify arithmetic excess return. In Chapter 3 an alternative geometric definition of excess return was proposed to measure the added value of portfolio managers.

A number of geometric excess return attribution models (*geometric methods*) have been developed over the years (Allen, 1991; Bain, 1996; Burnie et al., 1998; Bacon, 2002). These methods are similar and in most cases were in use long before being published externally.

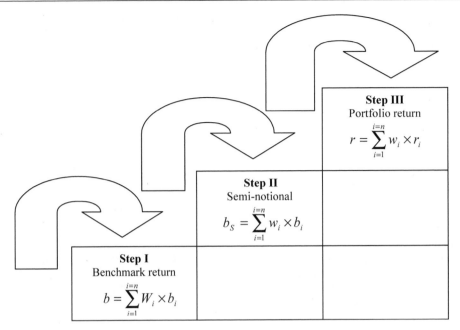

Figure 5.5 Brinson steps.

The Brinson model can be easily adapted to break down the geometric excess return:

$$\frac{(1+r)}{(1+b)} - 1 \tag{3.3}$$

Asset allocation

To identify the contribution from asset allocation we can use the same intermediate or semi-notional fund we used in the Brinson method, but this time using the geometric rather than the arithmetic difference:

$$\frac{(1+b_S)}{(1+b)} - 1 \tag{5.23}$$

The contribution to geometric asset allocation in the ith category is now:

$$A_i^G = (w_i - W_i) \times \left(\frac{1+b_i}{1+b} - 1 \right) \tag{5.24}$$

Note that the total geometric asset allocation A^G:

$$A^G = \sum_{i=1}^{i=n} A_i^G = \frac{(1+b_S)}{1+b} - 1 \tag{5.25}$$

Equation (5.24) is analogous to Equation (5.18); the geometric difference of the category return against the overall benchmark is used rather than the arithmetic difference. A more detailed proof can be found in Appendix A.

Stock selection

Similarly, to identify the total contribution to stock selection we can use the ratio between the portfolio return and the semi-notional return:

$$\frac{(1+r)}{(1+b_S)} - 1 \tag{5.26}$$

The contribution to geometric stock selection in the ith category is now:

$$S_i^G = w_i \times \left(\frac{1+r_i}{1+b_i} - 1\right) \times \frac{(1+b_i)}{(1+b_S)} \tag{5.27}$$

Equation (5.27) is not quite as expected on extension from Equation (5.22): there is an unexpected term $(1+b_i)/(1+b_S)$. This term is required because outperformance in a category whose benchmark return is already performing well will add more value geometrically than the equivalent outperformance in a category whose benchmark return is not performing well. Again a more detailed proof can be found in Appendix A.

Equation (5.27) simplifies to Equation (5.28) the arithmetic difference divided by the semi-notional fund preferred by Burnie et al.:

$$S_i^G = w_i \times \frac{(r_i - b_i)}{(1+b_S)} \tag{5.28}$$

Note that the total geometric stock selection S^G:

$$S^G = \sum_{i=1}^{i=n} S_i^G = \frac{(1+r)}{(1+b_S)} - 1 \tag{5.29}$$

Stock selection and asset allocation compound together to produce the geometric excess return:

$$\frac{(1+r)}{(1+b_S)} \times \frac{(1+b_S)}{(1+b)} - 1 = \frac{(1+r)}{(1+b)} - 1 \tag{5.30}$$

or

$$(1+S^G) \times (1+A^G) - 1 = \frac{(1+r)}{(1+b)} - 1 = g \tag{5.31}$$

The contribution to geometric excess return from asset allocation is calculated in Exhibit 5.7:

Exhibit 5.7   Geometric asset allocation

Geometric *asset allocation* for data in Table 5.1 is:

$$\frac{(1+b_S)}{(1+b)} - 1 = \frac{1.052}{1.064} - 1 = -1.13\%$$

Individual country asset allocation effects are:

$$\text{UK equities} \quad (40\% - 40\%) \times \left(\frac{1.10}{1.064} - 1\right) = 0.0\%$$

$$\text{Japanese equities} \quad (30\% - 20\%) \times \left(\frac{0.96}{1.064} - 1\right) = -0.98\%$$

$$\text{US equities} \quad (30\% - 40\%) \times \left(\frac{1.08}{1.064} - 1\right) = -0.15\%$$

$$Total \quad 0.0\% - 0.98\% - 0.15\% = -1.13\%$$

Given that the benchmark return is positive the geometric excess return is less than the arithmetic excess return. The contributions to asset allocation are of the same order but slightly less than the arithmetic asset allocation. The sign will always be the same. The contribution to geometric excess return from stock selection is calculated in Exhibit 5.8:

Exhibit 5.8   Geometric stock selection

Geometric stock selection including interaction for data in Table 5.1 is:

$$\frac{(1+r)}{(1+b_S)} - 1 = \frac{1.083}{1.052} - 1 = 2.95\%$$

Individual country stock selection effects are:

$$\text{UK equities} \quad 40\% \times \left(\frac{1.20}{1.10} - 1\right) \times \frac{1.10}{1.052} = 3.80\%$$

$$\text{Japanese equities} \quad 30\% \times \left(\frac{0.94}{0.95} - 1\right) \times \frac{0.95}{1.052} = -0.29\%$$

$$\text{US equities} \quad 30\% \times \left(\frac{1.06}{1.08} - 1\right) \times \frac{1.08}{1.052} = -0.57\%$$

$$Total \quad 3.80\% - 0.28\% - 0.57\% = 2.95\%$$

Again, as expected, the geometric stock selection effects are similar to the arithmetic stock selection effects but slightly smaller in magnitude. The geometric attribution effects are summarized in Table 5.5.

SECTOR WEIGHTS

In Brinson-type models (arithmetic or geometric) we have assumed from Equation (5.1) that the sum of the weights and returns for each asset category will equal the total portfolio return and that the weights will sum to 100%.

Table 5.5 Geometric attribution (stock selection and interaction combined)

	Portfolio weight w_i	Benchmark weight W_i	Portfolio return r_i	Benchmark return b_i	Asset allocation $(w_i - W_i) \times \left(\dfrac{1+b_i}{1+b} - 1\right)$	Stock selection $w_i \times \left(\dfrac{1+r_i}{1+b_i} - 1\right) \times \dfrac{(1+b_i)}{(1+b_S)}$
	(%)	(%)	(%)	(%)	(%)	(%)
UK equities	40	40	20	10	0.0	3.8
Japanese equities	30	20	−5	−4	−0.98	−0.29
US equities	30	40	6	8	−0.15	−0.57
Total	100	100	8.3	6.4	−1.13	2.95

To ensure Equation (5.1) holds we must use return calculation methodologies from Chapter 2 that can be disaggregated (i.e., broken down into the contributions to return from each active decision of the investment process).

The return methodology for each category, segment or sector must be identical to that used for the overall return. Because internal rates of return assume a single constant force of return throughout the period of measurement this methodology is not suitable for attribution.

The Dietz methodologies readily fit into the Brinson model since the returns can be disaggregated. Although the total return will be completely explained, transactions during the period of measurement may result in the contributions to asset allocation and stock selection being calculated incorrectly due to Dietz method weighting assumptions. The more detailed analysis of our standard attribution in Table 5.6 illustrates this point.

The portfolio returns used to calculate the attribution effects summarized in Table 5.5 have actually been calculated using a simple Dietz formula. Using time-weighted returns, summarized for each sub-period in Table 5.6, it would appear that US equities outperform rather than underperform the benchmark.

To calculate the true attribution we must calculate attribution effects for the period immediately before the cash flow and then after the cash flow, summarized in Table 5.7.

Table 5.6 More detailed analysis of our standard attribution

	UK equities	Japanese equities	US equities
Start value	£400	£400	£200
End value	£480	£185	£418
Cash flow	£0	−£200	£200
Market value at time of cash flow	N/A	£420	£220
Simple Dietz	$\dfrac{480 - 400}{400} = 20.0\%$	$\dfrac{185 - 400 + 200}{400 - \dfrac{200}{2}} = -5\%$	$\dfrac{418 - 200 - 200}{200 + \dfrac{200}{2}} = 6.0\%$
Time-weighted	$\dfrac{480}{400} - 1 = 20.0\%$	$\dfrac{420}{400} \times \dfrac{185}{220} - 1 = -11.7\%$	$\dfrac{220}{200} \times \dfrac{418}{420} - 1 = 9.48\%$

Table 5.7 Attribution effects for the period before and after the cash flow

	Portfolio weight (%)	Benchmark weight (%)	Portfolio return (%)	Benchmark return (%)	Asset allocation (%)	Stock selection (%)
1st period						
UK equities	40	40	10	10	0.0	0.0
Japanese equities	40	20	5	10	0.0	−1.8
US equities	20	40	10	10	0.0	0.0
Total	*100*	*100*	*8.0*	*10.0*	*0.0*	*−1.8*
2nd period						
UK equities	40.74	40	9.1	0.0	0.0	3.8
Japanese equities	20.37	20	−15.9	−12.7	−0.0	−0.7
US equities	38.89	40	−0.48	−1.8	−0.0	0.5
Total	*100*	*100*	*0.3*	*−3.3*	*−0.00*	*3.7*
Combined period						
UK equities	N/A	N/A	20.0	10	0.0	3.8
Japanese equities	N/A	N/A	−11.7	−4.0	0.0	−2.5
US equities	N/A	N/A	9.48	8.0	0.0	0.5
Total			*8.3*	*6.4*	*−0.0*	*1.8*

Over the entire period, asset allocation effects are minimal; all markets performed equally well in the first period and the bet sizes were small for the second period.

Our first attribution did not capture the portfolio's move to a neutral asset allocation position at the time of the cash flow. Although the original attribution reconciled, in this example Dietz-type returns do not provide the full picture as there has been a transfer of effects between asset allocation and stock selection caused by the choice of methodology.

In reality, US stock selection is much better than initially presented and Japanese stock selection much worse. The more frequent the attribution, ideally daily, the more accurate the result.

Illmer and Marty (2003) offer an alternative approach to time-weighted returns which decomposes the money-weighted return while capturing the effect of asset allocation decisions during the period; in particular, this approach captures the impact of external cash flows directed by the client. This allows the continued use of the money-weighted return with the impact of external cash flow isolated and defined as timing. To achieve this they calculate a benchmark return using a money-weighted methodology applying the cash flow enjoyed by the portfolio – an approach very similar in concept to the analyst's test method in Chapter 2. The chief advantage of this method is that it allows the continued use of money-weighted returns without the disruption often caused by large external or internal (between categories) cash flows.

Buy-and-hold (or holding-based) attribution

To simplify the attribution process some practitioners suggest an approximate approach to attribution which ignores the impact of transactions during the period of measurement called buy-and-hold attribution.

In this approach the beginning weights of securities and sectors together with their returns are used to calculate attribution effects. The returns are usually derived from another source and not derived from the actual portfolio return.

The advantage of this method is the ease of implementation; only the holdings need to be input into the attribution system. Proponents argue that returns are only estimates anyway, and valuations are uncertain and cannot be achieved if the portfolio manager wished to sell. Why worry too much about the accuracy of the methodology if the valuation is incorrect?

The big disadvantage of this approach is that the buy-and-hold return will not reconcile with the real return (good estimate or not) of the portfolio. This will lead to a residual between the real portfolio return and the return explained by attribution. A small residual will be of no concern, but often the residual will grow over time to become the single largest factor, thus invalidating the entire analysis. Residuals will tend to be larger for:

 (i) More active managers.
 (ii) If initial public offerings (IPOs) are a key part of the portfolio manager's strategy. The buy-and-hold approach tends to pick up the end-of-day price, not the float price.
(iii) Large cash flows.
(iv) Illiquid assets.
 (v) Longer measurement periods. The smaller the measurement period the better; but, even daily analysis can result in significant residuals.

If transaction information is not captured there is no opportunity to investigate the value added by the trading department. Since performance analysts using buy-and-hold attribution are not expecting the attribution to reconcile to the portfolio return, operational errors will not be spotted.

Spaulding (2003) provides a more balanced perspective on the various approaches. The alternative to buy-and-hold is transaction-based attribution in which holdings and transaction information is used to replicate the portfolio return.

The decision on whether to use buy-and-hold or transaction-based attribution will ultimately depend on the purpose for which the attribution will be used and the requirements of the asset manager. Buy-and-hold attribution may be acceptable for the exclusive internal use of the portfolio manager, but clients are not always tolerant of attribution residuals. Pragmatism is a key tool in the performance measurer's armoury; however, in this instance I would not compromise. Performance measurers rely on good-quality data, reconciled transaction-based attribution improves the quality of back office processes by providing a tool that quickly identifies operational errors and improves the general risk control environment of the firm.

Security-level attribution

If the investment decision process is genuinely bottom up, then it is not appropriate to calculate asset allocation effects. For security-level attribution the asset allocation process is effectively over- or underweighting an individual security. Traditional stock selection calculations effectively measure the ability to add value within that security by timing trades.

MULTI-PERIOD ATTRIBUTION

We observed in Chapter 3 that the sum of the arithmetic excess return for each finite period does not equal the total arithmetic excess return for the total period:

$$R - \bar{R} \neq \sum (R_t - \bar{R}_t) \tag{5.32}$$

Therefore, over multiple periods we should not expect our arithmetic attribution factors which add over single periods to add up for the total period under analysis.

SMOOTHING ALGORITHMS

Accepting that it is desirable for multiple period arithmetic attribution factors to add up over time, a number of methodologies (known as smoothing algorithms) have been developed to achieve this.

Carino

Carino (1999) suggests the results for the single period can be transformed into results that naturally cumulate over time. Continuously compounded returns may be summed as demonstrated in Equation (2.29). Using this relationship Carino introduces the factor:

$$k_t = \ln(1 + r_t) - \ln(1 + b_t) \tag{5.33}$$

If $r_t = b_t$ set:

$$k_t = \frac{1}{(1 + r_t)}$$

Since from Chapter 2 for continuously compounded returns we know that:

$$\ln(1 + r) = \ln(1 + r_1) + \ln(1 + r_2) + \cdots + \ln(1 + r_n) \tag{2.29}$$

and similarly for the benchmark:

$$\ln(1 + b) = \ln(1 + b_1) + \ln(1 + b_2) + \cdots + \ln(1 + b_n) \tag{5.34}$$

Subtracting Equation (5.34) from Equation (2.29):

$$\ln(1 + r) - \ln(1 + b) = \ln(1 + r_1) - \ln(1 + b_1) + \cdots + \ln(1 + r_n) - \ln(1 + b_n) \tag{5.35}$$

Substituting Equation (5.33) into Equation (5.35) and simplifying:

$$\ln(1+r) - \ln(1+b) = \sum_{t=1}^{T} k_t \times (r_t - b_t) \tag{5.36}$$

To transform back to the desired arithmetic difference Carino introduced a similar factor for the entire period:

$$k = \frac{\ln(1+r) - \ln(1+b)}{r - b} \tag{5.37}$$

Therefore, substituting Equation (5.37) into Equation (5.36):

$$r - b = \sum_{t=1}^{t=n} \frac{k_t}{k} \times (r_t - b_t) \tag{5.38}$$

It follows that:

$$r - b = \sum_{t=1}^{t=n} \frac{k_t}{k} \times A_t + \sum_{t=1}^{t=n} \frac{k_t}{k} \times S_t + \sum_{t=1}^{t=n} \frac{k_t}{k} \times I_t \tag{5.39}$$

Table 5.8 extends the example data in Table 5.1 over four quarters. The portfolio return for the year is now 3.86% and the benchmark return is −9.41%. The objective is to calculate annual attribution effects that add to the arithmetic excess return of 13.27%.

Carino factors are calculated for each period and the overall period in Exhibit 5.9:

Table 5.8 Data from Table 5.1 extended over four quarters

	Portfolio weight (%)	Benchmark weight (%)	Portfolio return (%)	Benchmark return (%)	Asset allocation (%)	Stock selection (%)
1st quarter						
UK equities	40	40	20	10	0.0	4.0
Japanese equities	30	20	−5	−4	−1.04	−0.3
US equities	30	40	6	8	−0.16	−0.6
Total	100	100	8.3	6.4	−1.2	3.1
2nd quarter						
UK equities	70	40	−5	−7	−0.72	1.4
Japanese equities	20	30	3	4	−0.86	−0.2
US equities	10	30	−5	10	1.08	0.5
Total	100	100	−3.4	−4.6	−0.5	1.7
3rd quarter						
UK equities	30	50	−20	−25	2.5	1.5
Japanese equities	50	40	8	5	1.75	1.5
US equities	20	10	−15	−20	−0.75	1.0
Total	100	100	−5.0	−12.5	3.5	4.0
4th quarter						
UK equities	30	40	10	5	−0.3	1.5
Japanese equities	50	40	−7	−5	−0.7	−1.0
US equities	20	20	25	10	0.0	3.0
Total	*100*	*100*	*4.5*	*2.0*	*−1.0*	*3.5*
Annual total			**3.86**	**−9.41**		

Exhibit 5.9   Carino factors

$$k_t = \frac{\ln(1 + r_t) - \ln(1 + b_t)}{r_t - b_t}$$

1st quarter $k_1 = \dfrac{(\ln 1.083 - \ln 1.064)}{(8.3\% - 6.4\%)} = 0.931\,56$

2nd quarter $k_2 = \dfrac{(\ln 0.966 - \ln 0.954)}{(-3.4\% + 4.6\%)} = 1.041\,68$

3rd quarter $k_3 = \dfrac{(\ln 0.95 - \ln 0.875)}{(-5.0\% + 12.5\%)} = 1.096\,51$

4th quarter $k_4 = \dfrac{(\ln 1.045 - \ln 1.02)}{(4.5\% - 2.0\%)} = 0.968\,57$

Year $k = \dfrac{(\ln 1.0386 - \ln 0.9059)}{(3.86\% + 9.41\%)} = 1.030\,13$

Using the Carino factors calculated in Exhibit 5.9 revised attribution effects can be calculated for the 1st quarter as shown in Exhibit 5.10:

Exhibit 5.10   Carino revised 1st-quarter attribution factors

UK asset allocation $0\% \times \dfrac{k_1}{k} = 0\% \times \dfrac{0.93156}{1.03013} = 0\%$

Japanese asset allocation $= -1.04\% \times \dfrac{0.93156}{1.03013} = -0.94\%$

US asset allocation $= -0.16\% \times \dfrac{0.93156}{1.03013} = -0.14\%$

UK stock selection $= 4.0\% \times \dfrac{0.93156}{1.03013} = 3.62\%$

Japanese stock selection $= -0.3\% \times \dfrac{0.93156}{1.03013} = -0.27\%$

US stock selection $= -0.6\% \times \dfrac{0.93156}{1.03013} = -0.54\%$

Extending the process in Exhibit 5.10 to all four quarters we can calculate revised attribution factors that sum to the arithmetic difference for the entire four-quarter period in Table 5.9.

The objective has been achieved in Table 5.9; our attribution factors are now additive. It should be noted that our revised attribution effects in each quarter are unique for that overall period. If we lengthen the period of analysis we will need to

Table 5.9 Revised attribution factors for the four-quarter period (Carino)

	Original arithmetic attribution		Revised Carino attribution	
	Asset allocation (%)	Stock selection (%)	Asset allocation (%)	Stock selection (%)
1st quarter				
UK equities	0.0	4.0	0.0	3.62
Japanese equities	−1.04	−0.3	−0.94	−0.27
US equities	−0.16	−0.6	−0.14	−0.54
Total	*−1.2*	*3.1*	*−1.09*	*2.80*
2nd quarter				
UK equities	−0.72	1.4	−0.73	1.42
Japanese equities	−0.86	−0.2	−0.87	−0.2
US equities	1.08	0.5	1.09	0.51
Total	*−0.5*	*1.7*	*−0.51*	*1.72*
3rd quarter				
UK equities	2.5	1.5	2.66	1.60
Japanese equities	1.75	1.5	1.86	1.60
US equities	−0.75	1.0	−0.8	1.06
Total	*3.5*	*4.0*	*3.73*	*4.26*
4th quarter				
UK equities	−0.3	1.5	−0.28	1.41
Japanese equities	−0.7	−0.1	−0.66	−0.94
US equities	0.0	3.0	0.0	2.82
Total	*−1.0*	*3.5*	*−0.94*	*3.29*
Four-quarter total				
UK equities			1.65	8.04
Japanese equities			−0.60	0.18
US equities			0.15	3.85
Total			*1.20*	*12.07*

	Portfolio return (%)	Benchmark return (%)	Asset allocation (%)	Stock selection (%)
Total	*3.86*	*−9.41*	*1.20*	*12.07*

recalculate new revised attribution effects for each quarter. This is both counter-intuitive and cumbersome, particularly if we wish to calculate attribution effects over a number of years.

Menchero

Menchero (2000) offers a similar if more sophisticated approach to Carino; he suggests the introduction of a constant factor M into Equation (5.32) that takes into account the characteristic scaling which arises from geometric compounding:

$$r - b \approx M \times \sum_{t=1}^{T}(r_t - b_t) \qquad (5.40)$$

Logically, Menchero chooses for M the ratio of the difference of the arithmetic average between portfolio and benchmark returns to the difference of the geometric average portfolio and benchmark returns:

$$M = \frac{(r - b)/T}{[(1+r)^{1/T} - (1+b)^{1/T}]} \qquad (5.41)$$

if $r = b$ set:

$$M = (1+r)^{(T-1)/T} \qquad (5.42)$$

Unfortunately, this still leaves a residual in Equation (5.40), which means we must calculate a corrective term α_t such that:

$$r - b = \sum_{t=1}^{t=T}(M + \alpha_t) \times (r_t - b_t) \qquad (5.43)$$

Calculating α_t as small as possible so that the linking coefficients $(M + \alpha_t)$ can be distributed as uniformly as possible to provide an "optimal solution", Menchero uses Lagrange multipliers to calculate:

$$\alpha_t = \left(\frac{r - b - M \times \sum_{t=1}^{t=T}(r_t - b_t)}{\sum_{t=1}^{t=T}(r_t - b_t)^2} \right) \times (r_t - b_t) \qquad (5.44)$$

It follows that:

$$r - b = \sum_{t=1}^{t=T}(M + \alpha_t) \times A_t + \sum_{t=1}^{t=T}(M + \alpha_t) \times S_t + \sum_{t=1}^{t=T}(M + \alpha_t) \times I_t \qquad (5.45)$$

Menchero factors are calculated for each period and the overall period for the data in Table 5.8 is shown in Exhibit 5.11:

Exhibit 5.11 Menchero factors

$$\alpha_t = \left(\frac{r - b - M \times \sum\limits_{t=1}^{t=T} (r_t - b_t)}{\sum\limits_{t=1}^{t=T} (r_t - b_t)^2} \right) \times (r_t - b_t)$$

$$M = \frac{(+3.86\% + 9.41\%)/4}{[(1.0386)^{1/4} - (0.9059)^{1/4}]} = 0.978\,13$$

$$\sum_{t=1}^{t=T} (r_t - b_t) = (8.3\% - 6.4\% - 3.4\% - 4.6\% - 5.0\% - 12.5\%$$

$$+ 4.5\% + 2\%) = 13.1\%$$

$$\sum_{t=1}^{t=T} (r_t - b_t)^2 = (1.9\%)^2 + (1.2\%)^2 + (7.5\%)^2 + (2.5\%)^2 = 0.6755\%$$

Therefore, for the data in Table in 5.8:

$$\alpha_t = \frac{(3.86\% + 9.41\% - 0.97813 \times 13.1\%)}{0.6755\%} \times (r_t - b_t) = 0.675\,79 \times (r_t - b_t)$$

1st quarter $\alpha_1 = 0.675\,79 \times (8.3\% - 6.4\%) = 0.012\,84$

2nd quarter $\alpha_2 = 0.675\,79 \times (-3.2\% + 4.6\%) = 0.009\,46$

3rd quarter $\alpha_3 = 0.675\,79 \times (-5.0\% + 12.5\%) = 0.050\,68$

4th quarter $\alpha_4 = 0.675\,79 \times (4.5\% - 2\%) = 0.016\,89$

Revised Menchero attribution effects for the 1st quarter are calculated in Exhibit 5.12.

Exhibit 5.12 Menchero revised attribution factors

UK asset allocation $= 0\% \times (M + \alpha_1) = 0\% \times (0.978\,13 + 0.012\,84) = 0\%$

Japanese asset allocation $= -1.04\% \times (0.978\,13 + 0.012\,84) = -1.03\%$

US asset allocation $= -0.16\% \times (0.978\,13 + 0.012\,84) = 0.16\%$

UK stock selection $= 4.0\% \times (0.978\,13 + 0.012\,84) = 3.96\%$

Japanese stock selection $= -0.3\% \times (0.978\,13 + 0.012\,84) = -0.3\%$

US stock selection $= -0.6\% \times (0.978\,13 + 0.012\,84) = -0.59\%$

Table 5.10 Revised attribution factors for the four-quarter period (Menchero)

	Original arithmetic attribution		Revised menchero attribution	
	Asset allocation (%)	Stock selection (%)	Asset allocation (%)	Stock selection (%)
1st quarter				
UK equities	0.0	4.0	0.0	3.96
Japanese equities	−1.04	−0.3	−1.03	−0.30
US equities	−0.16	−0.6	−0.16	−0.59
Total	*−1.2*	*3.1*	*−1.19*	*3.07*
2nd quarter				
UK equities	−0.72	1.4	−0.71	1.38
Japanese equities	−0.86	−0.2	−0.85	−0.2
US equities	1.08	0.5	1.07	0.49
Total	*−0.5*	*1.7*	*−0.49*	*1.68*
3rd quarter				
UK equities	2.5	1.5	2.57	1.54
Japanese equities	1.75	1.5	1.80	1.54
US equities	−0.75	1.0	−0.77	1.03
4th quarter				
UK equities	−0.3	1.5	−0.30	1.49
Japanese equities	−0.7	−1.0	−0.70	−0.99
US equities	0.0	3.0	0.0	2.98
Total	*−1.0*	*3.5*	*−0.99*	*3.48*
Four-quarter total				
UK equities			1.56	8.38
Japanese equities			−0.78	0.05
US equities			0.14	3.91
Total			*0.92*	*12.34*

	Portfolio return (%)	Benchmark return (%)	Asset allocation (%)	Stock selection (%)
Total	*3.86*	*−9.41*	*0.92*	*12.34*

Extending the process in Exhibit 5.12 to all four quarters we can calculate revised attribution factors that sum to the arithmetic difference for the entire four-quarter period in Table 5.10.

Again we have achieved our objective but with a slightly different solution from the Carino approach. Again it should be noted that our revised effects are unique for the overall period; it is necessary to recalculate each individual period's effects again as we lengthen the period of analysis. With the added disadvantage of complexity, this method is also counter-intuitive and cumbersome.

GRAP method

Carino and Menchero are examples of smoothing algorithms in which the natural residual of the multi-period arithmetic attribution is structurally distributed across all the contributions to performance.

GRAP (1997), a Paris-based working group of performance experts, proposed a different type of "linking" approach as follows: Let a_t = arithmetic excess return in period t. Then we have $r_1 = b_1 + a_1$ for period $t = 1$ and $r_2 = b_2 + a_2$ for period $t = 2$. The total return over the first two periods is therefore:

$$
\left.\begin{aligned}
(1 + r) &= (1 + b_1 + a_1) \times (1 + b_2 + a_2) \\
&= (1 + b_1 + a_1) \times (1 + b_2) + (1 + b_1 + a_1) \times a_2 \\
&= (1 + b_1) \times (1 + b_2) + a_1 \times (1 + b_2) + (1 + r_1) \times a_2 \\
&= (1 + b) + a_1 \times (1 + b_2) + (1 + r_1) \times a_2 \\
(r - b) &= a = a_1 \times (1 + b_2) + (1 + r_1) \times a_2
\end{aligned}\right\} \quad (5.46)
$$

In effect, the excess return for the 1st period is reinvested in the benchmark return of the 2nd period and the excess return of the 2nd period is compounded by the actual portfolio return in the 1st period.

Over n periods we can generalize:

$$
a = \sum_{T=1}^{n} a_T \times \prod_{t=1}^{T-1}(1 + r_t) \times \prod_{T+1}^{n}(1 + b_t) \quad (5.47)
$$

In effect, the excess return for period $t = T$ is compounded by the actual portfolio return up to period $t = T$ and reinvested in the benchmark thereafter.

It follows that:

$$
r - b = \sum_{T=1}^{n}(A_T + S_T + I_T) \times \prod_{t=1}^{T-1}(1 + r_t) \times \prod_{t=T+1}^{n}(1 + b_t) \quad (5.48)
$$

GRAP-revised 1st-quarter attribution effects are calculated in Exhibit 5.13:

Exhibit 5.13   GRAP-revised 1st-quarter attribution factors

UK asset allocation $= 0\% \times (1 + b_2) \times (1 + b_3) \times (1 + b_4) = 0\% \times 0.954$
$\times 0.875 \times 1.02 = 0\%$

Japanese asset allocation $= -1.04\% \times 0.954 \times 0.875 \times 1.02 = -0.89\%$

US asset allocation $= -0.16\% \times 0.954 \times 0.875 \times 1.02 = -0.14\%$

UK stock selection $= 4.0\% \times 0.954 \times 0.875 \times 1.02 = 3.41\%$

Japanese stock selection $= -0.3\% \times 0.954 \times 0.875 \times 1.02 = -0.26\%$

US stock selection $= -0.6\% \times 0.954 \times 0.875 \times 1.02 = -0.51\%$

GRAP-revised 2nd-quarter attribution effects are calculated in Exhibit 5.14:

Exhibit 5.14   GRAP-revised 2nd-quarter attribution factors

UK asset allocation $= -0.72\% \times (1 + r_1) \times (1 + b_3) \times (1 + b_4)$

$\qquad\qquad\qquad = -0.72\% \times 1.083 \times 0.875 \times 1.02 = -0.7\%$

Japanese asset allocation $= -0.86\% \times 1.083 \times 0.875 \times 1.02 = -0.83\%$

US asset allocation $= 1.08\% \times 1.083 \times 0.875 \times 1.02 = 1.04\%$

UK stock selection $= 1.4\% \times 1.083 \times 0.875 \times 1.02 = 1.35\%$

Japanese stock selection $= -0.2\% \times 1.083 \times 0.875 \times 1.02 = -0.19\%$

US stock selection $= 0.5\% \times 1.083 \times 0.875 \times 1.02 = 0.48\%$

Extending the process in Exhibits 5.13 and 5.14 to all four quarters we can calculate revised attribution factors that sum to the arithmetic difference for the entire four-quarter period as shown in Table 5.11.

Again the objective is achieved but with a different solution from either the Carino or Menchero approaches. Typically, GRAP is closer to Carino. Again, it should be noted that our revised effects are unique for the overall period; it is necessary to recalculate each individual period's effects again as we lengthen the period of analysis. Although still cumbersome I do find this approach slightly more intuitive.

Frongello

Frongello (2002) suggested a linking algorithm using the same concept as the GRAP method with:

$$f_T = a_T \times \prod_{t=1}^{t=T-1} (1 + r_t) + b_T \times \sum_{t=1}^{t=T-1} f_t \qquad (5.49)$$

where: $f_t =$ the revised Frongello attribution effect for period t.

The first part of this equation compounds the single-period arithmetic excess return a_T with the cumulative return of the actual portfolio up to the prior period, while the second part is the gain on the sum of the prior period Frongello-adjusted excess returns generated by the current benchmark return as demonstrated in Exhibit 5.15.

It follows that:

$$a = r - b = \sum_{T=1}^{T=n} (A_T + S_T + I_T) \times \prod_{t=1}^{t=T-1} (1 + r_t) + b_T \times \sum_{t=1}^{t=T-1} f_t$$

Table 5.11   Revised attribution factors for the entire four-quarter period

	Original arithmetic attribution		Revised GRAP attribution	
	Asset allocation (%)	Stock selection (%)	Asset allocation (%)	Stock selection (%)
1st quarter				
UK equities	0.0	4.0	0.0	3.41
Japanese equities	−1.04	−0.3	−0.89	−0.26
US equities	−0.16	−0.6	−0.14	−0.51
Total	*−1.2*	*3.1*	*−1.02*	*2.64*
2nd quarter				
UK equities	−0.72	1.4	−0.70	1.35
Japanese equities	−0.86	−0.2	−0.83	−0.19
US equities	1.08	0.5	1.04	0.48
Total	*−0.5*	*1.7*	*−0.48*	*1.64*
3rd quarter				
UK equities	2.5	1.5	2.67	1.60
Japanese equities	1.75	1.5	1.87	1.60
US equities	−0.75	1.0	−0.80	1.07
Total	*3.5*	*4.0*	*3.73*	*4.27*
4th quarter				
UK equities	−0.3	1.5	−0.30	1.49
Japanese equities	−0.7	−0.1	−0.70	−0.99
US equities	0.0	3.0	0.0	2.98
Total	*−1.0*	*3.5*	*−0.99*	*3.48*
Four-quarter total				
UK equities			1.67	7.85
Japanese equities			−0.55	0.16
US equities			0.11	4.02
Total			*1.24*	*12.03*

	Portfolio return (%)	Benchmark return (%)	Asset allocation (%)	Stock selection (%)
Total	*3.86*	*−9.41*	*1.24*	*12.03*

Exhibit 5.15   Frongello-revised 2nd-quarter attribution factors

Note Frongello 1st-period attribution effects are never adjusted:

UK asset allocation $= -0.72\% \times (1 + r_1) + b_2 \times f_1 = -0.72\%$

$$\times\ 1.083 - 0.046 \times 0.0\% = -0.78\%$$

Japanese asset allocation $= -0.86\% \times 1.083 - 0.046 \times -1.04\% = -0.88\%$

US asset allocation $= 1.08\% \times 1.083 - 0.046 \times -0.16\% = 1.18\%$

UK stock selection $= 1.4\% \times 1.083 - 0.046 \times 4.0\% = 1.33\%$

Japanese stock selection $= -0.2\% \times 1.083 - 0.046 \times -0.30\% = -0.2\%$

US stock selection $= 0.5\% \times 1.083 - 0.046 \times -0.6\% = 0.57\%$

Frongello-revised 3rd-quarter attribution effects are calculated in Exhibit 5.16:

Exhibit 5.16   Frongello-revised 3rd-quarter attribution factors

UK asset allocation $= 2.5\% \times (1 + r_1) \times (1 + r_2) + b_3 \times (f_2 + f_1) = 2.5\%$

$$\times 1.083 \times 0.966 - 0.125 \times (-0.78 + 0.0\%) = 2.71\%$$

Japanese asset allocation $= 1.75\% \times 1.083 \times 0.966 - 0.125 \times (-0.88\% - 1.04\%)$

$$= 2.07\%$$

US asset allocation $= -0.75\% \times 1.083 \times 0.966 - 0.125 \times (1.18\% - 0.16\%)$

$$= -0.91\%$$

UK stock selection $= 1.5\% \times 1.083 \times 0.966 - 0.125 \times (1.33\% + 4.0\%)$

$$= 0.9\%$$

Japanese stock selection $= 1.5\% \times 1.083 \times 0.966 - 0.125 \times (-0.2\% - 0.3\%)$

$$= 1.63\%$$

US stock selection $= 1.0\% \times 1.083 \times 0.966 - 0.125 \times (0.57\% - 0.6\%)$

$$= 1.05\%$$

Extending the process in Exhibits 5.15 and 5.16 to all four quarters we can calculate revised attribution factors that sum to the arithmetic difference for the entire four-quarter period in Table 5.12.

The Frongello method produces the same total period effects as the GRAP method for the total period. While 1st-quarter effects remain unaltered, subsequent quarters must be revised if the overall period is extended.

Davies and Laker

Davies and Laker (2001) refer back to Brinson et al.'s (1986) original article that suggested applying the Brinson model over multiple periods and also refer to the

Table 5.12   Revised attribution factors for the entire four-quarter period (Frongello)

	Original arithmetic attribution		Revised Frongello attribution	
	Asset allocation (%)	Stock selection (%)	Asset allocation (%)	Stock selection (%)
1st quarter				
UK equities	0.0	4.0	0.0	4.0
Japanese equities	−1.04	−0.3	−1.04	−0.3
US equities	−0.16	−0.6	−0.16	−0.6
Total	*−1.2*	*3.1*	*−1.2*	*3.1*
2nd quarter				
UK equities	−0.72	1.4	−0.78	1.33
Japanese equities	−0.86	−0.2	−0.88	−0.50
US equities	1.08	0.5	1.18	0.57
Total	*−0.5*	*1.7*	*−0.49*	*1.70*
3rd quarter				
UK equities	2.5	1.5	2.71	0.90
Japanese equities	1.75	1.5	2.07	1.63
US equities	−0.75	1.0	−0.91	1.05
Total	*3.5*	*4.0*	*3.87*	*3.58*
4th quarter				
UK equities	−0.3	1.5	−0.26	1.62
Japanese equities	−0.7	−1.0	−0.69	−0.97
US equities	0.0	3.0	0.0	3.00
Total	*−1.0*	*3.5*	*−0.95*	*3.65*
Four-quarter total				
UK equities			1.67	7.85
Japanese equities			−0.55	0.16
US equities			0.11	4.02
Total			*1.24*	*12.03*

	Portfolio return (%)	Benchmark return (%)	Asset allocation (%)	Stock selection (%)
Total	*3.86*	*−9.41*	*1.24*	*12.03*

work of Kirievsky and Kirievsky (2000). They suggest compounding each of the notional funds to derive the total attribution effects for multiple periods as follows:

$$\text{Arithmetic excess return over total period} \quad r - b = \prod_{t=1}^{t=n}(1 + r_t) - \prod_{t=1}^{t=n}(1 + b_t) \quad (5.50)$$

$$\text{Asset allocation} \quad \prod_{t=1}^{t=n}(1 + b_{S,t}) - \prod_{t=1}^{t=n}(1 + b_t) \quad (5.51)$$

where: $b_{S,t}$ = the semi-notional (allocation notional) fund in period t

$$b_S = \prod_{t=1}^{t=n}(1 + b_{S,t}) - 1.$$

$$\text{Stock selection} \quad \prod_{t=1}^{t=n}(1 + r_{S,t}) - \prod_{t=1}^{t=n}(1 + b_t) \qquad (5.52)$$

where: $r_{S,t}$ = the selection notional fund in period t

$$r_S = \prod_{t=1}^{t=n}(1 + r_{S,t}) - 1.$$

$$\text{Interaction} \quad \prod_{t=1}^{t=n}(1 + r_t) - \prod_{t=1}^{t=n}(1 + r_{S,t}) - \prod_{t=1}^{t=n}(1 + b_{S,t}) + \prod_{t=1}^{t=n}(1 + b_t) \qquad (5.53)$$

The Davies and Laker method establishes total contributions for allocation, selection and interaction. Their 2001 article did not address individual sector returns although it did hint at the use of a Carino-type algorithm to calculate individual sector contributions that add up to the total for each factor.

Using the data from Table 5.6 again, the Brinson notional fund is calculated for each quarter and compounded in Exhibit 5.17:

Exhibit 5.17   Brinson notional funds

Quarter 1

The allocation notional return $b_{S,1} = \sum_{i=1}^{i=n} w_i \times b_i$ for quarter 1 is:

$$b_{S,1} = 40\% \times 10\% + 30\% \times -4\% + 30\% \times 8\% = 5.2\%$$

The selection notional return $r_{S,1} = \sum_{i=1}^{i=n} W_i \times r_i$ for quarter 1 is:

$$r_{S,1} = 40\% \times 20\% + 20\% \times -5\% + 40\% \times 6\% = 9.4\%$$

Quarter 2

$$b_{S,2} = 70\% \times -7.0\% + 20\% \times 4.0\% + 10\% \times -10.0\% = -5.1\%$$
$$r_{S,2} = 40\% \times -5.0\% + 30\% \times 3.0\% + 30\% \times -5.0\% = -2.6\%$$

Quarter 3

$$b_{S,3} = 30\% \times -25\% + 50\% \times 5.0\% + 20\% \times -20.0\% = -9.0\%$$
$$r_{S,3} = 50\% \times -20.0\% + 40\% \times 8.0\% + 10\% \times -15\% = -8.3\%$$

Quarter 4

$$b_{S,4} = 30\% \times 5.0\% + 50\% \times -5.0\% + 20\% \times 10.0\% = 1.0\%$$

$$r_{S,4} = 40\% \times 10.0\% + 40\% \times -7.0\% + 20\% \times 25.0\% = 6.2\%$$

Compounded notional funds

$$\prod_{t=1}^{t=n}(1 + b_{S,t}) = 1.052 \times 0.949 \times 0.91 \times 1.01 = 0.9176$$

$$\prod_{t=1}^{t=n}(1 + r_{S,t}) = 1.094 \times 0.974 \times 0.917 \times 1.062 = 1.0377$$

Total or "exact" attribution effects are calculated for the entire period in Exhibit 5.18:

Exhibit 5.18   Exact attribution effects

$$r = \prod_{t=1}^{t=n}(1 + r_t) - 1 = 3.86\%$$

$$b = \prod_{t=1}^{t=n}(1 + b_t) - 1 = -9.41\%$$

$$r_S = \prod_{t=1}^{t=n}(1 + r_{S,t}) - 1 = 3.77\%$$

$$b_S = \prod_{t=1}^{t=n}(1 + b_{S,t}) - 1 = -8.24\%$$

Excess return   3.86% + 9.41% = 13.27%

Stock selection   3.77% + 9.41% = 13.18%

Asset allocation   − 8.24 + 9.41% = 1.16%

Interaction   3.86% − 3.77% + 8.24% − 9.41% = −1.07%

$$\underbrace{13.27\%}_{\text{Excess return}} = \underbrace{13.18\%}_{\text{Stock selection}} + \underbrace{1.17\%}_{\text{Asset allocation}} + \underbrace{-1.07\%}_{\text{Interaction}}$$

Only the total level attribution effect can be calculated this way. To establish the contribution from each category a smoothing algorithm must be used on each effect separately.

This method combines arithmetic and geometric concepts and is really an evolution stage between the arithmetic and full geometric methodologies.

The Davies and Laker method literally compounds the basic flaw of the Brinson model, interaction, with the result that this factor is even less meaningful. It is perhaps more sensible to combine interaction with stock selection defining stock selection as:

$$\prod_{t=1}^{t=n}(1 + r_t) - \prod_{t=1}^{t=n}(1 + b_{S,t}) \tag{5.54}$$

Therefore stock selection plus asset allocation fully explain excess return:

$$r - b = \underbrace{\prod_{t=1}^{t=n}(1 + r_t) - \prod_{t=1}^{t=n}(1 + b_{S,t})}_{\text{Stock selection}} + \underbrace{\prod_{t=1}^{t=n}(1 + b_{S,t}) - \prod_{t=1}^{t=n}(1 + b_t)}_{\text{Asset allocation}} \tag{5.55}$$

Multi-period geometric attribution

Multi-period geometric attribution does not suffer the same linking challenges as multi-period arithmetic attribution. Chapter 3 demonstrated that geometric excess returns compound over time. Geometric attribution effects also compound to provide the single-period excess return, therefore substituting Equation (5.31) into Equation (3.13):

$$\prod_{t=1}^{t=n}(1 + S_t^G) \times \prod_{t=1}^{t=n}(1 + A_t^G) - 1 = g \tag{5.56}$$

Table 5.13 summarizes the geometric attribution effects for all four quarters.

Unlike for multi-period arithmetic attribution there is no need to make continual adjustments as the total period of measurement extends. The total attribution effects compound as demonstrated in Exhibit 5.19:

Exhibit 5.19   Multi-period geometric attribution effects

Stock selection $1.0295 \times 1.0179 \times 1.044 \times 1.0347 - 1 = 13.19\%$

Asset allocation $0.9887 \times 0.9948 \times 1.04 \times 0.9902 - 1 = 1.29\%$

Geometric excess return $\dfrac{1.0386}{0.9059} - 1 = 1.1319 \times 1.0129 - 1 = 14.64\%$

In fact, the geometric total effects are the geometric equivalent of the Davies and Laker arithmetic effects as shown in Exhibit 5.20:

Exhibit 5.20   Geometric total effects

$$r = \prod_{t=1}^{t=n}(1 + r_t) - 1 = 3.86\%$$

$$b = \prod_{t=1}^{t=n}(1 + b_t) - 1 = -9.41\%$$

$$b_S = \prod_{t=1}^{t=n}(1 + b_{S,t}) - 1 = -8.24\%$$

$$\text{Excess return} \quad \frac{1+r}{1+b} - 1 = \frac{1.0386}{0.9059} - 1 = 14.64\%$$

$$\text{Stock selection} \quad \frac{1+r}{1+b_S} - 1 = \frac{1.0386}{0.9176} - 1 = 13.19\%$$

$$\text{Asset allocation} \quad \frac{1+b_S}{1+b} - 1 = \frac{0.9176}{0.9059} - 1 = 1.29\%$$

$$\underbrace{14.64\%}_{\text{Geometric excess return}} = \underbrace{1.1319}_{\text{Stock selection}} \times \underbrace{1.0129}_{\text{Asset allocation}} - 1$$

Table 5.13　Geometric attribution effects for all four quarters

	Geometric attribution	
	Asset allocation (%)	Stock selection (%)
1st quarter		
UK equities	0.0	3.8
Japanese equities	−0.98	−0.29
US equities	−0.15	−0.57
Total	*−1.13*	*2.95*
2nd quarter		
UK equities	−0.75	1.48
Japanese equities	−0.90	−0.21
US equities	1.13	0.53
Total	*−0.52*	*1.79*
3rd quarter		
UK equities	2.86	1.65
Japanese equities	2.00	1.65
US equities	−0.86	1.10
Total	*4.0*	*4.4*
4th quarter		
UK equities	−0.29	1.49
Japanese equities	−0.69	−0.99
US equities	0.0	2.97
Total	*−0.98*	*3.47*
Total	***1.29***	***13.19***

The total geometric attribution effects for each period need not be adjusted. Within each period the attribution effects for each category sum to the total geometric effect;

therefore, the unadjusted categories cannot be compounded in the same way as the totals. The individual category effects can be adjusted if desired so that they compound to the total effect by Equation (5.57):

$$\hat{S}_i + (1 + S_i) \times \left(\frac{1 + S}{\prod_{i=1}^{i=n}(1 + S_i)} \right)^{\left(|S_I| / \sum |S_i| \right)} - 1 \qquad (5.57)$$

where: $\hat{S}_i$ = adjusted geometric effect for category i.

Adjusted geometric effects for the first quarter are calculated for stock selection in Exhibit 5.21. The adjustments are quite small and need not be changed if the period of measurement is extended:

Exhibit 5.21   Adjusted stock selection

$$\prod_{i=1}^{i=n}(1 + S_i) = 1.038 \times 0.9971 \times 0.9943 = 1.02916$$

$$\sum |S_i| = 3.8\% + 0.29\% + 0.53\% = 4.62\%$$

$$\text{UK equities}\quad 1.038 \times \left(\frac{1.0295}{1.02916} \right)^{3.8\%/4.62\%} - 1 = 3.83\%$$

$$\text{Japanese equities}\quad 0.9971 \times \left(\frac{1.0295}{1.02916} \right)^{0.29\%/4.62\%} - 1 = -0.28\%$$

$$\text{US equities}\quad 0.9943 \times \left(\frac{1.0295}{1.02916} \right)^{0.57\%/4.62\%} - 1 = -0.57\%$$

$$\prod_{i=1}^{i=n}(1 + \hat{S}_i) = 1.0383 \times 0.9972 \times 0.9943 = 1.0295$$

For most scenarios the choice of linking method will not normally change the interpretation of results. I favour geometric excess returns and, therefore, I'm more comfortable with the geometric linking. For arithmetic excess returns I prefer the GRAP method.

RISK-ADJUSTED ATTRIBUTION

Brinson et al. (1991), in a follow-up article to their original, suggested that systematic risk measures such as beta or duration could be used in conjunction with their standard model. This is only appropriate if the portfolio manager is using systematic risk in the investment decision process. For example, an equity portfolio manager could choose to increase the beta of a category rather than or as well as going overweight to achieve an asset allocation effect. We can measure the impact of this decision in the standard Brinson model using the regression equation to calculate systematic risk-adjusted returns:

$$\text{Regression equation} \quad r_p - r_F = \alpha + \beta \times (b - r_F) + \varepsilon \tag{4.14}$$

Rearranging Equation (4.14) and ignoring the error term we can break down the return into selectivity or Jensen's alpha and the return derived from systematic risk:

$$r_p = \underbrace{\alpha}_{\text{Selectivity}} + \underbrace{r_F + \beta \times (b - r_F)}_{\text{Systematic risk}} \tag{5.58}$$

We can define an intermediate benchmark return adjusted for systematic risk b'_i:

$$b'_i = x_i + \beta_i \times (b_i - x_i) \tag{5.59}$$

where: x_i = risk-free rate in country i

b_i = benchmark return in country i

β_i = systematic risk in country i.

To identify the added value from asset allocation due to systematic risk we must calculate the return of an additional intermediate fund.

In this notional fund, adjusted for systematic risk, the asset allocation weights of the actual fund are applied to the risk-adjusted benchmark returns within each category:

$$\text{Systematic risk notional fund} \quad b'_S = \sum_{i=1}^{i=n} w_i \times b'_i \tag{5.60}$$

The total excess return is now the combination of three wealth ratios:

$$\frac{1+r}{1+b} - 1 = \underbrace{\frac{1+r}{1+b'_S}}_{\text{Selectivity}} \times \underbrace{\frac{1+b'_S}{1+b_S}}_{\text{Systematic risk}} \times \underbrace{\frac{1+b_S}{1+b}}_{\text{Asset allocation}} - 1 \tag{5.61}$$

Selectivity

To identify the total contribution to selectivity we can use the ratio between the portfolio return and the systematic risk-adjusted notional return:

$$\frac{(1+r)}{(1+b'_S)} - 1 \tag{5.62}$$

The contribution to selectivity in the ith category is now:

$$S'_i = w_i \times \left(\frac{1+r_i}{1+b'_i} - 1 \right) \times \frac{(1+b'_i)}{(1+b'_S)} \tag{5.63}$$

Table 5.14 Standard data example with risk-free rate and beta

	Portfolio weight (%)	Benchmark weight (%)	Portfolio return (%)	Benchmark return (%)	Risk-free rate (%)	β
UK equities	40	40	20	10	1.0	1.3
Japanese equities	30	20	−5	−4	0.1	1.0
US equities	30	40	6	8	0.2	0.8
Total	*100*	*100*	*8.3*	*6.4*		

To calculate the contribution from systematic risk we can use the ratio of the systematic risk notional fund with the semi-notional fund:

$$\frac{(1 + b'_S)}{(1 + b_S)} - 1 \tag{5.64}$$

The contribution from systematic risk in the ith category is now:

$$R_i = w_i \times \left(\frac{1 + b'_i}{1 + b_i} - 1 \right) \times \frac{(1 + b_i)}{(1 + b_S)} \tag{5.65}$$

The asset allocation term is unchanged.

Our standard data example is extended in Table 5.14 to include the risk-free rate for each market and the beta. We must make the assumption the portfolio manager is using beta as part of the asset allocation process.

Using the regression equation we can calculate risk-adjusted benchmark returns and, therefore, calculate the attribution effects for selectivity and systematic risk as shown in Exhibits 5.22, 5.23 and 5.24, respectively:

Exhibit 5.22 Return adjusted for systematic risk

Revised benchmark returns adjusted for systematic risk:

UK equities $x_i + \beta_i \times (b_i - x_i) = 1.0\% + 1.3 \times (10.0\% - 1.0\%) = 12.7\%$

Japanese equities $0.1\% + 1.0 \times (-4.0\% - 0.1\%) = -4.0\%$

US equities $0.2\% + 0.8 \times (8.0\% - 0.2\%) = 6.44\%$

Systematic risk notional fund:

$$b'_S = 40\% \times 12.7\% + 30\% \times -4\% + 30\% \times 6.44\% = 5.81\%$$

Exhibit 5.23   Selectivity

$$\frac{(1+r)}{(1+b'_S)} - 1 = \frac{1.083}{1.0581} - 1 = 2.35\%$$

Individual country selectivity effects are:

UK equities $40\% \times \left(\frac{1.20}{1.127} - 1\right) \times \frac{1.127}{1.052} = 2.76\%$

Japanese equities $30\% \times \left(\frac{0.94}{0.95} - 1\right) \times \frac{0.95}{1.052} = -0.28\%$

US equities $30\% \left(\frac{1.06}{1.08} - 1\right) \times \frac{1.08}{1.052} = -0.12\%$

Total $2.76\% - 0.28\% - 0.12\% = 2.35\%$

Exhibit 5.24   Systematic risk

$$\frac{(1+b'_S)}{(1+b_S)} - 1 = \frac{1.0581}{1.052} - 1 = 0.58\%$$

Individual country selectivity effects are:

UK equities $40\% \times \left(\frac{1.20}{1.127} - 1\right) \times \frac{1.127}{1.052} = 2.76\%$

Japanese equities $30\% \times \left(\frac{0.94}{0.95} - 1\right) \times \frac{0.95}{1.052} = -0.28\%$

US equities $30\% \times \left(\frac{1.06}{1.08} - 1\right) \times \frac{1.08}{1.052} = -0.12\%$

Total $2.76\% - 0.28\% - 0.12\% = 2.35\%$

Asset allocation effects are unchanged from before. The revised risk-adjusted attribution summary is shown in Table 5.15. The systematic risk asset allocation and asset allocation effects can be compounded to calculate the overall asset allocation effect. Note there is now a contribution to UK equity allocation of 1.03% due to the high beta greater than 1 in a rising market. In effect, part of the 20.0% return is due to high systematic risk and is therefore not entirely stock selection.

Since portfolios are rarely managed in this manner risk-adjusted attribution for equities is seldom used.

Table 5.15 Risk-adjusted attribution

	Portfolio weight w_i	Benchmark weight W_i	Portfolio return r_i	Benchmark return b_i	Asset allocation $(w_i - W_i)$ $\times \left(\dfrac{1+b_i}{1+b} - 1\right)$	Systematic risk allocation $w_i \times \left(\dfrac{1+b_i'}{1+b_i} - 1\right)$ $\times \dfrac{(1+b_i)}{(1+b_S)}$	Selectivity $w_i \times \left(\dfrac{1+r_i}{1+b_i'} - 1\right)$ $\times \dfrac{(1+b_i')}{(1+b_S')}$
	(%)	(%)	(%)	(%)	(%)	(%)	(%)
UK equities	40	40	20	10	0.0	1.03	2.76
Japanese equities	30	20	−5	−4	−0.98	0.0	−0.28
US equities	30	40	6	8	−0.15	−0.44	−0.12
Total	*100*	*100*	*8.3*	*6.4*	*−1.13*	*0.58*	*2.35*

MULTI-CURRENCY ATTRIBUTION

Ankrim and Hensel

Ankrim and Hensel (1992) recognized that the currency return is comprised of two components: the unpredictable "currency surprise" and the predictable interest-rate differential or "forward premium" between the appropriate currencies.

Let S_i^t = the spot rate of currency i at time t, and F_i^{t+1} = the forward exchange rate of currency i at time t for conversion through a forward contract at time $t+1$. Then, the return of currency i is:

$$c_i = \frac{S_i^{t+1} - S_i^t}{S_i^t} = \frac{S_i^{t+1}}{S_i^t} - 1 \tag{5.66}$$

Expanding Equation (5.66):

$$c_i = \frac{S_i^{t+1} - F_i^{t+1} + F_i^{t+1} - S_i^t}{S_i^t} \tag{5.67}$$

We can break down the currency return into:

$$\text{Currency surprise in currency } i \quad e_i = \frac{S_i^{t+1} - F_i^{t+1}}{S_i^t} \tag{5.68}$$

and

$$\text{Forward premium in currency } i \quad d_i = \frac{F_i^{t+1} - S_i^t}{S_i^t} = \frac{F_i^{t+1}}{S_i^t} - 1 \tag{5.69}$$

The currency return is the sum of the currency surprise plus the forward premium or interest-rate differential:

$$c_i = e_i + d_i \tag{5.70}$$

We can now expand Equation (5.1) as follows:

$$r = \sum_{i=1}^{i=n} w_i \times (r_i - e_i - d_i) + \sum_{i=1}^{i=n} w_i \times e_i + \sum_{i=1}^{i=n} w_i \times d_i \tag{5.71}$$

Isolating forward currency contracts separately in Equation (5.71):

$$r = \sum_{i=1}^{i=n} w_i \times (r_i - e_i - d_i) + \sum_{i=1}^{i=n} w_i \times e_i + \sum_{i=1}^{i=n} w_i \times d_i + \sum_{i=1}^{i=n} \tilde{w}_i \times f_i \qquad (5.72)$$

where: The return to forward currency contracts is:

$$f_i = \frac{S_i^{t+1} - F_i^{t+1}}{F_i^{t+1}} = \frac{S_i^{t+1}}{F_i^{t+1}} - 1 \qquad (5.73)$$

$\tilde{w}_i =$ weight of currency forward contact in currency i.

Note the forward return is linked to the currency surprise by the formula:

$$f_i = \frac{e_i}{(1 + d_i)} \qquad (5.74)$$

In effect, forward currency contracts economically consist of two currencies: one with a positive weight and one negative.

Assuming that the currency returns, currency forward returns, currency surprise and forward premiums are the same in both the portfolio and the benchmark, then it follows that the benchmark return can be constructed as:

$$b = \sum_{i=1}^{i=n} W_i \times (b_i - e_i - d_i) + \sum_{i=1}^{i=n} W_i \times e_i + \sum_{i=1}^{i=n} W_i \times d_i + \sum_{i=1}^{i=n} \tilde{W}_i \times f_i \qquad (5.75)$$

where: $\tilde{W}_i =$ benchmark weight of currency forward contact in currency i.

Applying the standard Brinson approach to Equations (5.72) and (5.75), we derive the following attribution effects:

$$\text{Asset allocation}\quad A_i = (w_i - W_i) \times (l_i - l) \qquad (5.76)$$

where: $l_i = b_i - e_i - d_i = b_i - c_i$ $\qquad (5.77)$

The arithmetic difference between the benchmark return in base currency and the currency return. Not quite the local return, which can only be derived by using the geometric difference.

$$l = \sum_{i=1}^{i=n} w_i \times l_i \qquad (5.78)$$

The revised weighted average benchmark return adjusting for currency.

$$\text{Security selection excluding interaction}\quad S_i = W_i \times (k_i - l_i) \qquad (5.79)$$

where: $k_i = r_i - e_i - d_i = r_i - c_i$ $\qquad (5.80)$

The arithmetic difference between the portfolio return in base currency and the currency return.

$$\text{Interaction}\quad I_i = (w_i - W_i) \times (k_i - l_i) \qquad (5.81)$$

Or, if you prefer security selection including stock selection:

$$S_i = w_i \times (k_i - l_i) \tag{5.82}$$

The contribution from currency is analogous to asset allocation:

$$C_i = \underbrace{(w_i - W_i) \times (e_i - e)}_{\text{Underlying assets}} + \underbrace{(\tilde{w}_i - \tilde{W}_i) \times (f_i - e)}_{\text{Currency forwards}} \tag{5.83}$$

where: C_i = contribution to currency from currency i

$$e = \sum_{i=1}^{i=n} W_i \times e_i \tag{5.84}$$

Weighted average benchmark currency surprise.

The final term, forward premium, is also analogous to asset allocation:

$$D_i = (w_i - W_i) \times (d_i - d) \tag{5.85}$$

where: D_i = contribution to forward premium in currency i

$$d = \sum_{i=1}^{i=n} W_i \times d_i \tag{5.86}$$

Weighted average benchmark forward premium.

Extending the basic data in Table 5.1 to Table 5.16 results in a multi-currency account including currency forward contracts and base currency of sterling.

Exhibit 5.25 calculates the portfolio and benchmark returns for the data in Table 5.16.

Table 5.16 Ankrim and Hensel

	Portfolio weight w_i (%)	Benchmark weight W_i (%)	Portfolio base return r_i (%)	Benchmark base return b_i (%)	Currency return c_i (%)	Currency surprise e_i (%)	Forward premium d_i (%)
UK equities	40	40	20	10.0	0	0	0
Japanese equities	30	20	4.5	5.6	10	9	1
US equities	30	40	27.2	29.6	20	18	2
	$\tilde{w}_i$ (%)	$\tilde{W}_i$ (%)		f_i (%)			
Sterling forward contracts	+20	+30		0			
Yen forward contracts	−15	−10		8.91			
US dollar forward contracts	−5	−20		17.65			
Total	*100*	*100*	*15.29*	*12.54*			

Exhibit 5.25   Return calculations for Ankrim and Hensel

Using Table 5.16 the portfolio return is:

$$r = 40\% \times 20\% + 30\% \times 4.5\% + 30\% \times 27.2\% - 15\%$$
$$\times 8.91\% - 5\% \times 17.65 = 15.29\%$$

The benchmark return is:

$$b = 40\% \times 10\% + 20\% \times 5.6\% + 40\% \times 29.6\% - 10\% \times 8.91 - 20\%$$
$$\times 17.65 = 12.54\%$$

The weighted average benchmark currency surprise is:

$$e = 40\% \times 0.0\% + 20\% \times 9.0\% + 40\% \times 18\% = 9.0\%$$

The weighted average benchmark forward premium is:

$$d = 40\% \times 0.0\% + 20\% \times 1.0\% + 40\% \times 2.0\% = 1.0\%$$

The revised weighted average benchmark return premium is:

$$l = 40\% \times (10.0\% - 0.0\%) + 20\% \times (5.6\% - 10.0\%) + 40\%$$
$$\times (29.6\% - 20.0\%) = 6.96\%$$

Ankrim and Hensel asset allocation effects are calculated in Exhibit 5.26. The asset allocation bets are exactly as before but the individual country returns and the revised benchmark return now include the compounding effect of market and currency returns, thus impacting the calculation of asset allocation effects. This compounding effect has changed the total asset allocation effect in Exhibit 5.5 from −1.2% to −1.4%.

Exhibit 5.26   Asset allocation (Ankrim and Hensel)

$$(w_i - W_i) \times (l_i - l)$$

UK equities $(40\% - 40\%) \times [(10.0\% - 0.0\%) - 6.96\%] = 0.0\%$

Japanese equities $(30\% - 20\%) \times [(5.6\% - 10.0\%) - 6.96\%] = -1.14\%$

US equities $(30\% - 40\%) \times [(29.6\% - 20.0\%) - 6.96\%] = -0.26\%$

Total $0.0\% - 1.14\% - 0.26\% = -1.4\%$

Security selection effects are calculated in Exhibit 5.27. There is no compounding effect for UK equities; therefore, the result is the same as in Exhibit 5.6. However, the Japanese and US equities stock selection has been impacted by currency compounding, dramatically in the case of US equities changing the effect from −0.6% to −0.96. For completeness the revised interaction effects are shown in Exhibit 5.28.

Exhibit 5.27   Stock selection (Ankrim and Hensel)

$$W_i \times (k_i - l_i)$$

UK equities $40\% \times [(20.0\% - 0.0\%) - (10.0\% - 0.0\%)] = 4.0\%$

Japanese equities $20\% \times [(4.5\% - 10.0\%) - (5.6\% - 10.0\%)] = -0.22\%$

US equities $40\% \times [(27.2\% - 20.0\%) - (29.6\% - 20.0\%)] = -0.96\%$

Total $4.0\% - 0.22\% - 0.96\% = 2.82\%$

Exhibit 5.28   Interaction (Ankrim and Hensel)

$$(w_i - W_i) \times (k_i - l_i)$$

UK equities $(40\% - 40\%) \times [(20\% - 0.0\%) - (10.0\% - 0.0\%)] = 0.0\%$

Japanese equities $(30\% - 20\%) \times [(4.5\% - 10\%) - (5.6\% - 10.0\%)] = -0.11\%$

US equities $(30\% - 40\%) \times [(27.2\% - 20\%) - (29.6\% - 20\%)] = 0.24\%$

Total $0.0\% - 0.11\% + 0.24\% = 0.13\%$

Currency allocation is calculated in Exhibit 5.29. From the underlying assets there is no contribution from sterling since there is no bet and no contribution from yen since, although there is a 10% overweight position, the currency surprise in yen is equal to the weighted average benchmark surprise. There is, however, a −0.9% contribution from a 10% underweight position in the strongly performing US dollar.

Currency forward contracts also contribute to the added value from currency management. Even though this is a sterling-based account it is possible to add value by being underweight sterling, in this example caused by being 10% underweight the benchmark hedged position, sterling underperforming both the yen and US dollar. In the benchmark the currency positions caused by the index weights in the underlying markets has been 50% hedged. Very little impact is caused by the underweight yen bet, but the overweight US dollar forward contract more than offsets the underweight underlying assets position and contributes +1.3%.

Exhibit 5.29   Currency management (Ankrim and Hensel)

Underlying assets $(w_i - W_i) \times (e_i - e)$

Sterling $(40\% - 40\%) \times (0.0\% - 9.0\%) = 0.0\%$

Yen $(30\% - 20\%) \times (9.0\% - 9.0\%) = 0.0\%$

US dollar $(30\% - 40\%) \times (18.0\% - 9.0\%) = -0.9\%$

$$\text{Currency forwards} \quad (\tilde{w}_i - \tilde{W}_i) \times (f_i - e)$$
$$\text{Sterling} \quad (20\% - 30\%) \times (0.0\% - 9.0\%) = 0.9\%$$
$$\text{Yen} \quad (-15\% + 10\%) \times (8.91\% - 9.0\%) = 0.0\%$$
$$\text{US dollar} \quad (-5\% + 20\%) \times (17.65\% - 9.0\%) = 1.3\%$$
$$\textit{Total} \quad 0.0\% + 0.0\% - 0.9\% + 0.9\% + 0.0\% + 1.3\% = 1.3\%$$

Forward premium effects tend to be small, particularly over short periods. In Exhibit 5.30 the impact of being underweight the US dollar caused by the underlying asset allocations contributes −0.1%.

Exhibit 5.30   Forward premium (Ankrim and Hensel)

$$(w_i - W_i) \times (d_i - d)$$
$$\text{Sterling} \quad (40\% - 40\%) \times (0.0\% - 1.0\%) = 0.0\%$$
$$\text{Yen} \quad (30\% - 20\%) \times (1.0\% - 1.0\%) = 0.0\%$$
$$\text{US dollar} \quad (30\% - 40\%) \times (2.0\% - 1.0\%) = -0.1\%$$
$$\textit{Total} \quad 0.0\% + 0.0\% - 0.1\% = -0.1\%$$

Total attribution effects are summarized in Table 5.17.

Table 5.17   Ankrim and Hensel attribution

	Asset allocation $(w_i - W_i)$ $\times (l_i - l)$ (%)	Stock selection $W_i \times (k_i - l_i)$ (%)	Forward premium $(w_i - W_i)$ $\times (d_i - d)$ (%)	Currency management $(w_i - W_i)$ $\times (e_i - e)$ (%)	Interaction $(w_i - W_i)$ $\times (k_i - l_i)$ (%)
UK equities	0.0	4.0	0.0	0.0	0.0
Japanese equities	−1.14	−0.22	0.0	0.0	−0.11
US equities	−0.26	−0.96	−0.10	−0.9	0.24
				$(\tilde{w}_i - \tilde{W}_i)$ $\times (f_i - e)$ (%)	
Sterling forward contracts				0.9	
Yen forward contracts				0.0	
US dollar forward contracts				1.3	
Total	*−1.40*	*2.82*	*−0.10*	*1.30*	*0.13*
Total excess return					**2.75**

There are a number of problems with the Ankrim and Hensel approach:

(i) The main problem is the use of an arithmetic return premium k. This ignores the compounding effect between market and currency returns and distributes this effect across asset allocation, stock selection and interaction.

(ii) The forward premium returns are isolated as a separate factor. In reality, this effect is always a consequence of asset allocation decisions. The asset allocator should be cognizant of forward premiums' effects; to avoid abuse, these effects should always be included with asset allocation.

(iii) The reference benchmark currency effect e is unaffected by hedging changes to the benchmark.

Karnosky and Singer

Karnosky and Singer (1994) resolved the issue of compounding by using continuously compounded returns in their model and solved the forward premium concern by thinking in terms of "return premium" above local interest rates.

They defined the total return on the portfolio as:

$$r = \sum_{i=1}^{i=n} w_i \times r_{Li} + \sum_{i=1}^{i=n} w_i \times c_i \qquad (5.87)$$

where: $r_{Li} =$ return in local currency for currency i.

Expanding Equation (5.87):

$$r = \sum_{i=1}^{i=n} w_i \times (r_{Li} - x_i) + \sum_{i=1}^{i=n} w_i \times (c_i + x_i) \qquad (5.88)$$

where: $x_i =$ interest rate in currency i.

Isolating forward currency contracts separately in Equation (5.88):

$$r = \sum_{i=1}^{i=n} w_i \times (r_{Li} - x_i) + \sum_{i=1}^{i=n} w_i \times (c_i + x_i) + \sum_{i=1}^{i=n} \tilde{w}_i \times f_i \qquad (5.89)$$

Note, using continuously compounded returns, that:

$$f_i = c_i + x_i - x_B$$

where: $x_B =$ interest rate in base currency.

If $\sum_{i=1}^{i=n} \tilde{w}_i = 0$, then $\sum_{i=1}^{i=n} \tilde{w}_i \times f_i = \sum_{i=1}^{i=n} c_i + x_i$ and Equation (5.89) simplifies to:

$$r = \sum_{i=1}^{i=n} w_i \times (r_{Li} - x_i) + \sum_{i=1}^{i=n} (w_i + \tilde{w}_i) \times (c_i + x_i) \qquad (5.90)$$

It follows that:

$$b = \sum_{i=1}^{i=n} W_i \times (b_{Li} - x_i) + \sum_{i=1}^{i=n} (W_i + \tilde{W}_i) \times (c_i + x_i) \qquad (5.91)$$

where: b_{Li} = benchmark return in local currency for currency i.

Applying the standard Brinson approach to Equations (5.90) and (5.91) we derive the following attribution effects:

$$\text{Asset allocation} \quad A_i = (w_i - W_i) \times (l'_i - l') \qquad (5.92)$$

where: $l'_i = b_{Li} - x_i$ is the benchmark return premium

$$l' = \sum_{i=1}^{i=n} W \times l'_i \text{ is the average benchmark return premium} \qquad (5.93)$$

This definition of asset allocation includes the forward premium effect in the benchmark return premium.

Security selection excluding interaction:

$$S_i = W_i \times (k'_i - l'_i) \qquad (5.94)$$

where: $k'_i = r_{Li} - x_i$ is the portfolio return premium $\qquad (5.95)$

$$\text{Interaction} \quad I_i = (w_i - W_i) \times (k'_i - l'_i) \qquad (5.96)$$

Or if you prefer security selection including interaction:

$$S_i = w_i \times (k'_i - l'_i) \qquad (5.97)$$

The contribution from currency is analogous to asset allocation:

$$C_i = \underbrace{(w_i - W_i) \times (c_i + x_i - c')}_{\text{Underlying assets}} + \underbrace{(\tilde{w}_i - \tilde{W}_i) \times (c_i + x_i - c')}_{\text{Currency forwards}} \qquad (5.98)$$

where: $c' = \sum_{i=1}^{i=n} (w_i + \tilde{W}_i) \times (c_i + x_i) \qquad (5.99)$

The example data in Table 5.16 is adapted for use by Karnosky and Singer in Table 5.18.

Total portfolio and benchmark returns are verified and the local benchmark return premium and currency benchmark calculated in Exhibit 5.31:

Exhibit 5.31   Total portfolio and benchmark returns for Karnosky and Singer

Using Table 5.18 the portfolio return is:

$r = 40\% \times (20.0\% + 0.0\%) + 30\% \times (-5.0\% + 10.0) + 30\% \times (6.0\% + 20.0\%)$

$\quad + 20\% \times (4.0\% + 0.0\%) - 15\% \times (3.0\% + 10.0\%) - 10\%$

$\quad \times (2.0\% + 20.0\%) = 15.05\%$

Note that these are continuously compounded returns and hence we use slightly different data from the standard example. Local market and currency returns are added, not compounded. The benchmark return is:

$$b = 40\% \times (10.0\% + 0.0\%) + 20\% \times (-4.0\% + 10.0\%) + 40\%$$
$$\times (8.0\% + 20.0\%)$$
$$+ 40.0\% \times (4.0\% + 0.0\%) - 10\% \times (3.0\% + 10.0\%) - 20\%$$
$$\times (2.0\% + 20.0\%) = 11.9\%$$

The average local benchmark return premium is:

$$l' = 40\% \times (10.0\% - 4.0\%) + 20\% \times (-4.0\% - 3.0\%) + 40\%$$
$$\times (8.0\% - 2.0\%) = 3.4\%$$

The currency plus interest benchmark return is:

$$c' = 40\% \times (4.0\% + 0.0\%) + 20\% \times (3.0\% + 10.0\%)$$
$$+ 40\% \times (2.0\% + 20\%)$$
$$= 8.5\%$$

Table 5.18 Karnosky and Singer

	Portfolio weight w_i (%)	Benchmark weight W_i (%)	Portfolio local return r_{Li} (%)	Benchmark local return b_{Li} (%)	Local interest rates x_i (%)	Currency return c_i (%)
UK equities	40	40	20	10.0	4.0	0
Japanese equities	30	20	−5.0	−4.0	3.0	10
US equities	30	40	6.0	8.0	2.0	20
	$\tilde{w}_i$ (%)	$\tilde{W}_i$ (%)				
Sterling forward contracts	+20	+30			4.0	0
Yen forward contracts	−15	−10			3.0	10
US dollar forward contracts	−5	−20			2.0	20
Total	*100*	*100*	*8.3*	*6.4*		
Total base currency return			**15.05**	**11.9**		

Asset allocation effects using the return premium are calculated in Exhibit 5.2:

Exhibit 5.32   Asset allocation (Karnosky and Singer)

$$(w_i - W_i) \times (l_i' - l')$$

UK equities $(40\% - 40\%) \times [(10.0\% - 4.0\%) - 3.4\%] = 0.0\%$

Japanese equities $(30\% - 20\%) \times [(-4.0\% - 3.0\%) - 3.4\%] = -1.04\%$

US equities $(30\% - 40\%) \times [(8.0\% - 2.0\%) - 3.4\%] = -0.26\%$

$Total$ $0.0\% - 1.04\% - 0.26\% = -1.3\%$

Stock selection effects based on local portfolio returns are calculated in Exhibit 5.33:

Exhibit 5.33   Stock selection including interaction (Karnosky and Singer)

$$w_i \times (k_i' - l_i')$$

UK equities $40\% \times [(20.0\% - 4.0\%) - (10.0\% - 4.0\%)] = 4.0\%$

Japanese equities $30\% \times [(-5.0\% - 3.0\%) - (-4.0\% - 3.0\%)] = -0.3\%$

US equities $30\% \times [(6.0\% - 2.0\%) - (8.0\% - 2.0\%)] = -0.6\%$

$Total$ $4.0\% - 0.3\% - 0.6\% = 3.1\%$

The currency management effect including forward currency contracts is calculated in Exhibit 5.34 (note the currency benchmark is essentially currency plus cash):

Exhibit 5.34   Currency management (Karnosky and Singer)

Underlying assets $(w_i - W_i) \times (c_i + x_i - c')$

Sterling $(40\% - 40\%) \times [(4.0\% + 0.0\%) - 8.5\%] = 0.0\%$

Yen $(30\% - 20\%) \times [(3.0\% + 10.0\%) - 8.5\%] = 0.45\%$

US dollar $(30\% - 40\%) \times [(2.0\% + 20.0\%) - 8.5\%] = -1.35\%$

Currency forwards $(\tilde{w}_i - \tilde{W}_i) \times (c_i + x_i - c')$

Sterling $(20\% - 30\%) \times [(4.0\% + 0.0\%) - 8.5\%] = 0.45\%$

Yen $(-15\% - 10\%) \times [(3.0\% + 10.0\%) - 8.5\%] = -0.23\%$

US dollar $(-5\% - 20\%) \times [(2.0\% + 20.0\%) - 8.5\%] = 2.03\%$

$Total$ $0.0\% + 0.45\% - 1.35\% + 0.45\% - 0.23\% + 2.03\% = 1.35\%$

Table 5.19 Karnosky and Singer attribution

	Asset allocation $(w_i - W_i) \times (l'_i - l')$ (%)	Stock selection $w_i \times (k'_i - l'_i)$ (%)	Currency management $(w_i - W_i) \times (c_i + x_i - c')$ (%)
UK equities	0.0	4.0	0.0
Japanese equities	−1.04	−0.30	0.45
US equities	−0.26	−0.60	−1.35
			$(\tilde{w}_i - \tilde{W}_i) \times (c_i + x_i - c')$ (%)
Sterling forward contracts			0.45
Yen forward contracts			−0.23
US dollar forward contracts			2.03
Total	*−1.30*	*3.1*	*+1.35*
Total excess return			**3.15**

The Karnosky and Singer attribution effects are summarized in Table 5.19.

GEOMETRIC MULTI-CURRENCY ATTRIBUTION

Because of the geometric relationship between market and currency returns it is essential to continue to use the geometric definition of excess return for multi-currency attribution.

Naive currency attribution

Attributing all the factors impacting multi-currency performance is quite complex. Fortunately, there is a simple short-hand, but incomplete method for calculating currency attribution: I call this "naive currency attribution".

We have already established the total portfolio returns in the base currency as:

$$r = \sum_{i=1}^{i=n} w_i \times r_i \qquad (2.33 \text{ or } 5.1)$$

and in local currency:

$$r_L = \sum_{i=1}^{i=n} w_i \times r_{Li} \qquad (2.37)$$

Similarly for the benchmark:

$$b = \sum_{i=1}^{i=n} W_i \times b_i \qquad (5.2)$$

and in local currency the "weighted average local benchmark return":

$$b_L = \sum_{i=1}^{i=n} W_i \times b_{Li} \qquad (5.100)$$

and defining in local currency the semi-notional local return:

$$b_{SL} = \sum_{i=1}^{i=n} w_i \times b_{Li} \qquad (5.101)$$

By definition, the currency performance of the portfolio must be the relative difference between the portfolio performance in base currency and the weighted total local return of the portfolio:

$$r'_C = \frac{1+r}{1+r_L} - 1 \qquad (5.102)$$

Likewise, the currency performance of the benchmark is defined as the relative difference between the performance of the benchmark in base currency and the performance of the benchmark in local currency:

$$b'_C = \frac{1+b}{1+b_L} - 1 \qquad (5.103)$$

The naive currency attribution is the ratio of the currency return of the portfolio relative to the currency return of the benchmark:

$$\left(\frac{\dfrac{1+r}{1+r_L}}{\dfrac{1+b}{1+b_L}}\right) - 1 \qquad (5.104)$$

which can be rewritten as:

$$\left(\frac{1+r}{1+r_L}\right) \times \left(\frac{1+b_L}{1+b}\right) - 1 \qquad (5.105)$$

In this naive version of currency attribution we can calculate our normal attribution effects of stock selection and allocation in local currency as follows:

$$\text{Stock selection} \quad \frac{1+r_L}{1+b_{SL}} - 1 \qquad (5.106)$$

$$\text{Asset allocation} \quad \frac{1+b_{SL}}{1+b_L} - 1 \qquad (5.107)$$

$$\text{Total currency effects} \quad \left(\frac{1+r}{1+r_L}\right) \times \left(\frac{1+b_L}{1+b}\right) - 1 \qquad (5.108)$$

We can then see that these factors compound to give:

$$\left(\frac{1+r_L}{1+b_{SL}}\right) \times \left(\frac{1+b_{SL}}{1+b_L}\right) \times \left(\frac{1+r}{1+r_L}\right) \times \left(\frac{1+b_L}{1+b}\right) - 1 = \frac{1+r}{1+b} - 1 \qquad (5.109)$$

Extending our existing example to Table 5.20, including currency but with no forward currency contracts for the time being and expressed in the base currency of sterling, base currency returns are calculated in Exhibit 5.35:

Table 5.20 Multi-currency geometric

	Portfolio weight w_i (%)	Benchmark weight W_i (%)	Portfolio local return r_{Li} (%)	Benchmark local return b_{Li} (%)	Portfolio base return r_i (%)	Benchmark base return b_i (%)	Currency return c_i (%)
UK equities	40	40	20	10	20	10.0	0
Japanese equities	30	20	−5	−4	4.5	5.6	10
US equities	30	40	6	8	27.2	29.6	20
Total	*100*	*100*	*8.3*	*6.4*	*17.5*	*17.0*	

Exhibit 5.35 Multi-currency attribution returns

Using Table 5.20 the local portfolio return is:

$$r_L = 40\% \times 20\% + 30\% \times -5\% + 30\% \times 6\% = 8.3\%$$

The weighted average local benchmark return is:

$$b_L = 40\% \times 10\% + 20\% \times -4\% + 40\% \times 8\% = 6.4\%$$

The local semi-notional return is:

$$b_{SL} = 40\% \times 10\% + 30\% \times -4\% + 30\% \times 8\% = 5.2\%$$

The base currency (£) return of the portfolio:

$$r = 40\% \times 20\% + 30\% \times 4.5\% + 30\% \times 27.2\% = 17.51\%$$

The base currency (£) return of the benchmark:

$$b = 40\% \times 10\% + 20\% \times 4.6\% + 40\% \times 29.6\% = 16.96\%$$

Exhibit 5.36 Naive currency attribution

The currency return in the portfolio is:

$$r'_C = \frac{1+r}{1+r_L} - 1 = \frac{1.1751}{1.083} - 1 = 8.50\%$$

The currency return in the benchmark is:

$$b'_C = \frac{1+b}{1+b_L} - 1 = \frac{1.1696}{1.064} - 1 = 9.92\%$$

The *naive currency allocation* is therefore:

$$\frac{1+r'_C}{1+b'_C} - 1 = \frac{\dfrac{1+r}{1+r_L}}{\dfrac{1+b}{1+b_L}} - 1 = \frac{1.0850}{1.0992} - 1 = -1.29\%$$

Naive currency attribution is a fairly straightforward calculation geometrically, as shown in Exhibit 5.36. Using the data in Table 5.20 the return from currency in the portfolio is 8.5% and the return from currency in the benchmark is 9.92%; therefore, the added value from currency management must be the ratio between the portfolio currency return with the benchmark currency return: -1.29%.

Exhibit 5.37   Multi-currency stock selection

From before (Exhibit 5.8) total *stock selection* in local currency is:

$$\frac{1+r_L}{1+b_{SL}} - 1 = \frac{1.083}{1.052} - 1 = 2.95\%$$

Individual country stock selection effects are:

UK equities $w_i \times \left(\frac{1+r_{Li}}{1+b_{Li}} - 1\right) \times \frac{1+b_{Li}}{1+b_S} = 30\% \times \left(\frac{1.2}{1.1} - 1\right) \times \frac{1.1}{1.052} = 3.8\%$

Japanese equities $30\% \times \left(\frac{0.95}{0.96} - 1\right) \times \frac{0.96}{1.052} = -0.29\%$

US equities $40\% \times \left(\frac{1.06}{1.08} - 1\right) \times \frac{1.08}{1.052} = -0.57\%$

Total $3.8\% - 0.29\% - 0.57\% = 2.95\%$

The asset allocation shown in Exhibit 5.38 is unchanged from Exhibit 5.7. It is labelled "naive" because it does not include the interest differential effects identified by Ankrim and Hensel and Karnosky and Singer.

Exhibit 5.38   Multi-currency asset allocation (naive)

From Exhibit 5.7 asset allocation is:

$$\frac{(1+b_S)}{(1+b)} - 1 = \frac{1.052}{1.064} - 1 = -1.13\%$$

Individual country asset allocation effects are:

UK equities $(w_i - W_i) \times \left(\frac{1+b_{Li}}{1+b_L} - 1\right) = (40\% - 40\%)$

$$\times \left(\frac{1.10}{1.064} - 1\right) = 0.0\%$$

Japanese equities $(30\% - 20\%) \times \left(\frac{0.96}{1.064} - 1\right) = -0.98\%$

US equities $(30\% - 40\%) \times \left(\frac{1.08}{1.064} - 1\right) = -0.15\%$

Total $0.0\% - 0.98\% - 0.15\% = -1.13\%$

The naive currency attribution results are summarized in Table 5.21.

Table 5.21 Naive currency attribution

	Portfolio weight w_i	Benchmark weight W_i	Portfolio return r_i	Benchmark return b_i	Asset allocation $(w_i - W_i)$ $\times\left(\dfrac{1+b_{Li}}{1+b_L} - 1\right)$	Stock selection $w_i \times \left(\dfrac{1+r_{Li}}{1+b_{Li}} - 1\right)$ $\times \dfrac{1+b_{Li}}{1+b_S}$	Naive currency allocation $\left(\dfrac{1+r}{1+r_L}\right)$ $\times\left(\dfrac{1+b_L}{1+b}\right) - 1$
	(%)	(%)	(%)	(%)	(%)	(%)	(%)
UK equities	40	40	20	10	0.0	3.8	
Japanese equities	40	20	4.7	5.6	−0.98	−0.28	
US equities	30	40	28.0	29.6	−0.15	−0.57	
Total	*100*	*100*	*17.51*	*16.96*	*−1.13*	*2.95*	*−1.29*

Compounding effects

An unavoidable but calculable complication in multi-currency portfolios is the impact of changing currency exposure due to the changing market values of the underlying assets.

Genuine "currency overlay" managers are unaware of changing market values (either in the portfolio or benchmark) and are only obliged to respond when they are informed of market value changes. Therefore, if the currency management is independent we must isolate these compounding effects.

The currency return of the benchmark in the ith currency can be calculated as follows:

$$c_i = \frac{1+b_i}{1+b_{Li}} - 1 \tag{5.110}$$

Because most commercial international indexes use the same spot rates,* benchmark currency returns for each currency will be consistent and equivalent to Equation (5.66).

Currency returns from Table 5.20 are calculated in Exhibit 5.39. For simplicity, note that in Table 5.20 the currency returns in the portfolio are identical to the currency returns in our benchmark.

Exhibit 5.39 Currency returns

The currency returns of the data in Table 5.20 are therefore:

$$\text{Sterling} \quad \frac{1.1}{1.1} - 1 = 0\% \quad \textit{(clearly, since this is a sterling-based account)}$$

$$\text{Japanese yen} \quad \frac{1.056}{0.96} - 1 = 10\%$$

$$\text{US dollar} \quad \frac{1.296}{1.08} - 1 = 20\%$$

---

*WM Reuters 4 o'clock London close.

Constructing the total currency return from the weights and returns of the benchmark we establish:

$$b_C = \sum W_i \times c_i \qquad (5.111)$$

Exhibit 5.40   Currency benchmark

$$b_C = 40\% \times 0\% + 20\% \times 10.0\% + 40\% \times 20.0\% = 10.0\%$$

The currency benchmark calculated in Exhibit 5.40 differs from the defined benchmark currency return in Exhibit 5.36 of 9.92%. This is caused by the changing market values of the underlying assets during the period of measurement. In this example the falling Japanese market reduces exposure to the raising yen, which is only partially offset, by the increased exposure to the US dollar caused by the rising US market.

The total impact of compounding within the benchmark is:

$$\frac{1.1}{1.0992} - 1 = 0.07\%$$

Constructing the total currency return of the portfolio we get:

$$r_C = \sum w_i \times c_i \qquad (5.112)$$

Exhibit 5.41   Calculated portfolio currency

$$r_C = 40\% \times 0\% + 30\% \times 10.0\% + 30\% \times 20.0\% = 9.0\%$$

The calculated portfolio currency in Exhibit 5.41 also differs from the defined portfolio currency in Exhibit 5.36 of 8.5%. The impact of compounding within the portfolio is therefore:

$$\frac{1.085}{1.09} - 1 = -0.46\%$$

The combined compounding impact in both the portfolio and benchmark is therefore:

$$0.9954 \times 1.0007 = -0.39\%$$

Clearly, it is inappropriate to allocate this effect to currency overlay managers unaware of market movements between points of measurement. The effects in this example portfolio are unusually large and normally only amount to a few basis points, particularly if measurement periods are maintained as short as possible, preferably daily.

Other geometric attribution multi-currency methodologies (Bain, 1996; McLaren, 2001) recognize this impact but suggest addressing this issue by adjusting market weights to calculate revised stock and allocation effects.*

---

* McLaren provides a choice of which factor to impact, determined by the order of the investment decision processes.

Interest-rate differentials

A further complicating factor in multi-currency portfolios is the exposure of currency managers to interest-rate differentials between currencies as they take currency "bets".

Ankrim and Hensel recognize the impact of interest-rate differentials by identifying a separate forward premium effect, while Karnosky and Singer recognize this effect by using the return premium of the local market return above local interest rates.

From a practical perspective I differ from Karnosky and Singer in taking the view that interest-rate differentials need only be used when the portfolio manager has deviated from the benchmark. The benchmark position is a given, the client may have already taken into account the return premium in allocating that benchmark to the portfolio manager.

The key point of understanding from a practical perspective is that a currency manager can only change the currency allocation of a portfolio by using currency forward contracts or similar instruments exposed to interest-rate differentials.

Forward currency contracts are priced by reference to the interest-rate differential between the relevant currencies. Therefore, any currency manager wishing to take a currency allocation "bet" must be exposed to the costs (or benefits) of these interest-rate differentials. In other words, the forward currency return rather than the spot currency return must be used to measure currency allocation effects.

Currency managers will have to respond to the decisions of country allocators. When country allocators take overweight or underweight country bets they generate currency positions. To maintain a neutral currency position these overweight and underweight positions should be "hedged to neutral". Because there is a cost (or benefit) associated with the forward currency contacts required to hedge to neutral, this cost or benefit should be borne by the country allocator, not the currency manager.

The currency return between spot rates can be broken down to the forward currency return and the forward premium (or interest-rate differential) as follows:

$$c_i = \frac{S_i^{t+1}}{S_i^t} - 1 \qquad (5.53)$$

Defining the return on a forward currency contract as:

$$f_i = \frac{S_i^{t+1}}{F_i^{t+1}} - 1 \qquad (5.59)$$

The interest-rate differential or forward premium in currency i:

$$d_i = \frac{F_i^{t+1}}{S_i^t} - 1 \qquad (5.55)$$

The currency return is therefore:

$$\frac{S_i^{t+1}}{S_i^t} = \frac{S_i^{t+1}}{F_i^{t+1}} \times \frac{F_i^{t+1}}{S_i^t} = (1 + f_i) \times (1 + d_i) \qquad (5.113)$$

Currency allocation

True currency allocation from the currency overlay manager's perspective should ignore the compounding effects of currency with market returns, focusing on the measured currency returns ignoring compounding.

The total relative measured currency performance is:

$$\frac{1 + r_C}{1 + b_C} - 1 \qquad (5.114)$$

r_C and b_C can now be redefined to include forward currency contracts:

$$r_C = \sum w_i \times c_i + \sum \tilde{w}_i \times f_i \qquad (5.115)$$

$$b_C = \sum_{i=1}^{i=n} W_i \times c_i + \sum_{i=1}^{i=n} \tilde{W}_i \times f_i \qquad (5.116)$$

Recognizing that, from the currency manager's perspective, any variation in the underlying asset position from the benchmark should be notionally represented by a forward return, not a spot return, the semi-notional currency return including notional forward returns for underlying asset allocation is:

$$c_{SH} = \sum_{i=1}^{i=n} W_i \times c_i + \sum (w_i - W_i + \tilde{w}_i) \times f_i \qquad (5.117)$$

Note that in Equation (5.117) for any currency bet the forward rate is used, while the benchmark is derived using spot rates.

Total currency allocation is therefore the ratio between currency semi-notional fund including notional forward returns and the measured benchmark currency return:

$$\frac{1 + c_{SH}}{1 + b_C} - 1 \qquad (5.118)$$

Any "bet" caused by the currency manager must be generated by a forward currency contract (notional or actual); then, the forward currency rate must be used to measure the contribution of that decision.

Currency allocation is analogous to country allocation, and we use a similar formula to calculate currency allocation attributing relative performance to currency in the ith currency as follows:

$$(w_i + \tilde{w}_i - W_i - \tilde{W}_i) \times \left(\frac{1 + f_i}{1 + c_i} - 1 \right) \qquad (5.119)$$

Extending Table 5.20 to include forward currency contracts in Table 5.22, we can calculate revised currency returns in Exhibit 5.42.

In the benchmark currency return, spot-rate returns are used for equity market exposures – physical assets generate the exposure, not forward currency contracts. Forward currency rates are only used if there is an element of hedging in the benchmark description. This differs from the Karnosky and Singer method, which assumes any investment in overseas assets generates a return premium (i.e., must be hedged back to the base currency). Only the variance from benchmark is exposed to interest-rate differentials.

Table 5.22 Multi-currency geometric

	Portfolio weight w_i (%)	Benchmark weight W_i (%)	Benchmark currency return c_i (%)	Benchmark hedged return b_{Hi} (%)
UK equities	40	40	0	10.0
Japanese equities	30	20	10	−3.0
US equities	30	40	20	10.0

	$\tilde{w}_i$ (%)	$\tilde{W}_i$ (%)	Forward currency return f_i (%)	
Sterling forward contracts	+20	+30	0	
Yen forward contracts	−15	−10	8.9	
US dollar forward contracts	−5	−20	17.8	
Total	*100*	*100*	*5.55*	

Exhibit 5.42 Revised currency returns

The revised benchmark currency return including forward contracts from Table 5.22 is:

$$b_C = 40\% \times 0\% + 20\% \times 10.0\% + 40\% \times 20.0\%$$
$$+ 30\% \times 0\% - 10\% \times 8.9\% - 20\% \times 17.8\% = 5.55\%$$

Currency semi-notional hedged to neutral:

$$c_{SH} = 40\% \times 0\% + 20\% \times 10.0\% + 40\% \times 20.0\% + (40\% - 40\% + 20\%)$$
$$\times 0.0\% + (30\% - 20\% - 15\%) \times 8.9\% + (30\% - 40\% - 5\%)$$
$$\times 17.9\% = 6.88\%$$

Currency allocation is calculated using forward currency rates for real forward currency positions and currency positions caused by country "bets" in Exhibit 5.43:

Exhibit 5.43 Currency allocation

$$\frac{1 + c_{SH}}{1 + b_C} - 1 = \frac{1.0688}{1.0555} = 1.26\%$$

Calculating for individual currencies:

$$\text{Sterling} \quad (60\% - 70\%) \times \left(\frac{1.0}{1.0555} - 1 \right) = 0.53\%$$

$$\text{Yen} \quad (15\% - 10\%) \times \left(\frac{1.089}{1.0555} - 1 \right) = 0.16\%$$

$$\text{US dollar} \quad (25\% - 20\%) \times \left(\frac{1.178}{1.0555} - 1 \right) = 0.58\%$$

$$\textit{Total} \quad 0.53\% + 0.16\% + 0.58\% = 1.26\%$$

In Exhibit 5.43 we have assumed all currency positions are created by forward currency contacts and hence used currency forward returns rather than spot returns to measure currency attribution.

In this exhibit the portfolio has benefited from being underweight sterling and overweight both the US dollar and Japanese yen.

Cost of hedging

The cost or benefit caused by physical currency positions must be borne by the country allocator. To do this we can use hedged indexes rather than local indexes to measure the true impact of the country allocator. The cost or benefit is in effect transferred from currency allocation because forwards have already been used to reflect the underlying assets bet.

Revised semi-notional return including hedge to neutral:

$$b_{SH} = \sum_{i=1}^{i=n} W_i \times b_{Li} + \sum_{i=1}^{i=n} (w_i - W_i) \times b_{Hi} \tag{5.120}$$

The revised semi-notional return including hedging caused by country bets is calculated in Exhibit 5.44 and revised country allocation is calculated in Exhibit 5.45.

The approach in Equation (5.120) is clearly designed for top-down investment decision processes including country allocation. It is possible to use a similar approach for bottom-up security selection processes, and industry sector allocation investment decision processes, assuming currency is not part of the security selection process.

The added value from country allocation has fallen from -1.13% to -1.22% because it "costs" 0.09% to hedge the exposed currency positions caused by the asset allocator's decision. The currency manager does not bear this cost, but it is reflected for the country allocator in the revised semi-notional return "hedged to neutral".

Exhibit 5.44   Semi-notional "hedged to neutral"

$$b_{SH} = 40\% \times 10.0\% + 20\% \times -4.0\% + 40\% \times 8.0\%$$
$$+ (40\% - 40\%) \times 10\% + (30\% - 20\%) \times -3.0\% + (30\% - 40\%)$$
$$\times 10.0\% = 5.1\%$$

Exhibit 5.45   Revised country allocation

$$\frac{1+b_{SH}}{1+b_L} - 1 = \frac{1.051}{1.064} - 1 = -1.22\%$$

UK allocation $(40\% - 40\%) \times \left(\frac{1.1}{1.064} - 1\right) = 0.0\%$

Japanese allocation $(30\% - 40\%) \times \left(\frac{0.97}{1.064} - 1\right) = -0.88\%$

US allocation $(30\% - 40\%) \times \left(\frac{1.1}{1.064} - 1\right) = -0.34\%$

Total $0.0\% - 0.88\% - 0.34\% = -1.22\%$

Forward currency contracts will impact the portfolio and benchmark market values, and therefore change the impact of compounding as shown in Exhibit 5.46:

Exhibit 5.46   Revised compounding effects

The implied portfolio currency return in Table 5.22 is:

$$r'_C = \frac{1+r}{1+r_L} - 1 = \frac{1.153}{1.083} - 1 = 6.45\%$$

The measured currency return (not adjusting for notional currency bets):

$$r_C = 40\% \times 0\% + 30\% \times 10.0\% + 30\% \times 20.0\%$$
$$+ 20\% \times 0\% - 15\% \times 8.9\% + -5\% \times 17.8\% = 6.78\%$$

The compounding impact within the portfolio is therefore:

$$\frac{1+r'_C}{1+r_C} = \frac{1.0645}{1.0678} - 1 = -0.30\%$$

The implied currency return in the benchmark is:

$$b'_C = \frac{1+b}{1+b_L} - 1 = \frac{1.125}{1.064} - 1 = 5.74\%$$

The compounding impact within the benchmark is therefore:

$$\frac{1+b_C}{1+b'_C} = \frac{1.0555}{1.0574} - 1 = -0.18\%$$

Total compounding effect:

$$\frac{1.0645}{1.0678} \times \frac{1.0555}{1.0574} - 1 = -0.49\%$$

Updated portfolio returns are shown in Table 5.23, leading to the revised attribution in Table 5.24.

Table 5.23   Updated portfolio returns

	Portfolio weight w_i (%)	Benchmark weight W_i (%)	Portfolio local return r_{Li} (%)	Benchmark local return b_{Li} (%)	Portfolio base return r_i (%)	Benchmark base return b_i (%)	Currency return c_i (%)
UK equities	40	40	20	10	20	10.0	0
Japanese equities	30	20	−5	−4	4.5	5.6	10
US equities	30	40	6	8	27.2	29.6	20
	$\tilde{w}_i$ (%)	$\tilde{W}_i$ (%)				Forward currency return f_i (%)	
Sterling forward contracts	+20	+30	N/A	N/A		0	
Yen forward contracts	−15	−10	N/A	N/A		8.9	
US dollar forward contracts	−5	−20	N/A	N/A		17.9	
Total	*100*	*100*	*8.3*	*6.4*	*15.3*	*12.5*	

Table 5.24   Multi-currency geometric attribution

	Asset allocation (%)	Stock selection (%)	Currency allocation (%)	Compounding (%)	
UK equities	0	3.8	0.53		
Japanese equities	−0.88	−0.29	0.16		*Total excess*
US equities	−0.34	−0.57	0.58		*return* *(%)*
Total	*−1.22*	*2.95*	*1.26*	*−0.49*	*2.47*

Currency timing (or currency selection)

Up to this point we have assumed that the currency return for each currency in the portfolio is the same as the benchmark currency return; in real portfolios this is rarely the case. Transactions will take place at exchange rates other than the exchange rates used to calculate indexes. This effect is analogous to stock selection and is called currency selection or currency timing.

The portfolio currency return in currency i is:

$$c'_i = \frac{1 + r_i}{1 + r_{Li}} - 1 \tag{5.121}$$

Let the portfolio forward currency return in currency i be f'_i.

We must redefine the portfolio measured currency return r_C again to include actual portfolio currency and forward returns:

$$r_C = \sum_{i=1}^{i=n} w_i \times c'_i + \sum_{i=1}^{i=n} \tilde{w}_i \times f'_i \tag{5.122}$$

To measure the impact of timing we need to compare it with a currency semi-notional fund utilizing benchmark currency and forward returns:

able 5.25   Revised attribution data

	Portfolio weight w_i (%)	Benchmark weight W_i (%)	Portfolio local return r_{Li} (%)	Benchmark local return b_{Li} (%)	Portfolio base return r_i (%)	Benchmark base return b_i (%)	Currency return c_i (%)
K equities	40	40	20	10	20	10.0	0
panese equities	30	20	−5	−4	4.7	5.6	10
S equities	30	40	6	8	28.0	29.6	20
	$\tilde{w}_i$ (%)	$\tilde{W}_i$ (%)			Forward return f'_i (%)	Forward return f_i (%)	
erling forward contracts	+20	+30	N/A	N/A	0	0	
en forward contracts	−15	−10	N/A	N/A	9.5	8.9	
S dollar forward contracts	−5	−20	N/A	N/A	17.0	17.9	
tal	*100*	*100*	*8.3*	*6.4*	*15.5*	*12.5*	

$$c_S = \sum_{i=1}^{i=n} w_i \times c_i + \sum_{i=1}^{i=n} \tilde{w}_i \times f_i \tag{5.123}$$

We attribute relative performance to currency timing in the ith currency for underlying assets as follows:

$$\tilde{w}_i \times \left(\frac{1 + c'_i}{1 + c_i} - 1\right) \times \left(\frac{1 + c_i}{1 + c_S}\right) \tag{5.124}$$

We attribute relative performance to currency timing in the ith currency for currency forwards as follows:

$$\tilde{w}_i \times \left(\frac{1 + f'_i}{1 + f_i} - 1\right) \times \left(\frac{1 + f_i}{1 + c_S}\right) \tag{5.125}$$

Extending our example to include timing effects in currencies and forward contracts, we get Table 5.25.

Real portfolio currency returns are calculated in Exhibit 5.47 and currency timing effects in each currency in Exhibit 5.48. The dollar return in the portfolio is greater than the benchmark dollar return, adding 0.21% of value. The yen return in the portfolio was also better than the benchmark yen, add a further 0.06%.

Exhibit 5.47   Portfolio currency returns

Note that in Table 5.24 the portfolio currency return in Japanese equities is now:

$$c'_i = \frac{1.056}{1.047} - 1 = 10.2\%$$

differing from the benchmark currency of 10.0%.

Likewise the portfolio currency in US dollars is:

$$\frac{1.28}{1.06} - 1 = 20.8\%$$

differing from the benchmark currency of 20.0%.

The measured portfolio currency return is now:

$$r_C = 40\% \times 0\% + 30\% \times 10.2\% + 30\% \times 20.8\%$$
$$+ 20\% \times 0\% - 15\% \times 9.5\% + -5\% \times 17.0\% = 7.01\%$$

Exhibit 5.48   Currency timing

Therefore, the total currency timing effect is:

$$\frac{1+r_C}{1+c_S} - 1 = \frac{1.0701}{1.0678} - 1 = 0.22\%$$

Calculating the impact per currency:

Sterling $w_i \times \left(\frac{1+c_i'}{1+c_i} - 1\right) \times \left(\frac{1+c_i}{1+c_s}\right) = 30\% \times \left(\frac{1.0}{1.0} - 1\right)$

$$\times \frac{1.0}{1.0678} = 0\%$$

Yen $30\% \times \left(\frac{1.102}{1.10} - 1\right) \times \frac{1.10}{1.0678} = 0.06\%$

US dollar $40\% \times \left(\frac{1.208}{1.20} - 1\right) \times \frac{1.20}{1.0678} = 0.21\%$

Sterling forwards $\tilde{w}_i \times \left(\frac{1+f_i'}{1+f_i} - 1\right) \times \left(\frac{1+f_i}{1+c_S}\right) = 20\% \times \left(\frac{1.0}{1.0} - 1\right)$

$$\times \frac{1.0}{1.0678} = 0\%$$

Yen forwards $-15\% \times \left(\frac{1.095}{1.089} - 1\right) \times \frac{1.089}{1.0678} = -0.99\%$

US dollar forwards $-5\% \times \left(\frac{1.17}{1.178} - 1\right) \times \frac{1.17}{1.0678} = 0.04\%$

Total $0\% + 0.06\% + 0.21\% + 0\% - 0.09\% + 0.04\% = 0.22\%$

Compounding effects need to be recalculated yet again, as shown in Exhibit 5.49:

Exhibit 5.49   Revised compounding effects

New implied portfolio currency:

$$\frac{1.155}{1.083} - 1 = 6.68\%$$

The total impact of compounding within the portfolio is:

$$\frac{1.0668}{1.0701} - 1 = -0.31\%$$

From before, the implied compounding impact in the benchmark is:

$$\frac{1.0555}{1.0574} - 1 = -0.18\%$$

Total impact from compounding:

$$\frac{1.0668}{1.0701} \times \frac{1.0555}{1.0574} - 1 = -0.50\%$$

Summarizing

We now have attributed relative performance to the following factors:

$$\text{Stock selection} \quad \frac{1+r_L}{1+b_{SL}} - 1 = \frac{1.083}{1.052} - 1 = 2.95\%$$

$$\text{Asset allocation} \quad \frac{1+b_{SH}}{1+b_L} - 1 = \frac{1.051}{1.064} - 1 = -1.22\%$$

$$\text{Total currency effects} \quad \frac{1+b_{SL}}{1+b_{SH}} \times \frac{1+r'_C}{1+b'_C} - 1 \quad \text{or} \quad \frac{1+b_{SL}}{1+r_L} \times \frac{1+r}{1+r_L} \times \frac{1+b_L}{1+b} - 1$$

$$\frac{1.052}{1.051} \times \frac{1.155}{1.083} \times \frac{1.064}{1.125} - 1 = 0.98\%$$

We can then see that these factors compound to give:

$$\underbrace{\frac{1+r_L}{1+b_{SL}}}_{\text{Stock}} \times \underbrace{\frac{1+b_{SH}}{1+b_L}}_{\text{Asset}} \times \underbrace{\frac{1+b_{SL}}{1+b_{SH}}}_{\text{Hedging cost transferred}} \times \underbrace{\frac{1+r}{1+r_L} \times \frac{1+b_L}{1+b}}_{\text{Naive currency attribution}} -1 = \frac{1+r}{1+b} - 1$$

$$\underbrace{\frac{1.083}{1.052}}_{\text{Stock}} \times \underbrace{\frac{1.051}{1.064}}_{\text{Asset}} \times \underbrace{\frac{1.052}{1.051}}_{\text{Hedging cost transferred}} \times \underbrace{\frac{1.155}{1.083} \times \frac{1.064}{1.125}}_{\text{Naive currency attribution}} -1 = \frac{1.155}{1.125} - 1 = 2.69\%$$

The total currency effects can be broken down further to:

$$\underbrace{\frac{1+r_C}{1+c_S} \times \frac{1+c_{SH}}{1+b_C}}_{\text{Currency overlay}} \times \underbrace{\frac{1+b_{SL}}{1+b_{SH}} \times \frac{1+c_S}{1+c_{SH}}}_{\text{Hedging mismatch}} \times \underbrace{\frac{1+r'_C}{1+r_C} \times \frac{1+b_C}{1+b'_C}}_{\text{Compounding}} -1$$

Hedging mismatch is an extremely small factor which represents the different perspective of the cost of hedging between the currency overlay manager and the asset allocator:

$$\underbrace{\times \frac{1.0701}{1.0678} \times \underbrace{\frac{1.0688}{1.0555}}_{} \times \underbrace{\frac{1.052}{1.051} \times \frac{1.0678}{1.0688}}_{} \times \underbrace{\frac{1.0668}{1.0701} \times \frac{1.0555}{1.0574}}_{}}_{} -1 = 0.98\%$$

$$\underbrace{\text{Timing} \qquad \text{Currency allocation} \qquad \text{Hedging mismatch} \qquad \text{Compounding}}$$

$$\underbrace{\qquad\qquad\qquad\qquad\qquad\qquad\qquad\qquad\qquad\qquad\qquad}_{\text{Currency overlay}}$$

Finally, we can summarize the currency attribution effects in Table 5.26 and overall attribution effects in Table 5.27.

Other currency issues

Unlike futures contracts in which gains and losses are channelled through the margin account, unrealized gains and losses build up in forward currency contracts. The practical consequence of this is that there will be a net forward position which damps performance in the event of unrealized gains and gears (provides leverage) performance

Table 5.26 Currency attribution

	Portfolio weight $w_i + \tilde{w}_i$	Benchmark weight $W_i + \tilde{W}_i$	Portfolio currency c'_i	Benchmark currency c_i	Portfolio forwards f'_i	Benchmark forwards f_i	Currency allocation $(w_i + \tilde{w}_i - w_i - \tilde{W}_i)$ $\times \left(\dfrac{1+f_i}{1+c_i} - 1\right)$	Timing
	(%)	(%)	(%)	(%)	(%)	(%)	(%)	(%)
Sterling	60	70	0.0	0.0	0.0	0.0	0.53	0.0
Yen	15	10	10.2	10.0	9.5	8.9	0.15	−0.03
US dollars	25	20	20.8	20.0	17.0	17.9	0.58	0.25
Total	100	100	7.01	5.55			1.26	0.22

Compounding	$\dfrac{1+r'_C}{1+r_C} \times \dfrac{1+b_C}{1+b'_C}$	−0.5
Hedging mismatch	$\dfrac{1+b_{SL}}{1+b_{SH}} \times \dfrac{1+c_S}{1+c_{SH}}$	0.0

Table 5.27 Multi-currency geometric attribution including timing

	Asset allocation (%)	Stock selection (%)	Currency allocation (%)	Currency timing (%)	Other effects* (%)	
UK equities	0	3.8	0.53	0		
Japanese equities	−0.88	−0.29	0.16	−0.03		
US equities	−0.34	−0.57	0.58	0.25		
						Total excess return
Total	−1.22	2.95	1.26	0.22	−0.5	2.69

*In real portfolios the other effects tend to no more than one or two basis points and are reduced if measurement periods are kept as short as possible, ideally daily.

in the event of unrealized losses. This net position is an attributable factor in its own right.

The denomination of a security does not necessarily coincide with the economic exposure of a security. A classic example is Japanese warrants and convertible bonds denominated in US$, Swiss francs and other currencies to encourage international investors, but linked ultimately to the yen price of a security. The prices of these instruments effectively adjust for the currency movements between the denomination currency and yen and, therefore, are economically exposed to yen.

FIXED INCOME ATTRIBUTION

The investment decision process for bond managers is very different from that of equity managers. Bonds are simply a series of defined future cash flows* which are relatively

---

* More complex instruments may contain some variability in future cash flows.

easy to price. Fixed income performance is therefore driven by changes in the yield curve (Campisi, 2000). Therefore, systematic risk in the form of duration is a key part of the investment process. Fixed income attribution is a specialist form of risk-adjusted attribution.

Weighted duration attribution

Van Breukelen (2000) suggested an approach to fixed interest attribution for top-down investment decision processes that focus on weighted duration bets. He used the following approximation formula for the return on bonds:

$$r_{Li} = x_i + D_i \times (-\Delta y_i) \qquad (5.126)$$

where: D_i = modified duration in bond category i

Δy_i = change in yield for category i.

Using the Karnosky and Singer definition of portfolio return:

$$r = \sum_{i=1}^{i=n} w_i \times (r_{Li} - x_i) + \sum_{i=1}^{i=n} w_i \times (c_i + x_i) \qquad (5.88)$$

It follows that:

$$b = \sum_{i=1}^{i=n} W_i \times (b_{Li} - x_i) + \sum_{i=1}^{i=n} W_i \times (c_i + x_i) \qquad (5.127)$$

Substituting Equation (5.126) into Equation (5.88):

$$r = \sum_{i=1}^{i=n} w_i \times D_i \times (-\Delta y_i) + \sum_{i=1}^{i=n} w_i \times (c_i + x_i) \qquad (5.128)$$

The factor $w_i \times D_i$ is equivalent to an equity weight, the bond manager can increase exposure by either increasing weight or increasing modified duration. It follows that the benchmark return can be described as:

$$b = \sum_{i=1}^{i=n} W_i \times D_{bi} \times (-\Delta y_{bi}) + \sum_{i=1}^{i=n} W_i \times (c_i + x_i) \qquad (5.129)$$

where: D_{bi} = benchmark modified duration for category i

Δy_{bi} = change in benchmark yield for category i.

Applying the standard Brinson approach to Equations (5.128) and (5.129), the excess return we wish to attribute is:

$$r - b = \sum_{i=1}^{i=n} w_i \times D_i \times -\Delta y_i - \sum_{i=1}^{i=n} W_i \times D_{bi} \times -\Delta y_{bi}$$

$$+ \sum_{i=1}^{i=n} w_i \times (c_i + x_i) - \sum_{i=1}^{i=n} W_i \times (c_i + x_i) \qquad (5.130)$$

Let:

$$c = \sum_{i=1}^{i=n} w_i \times (c_i + x_i) \qquad (5.131)$$

$$c' = \sum_{i=1}^{i=n} W_i \times (c_i + x_i) \qquad (5.99)$$

We are familiar with the last two terms which represent currency attribution in the Karnosky and Singer model (in this case without currency forwards which can easily be added).

Van Breukelen suggests creating two reference or notional funds to measure the contribution from fixed income management excluding currency (namely, overall duration, market selection and issue selection).

The overall duration notional fund is defined as:

$$b_D = \sum_{i=1}^{i=n} D_\beta \times D_{bi} \times W_i \times -\Delta y_{bi} + c' \qquad (5.132)$$

where: $D_\beta = D_r/D_b = $ duration beta $\qquad (4.63)$

$D_r = $ portfolio duration

$D_b = $ benchmark duration.

The duration beta is equivalent to an equity beta and can be used in the same way. *Therefore, the contribution from overall duration*:

$$b_D - b = \sum_{i=1}^{i=n} D_\beta \times D_{bi} \times W_i \times \Delta y_{bi} - \sum_{i=1}^{i=n} D_{bi} \times W_i \times \Delta y_{bi}$$

$$= \left(D_\beta \times \sum_{i=1}^{i=n} D_{bi} \times W_i - \sum_{i=1}^{i=n} D_{bi} \times W_i \right) \times \Delta y_b$$

$$= \sum_{i=1}^{i=n} D_{bi} \times W_i \times (D_\beta - 1) \times \Delta y_b \qquad (5.133)$$

The overall duration effect should only be measured if it is part of the investment decision process.

The duration-adjusted semi-notional fund is defined as:

$$r_S = \sum_{i=1}^{i=n} D_i \times w_i \times -\Delta y_{bi} + c' \qquad (5.134)$$

Therefore, the contribution from weighted duration allocation is:

$$r_S - b_D = \sum_{i=1}^{i=n} D_i \times w_i \times \Delta y_{bi} - \sum_{i=1}^{i=n} D_\beta \times D_{bi} \times W_i \times \Delta y_{bi} \qquad (5.135)$$

Table 5.28 Fixed income attribution

	Portfolio weight w_i (%)	Benchmark weight W_i (%)	Portfolio-modified duration D_i	Benchmark-modified duration D_{bi}	Portfolio return r_i (%)	Benchmark return b_i (%)	Risk-free rate x_i (%)
UK bonds	50	50	7.8	5.0	5.6	3.5	1.0
Japanese bonds	20	10	1.0	2.0	0.5	0.5	0.1
US bonds	30	40	4.0	3.0	3.2	3.0	0.2
Total	100	100	5.3	3.9	3.86	3.0	0.59

Applying the same Brinson and Fachler approach as in Equation (5.17):

$$r_S - b_D = \sum_{i=1}^{i=n}(D_i \times w_i - D_\beta \times D_{bi} \times W_i) \times (-\Delta y_{bi} + \Delta y_b) \tag{5.136}$$

Market allocation for category i is therefore:

$$A'_i = (D_i \times w_i - D_\beta \times D_{bi} \times W_i) \times (-\Delta y_{bi} + \Delta y_b) \tag{5.137}$$

If the overall duration is not part of the investment decision process, we can miss a step and move directly to:

$$r_S - b = \sum_{i=1}^{i=n}(D_i \times w_i - D_{bi} \times W_i) \times (-\Delta y_{bi} + \Delta y_b) \tag{5.138}$$

Market allocation for category i is therefore:

$$A_i = (D_i \times w_i - D_{bi} \times W_i) \times (-\Delta y_{bi} + \Delta y_b) \tag{5.139}$$

Issue selection is calculated by:

$$r - r_S - (c - c') = \sum_{i=1}^{i=n} D_i \times w_i \times (-\Delta y_{ri}) - \sum_{i=1}^{i=n} D_i \times w_i \times (-\Delta y_{bi}) - c + c' \tag{5.140}$$

Issue selection for category i is therefore:

$$S_i = D_i \times w_i \times (-\Delta y_{ri} + \Delta y_{bi}) \tag{5.141}$$

Currency allocation using Karnosky and Singer without forward contracts is:

$$C_i = (w_i - W_i) \times (c_i + x_i - c') \tag{5.98}$$

Table 5.28 provides the data for a simple numerical example of a three-category portfolio consisting of UK, Japanese and US bonds. Using these data the portfolio and benchmark total returns and durations are verified and the duration beta calculated in Exhibit 5.50:

Exhibit 5.50   Total returns and duration

Portfolio-modified duration $D = \sum_{i=1}^{i=n} w_i \times D_i$

$$= 50\% \times 7.8 + 20\% \times 1.0 + 30\% \times 4.0 = 5.3$$

Benchmark-modified duration $D_b = \sum_{i=1}^{i=n} W_i \times D_{bi}$

$$= 50\% \times 5.0 + 10\% \times 2.0 + 40\% \times 3.0 = 3.9$$

Duration beta $D_\beta = \dfrac{5.3}{3.9}$

Portfolio return $r = \sum_{i=1}^{i=n} w_i \times r_i$

$$= 50\% \times 5.6\% + 20\% \times 0.5\% + 30\% \times 3.2\%$$

$$= 3.86\%$$

Benchmark return $b = \sum_{i=1}^{i=n} W_i \times b_i$

$$= 50\% \times 3.5\% + 10\% \times 0.5\% + 40\% \times 3.0\%$$

$$= 3.0\%$$

Portfolio risk-free rate $x_r = \sum_{i=1}^{i=n} w_i \times x_i$

$$= 50\% \times 1.0\% + 20\% \times 0.1\% + 30\% \times 0.2\%$$

$$= 0.58\%$$

Or c if currency returns are 0

Benchmark risk-free rate $x_b = \sum_{i=1}^{i=n} W_i \times x_i$

$$= 50\% \times 1.0\% + 10\% \times 0.1\% + 40\% \times 0.2\%$$

$$= 0.59\%$$

Or c' if currency returns are 0.

Using equation (5.126) the implied yield changes are calculated directly from the portfolio and benchmark returns in Exhibits 5.51 and 5.52:

Exhibit 5.51   Implied portfolio yield changes

UK bonds $\Delta y_i = \dfrac{r_i - x_i}{D_i} = \dfrac{5.6\% - 1.0\%}{7.8} = -0.59\%$

Japanese bonds $\dfrac{0.5\% - 0.1\%}{1.0} = -0.4\%$

US bonds $\dfrac{3.2\% - 0.2\%}{4.0} = -0.75\%$

Total portfolio $\dfrac{3.86\% - 0.58\%}{5.3} = -0.62\%$

Exhibit 5.52   Implied benchmark yield changes

UK bonds $\dfrac{3.5\% - 1.0\%}{5.0} = -0.5\%$

Japanese bonds $\dfrac{0.5\% - 0.1\%}{2.0} = -0.2\%$

US bonds $\dfrac{3.0\% - 0.2\%}{3.0} = -0.93\%$

Total benchmark $\dfrac{3.00\% - 0.59\%}{3.9} = -0.62\%$

In this particular example the overall duration is part of the decision process. The overall duration notional fund and duration-adjusted semi-notional funds are calculated in Exhibit 5.53:

Exhibit 5.53   Notional funds

Overall duration notional fund:

$$b_D = \sum_{i=1}^{i=n} D_\beta \times D_{bi} \times W_i \times -\Delta y_{bi} + c'$$

$$= \frac{5.3}{3.9} \times (5.0 \times 50\% \times 0.5\% + 2.0 \times 10\% \times 0.2\% + 3.0 \times 40\% \times 0.93) + 0.59\%$$

$$= 3.87\%$$

Duration-adjusted semi-notional fund:

$$r_S = \sum_{i=1}^{i=n} D_i \times w_i \times -\Delta y_{bi} + c' = 7.8 \times 50\% \times 0.5\% + 1.0 \times 20\%$$

$$\times 0.2\% + 4.0 \times 30\% \times 0.93\% + 0.59\% = 3.70\%$$

The overall duration effect is calculated by taking the difference between the duration notional fund and the benchmark return as shown in Exhibit 5.54. It is one decision and, therefore, one allocation number is calculated. In this example the portfolio duration is much greater than the benchmark duration; since markets are rising this is a positive effect, adding 0.87% of value.

Exhibit 5.54   Overall duration allocation

$$b_D - b = 3.87\% - 3.0\% = 0.87\%$$

Exhibit 5.55 calculates the market allocation effects for each category. Since we have adjusted for the overall duration we must adjust the benchmark-weighted duration using the duration beta to ensure the correct effect is calculated. The portfolio is effectively overweight UK bonds which underperformed the overall index slightly losing 0.06%, underweight Japanese bonds which added 0.03% and underweight US bonds which lost 0.14% of value.

Exhibit 5.55   Market allocation

$$r_S - b_D = \sum_{i=1}^{i=n}(D_i \times w_i - D_\beta \times D_{bi} \times W_i) \times (-\Delta y_{bi} + \Delta y_b)$$

$$= 3.70\% - 3.87\% = -0.17\%$$

$$\text{UK bonds} = (D_i \times w_i - D_\beta \times D_{bi} \times W_i) \times (-\Delta y_{bi} + \Delta y_b)$$

$$= \left(7.8 \times 50\% - \frac{5.3}{3.9} \times 5.0 \times 50\%\right) \times (0.5 - 0.62)$$

$$= -0.06\%$$

$$\text{Japanese bonds} = \left(1.0 \times 20\% - \frac{5.3}{3.9} \times 2.0 \times 10\%\right) \times (0.2 - 0.62)$$

$$= 0.03\%$$

$$\text{US bonds} = \left(4.0 \times 30\% - \frac{5.3}{3.9} \times 3.0 \times 40\%\right) \times (0.93 - 0.62)$$

$$= -0.14\%$$

$$\textit{Total market allocation} = -0.06\% + 0.03\% - 0.14\% = -0.17\%$$

Exhibit 5.56 calculates the security or issue selection effects. The portfolio outperformed in UK and Japanese bonds evidenced by yield falls greater than benchmark but underperformed in US bonds. Currency effects are calculated in Exhibit 5.57. In this example currency returns are zero; therefore, currency allocation is measuring the local interest-rate allocation effects. The portfolio is overweight in low-yielding Japanese interest rates, losing value; but this is almost offset against an underweight exposure to low US interest rates.

Exhibit 5.56 Security (or issue) selection

$$r - r_S = \sum_{i=1}^{i=n} D_i \times w_i \times (-\Delta y_{ri}) - \sum_{i=1}^{i=n} D_i \times w_i \times (-\Delta y_{bi}) - c + c'$$

$$= 3.86\% - 3.70\% - 0.58\% + 0.59\% = 0.17\%$$

$$\text{UK bonds} = D_i \times w_i \times (-\Delta y_{ri} + \Delta y_{bi}) = 7.8 \times 50\% \times (0.59\% - 0.5\%)$$

$$= 0.35\%$$

$$\text{Japanese bonds} = 1.0 \times 20\% \times (0.4\% - 0.2\%)$$

$$= 0.04\%$$

$$\text{US bonds} = 4.0 \times 30\% \times (0.75\% - 0.93\%)$$

$$= -0.22\%$$

$$\textit{Total security selection} = 0.35\% + 0.04\% - 0.22\%$$

$$= 0.17\%$$

Exhibit 5.57 Currency allocation

$$c - c' = \sum_{i=1}^{i=n} w_i \times (c_i + x_i) - \sum_{i=1}^{i=n} W_i \times (c_i + x_i) = 0.58\% - 0.59\%$$

$$\text{UK bonds} = (w_i - W_i) \times (c_i + x_i - c')$$

$$= (50\% - 50\%) \times (0.0\% + 1.0\% - 0.59\%)$$

$$= 0.0\%$$

$$\text{Japanese bonds} = (20\% - 10\%) \times (0.0\% + 0.1\% - 0.59)$$

$$= -0.05\%$$

$$\text{US bonds} = (30\% - 40\%) \times (0.0\% + 0.2\% - 0.59)$$

$$= 0.04\%$$

$$\textit{Total currency allocation} = 0.0\% - 0.05\% + 0.04\%$$

$$= -0.01\%$$

The fixed income attribution effects are summarized in Table 5.29. This type of attribution is particularly suited for global bond portfolios and balanced portfolios. For

Table 5.29   Fixed income attribution

	Portfolio-weighted duration $w_i \times D_i$	Benchmark-weighted duration $W_i \times D_{bi}$	Portfolio change in yield Δy_i (%)	Benchmark change in yield Δy_{bi} (%)	Market allocation $(D_i \times w_i - D_\beta \times D_{bi} \times W_i \times (-\Delta y_{bi} + \Delta y_b))$ (%)	Issue selection $D_i \times w_i \times (-\Delta y_{ri} + \Delta y_{bi})$ (%)	Currency allocation $(w_i - W_i) \times (c_i + x_i - c')$ (%)
UK bonds	3.9	2.5	−0.59	−0.5	−0.06	0.35	0.0
Japanese bonds	0.2	0.2	−0.4	0.2	0.03	0.04	−0.05
US bonds	1.2	1.2	−0.75	−0.93	−0.14	−0.22	0.04
Total	*100*	*100*	*−0.62*	*−0.62*	*−0.17*	*0.17*	*−0.01*
					Overall duration $b_D - b$		*0.87*

balanced portfolios, essentially the same Brinson approach is employed but the impact of duration can be factored into the fixed income portion of the portfolio. The risk factor for equities is category weight and the risk factor for bonds weighted duration.

For single-currency bond portfolios more complex analysis is required to attribute the bond manager's yield curve positions and credit spread allocations.

ATTRIBUTION STANDARDS

Recently, there has been some discussion about the desirability of attribution standards. I'm not yet sure we have reached the point at which attribution standards would be useful. As demonstrated earlier in this chapter the development of attribution methodologies is gaining pace, but I believe it still has some way to go. Standards will have the effect of slowing down future developments.

The very nature of attribution does not lend itself to the application of standards; asset managers are constantly seeking ways of differentiating their products, implying the constant need to change attribution methodologies.

There are however a number of pitfalls that users of attribution analysis should avoid. I believe guidance to avoid these pitfalls by providing information to the users of attribution is much more appropriate and beneficial from an educational viewpoint.

The European Investment Performance Council (EIPC, 2002) has produced some basic guidance (reproduced here in Appendix C) and recently updated (EIPC, 2004) this guidance (reproduced here in Appendix D).

All asset managers should be able to answer the 22 questions posed in the EIPC's original guidance for their own attribution reports. Questions 14 and 15 are of particular interest (see p. 188).

Question 14 asks how the investment decision to invest outside the benchmark is measured. The answer depends on the investment decision process. If the portfolio manager wishes to buy an individual security in a country outside the benchmark, then this is a security selection decision and the performance of this security should be measured against the overall benchmark. If, however, the manager wishes to be overweight in the country, this is an asset allocation decision and should be measured accordingly. A representative index must be chosen to measure the impact of this overweight decision. There is a second decision to determine which securities to buy with the allocated cash; this will generate a security selection effect against the chosen representative index.

Question 15 asks if all transaction costs are included in the security selection effect. Almost all transaction-based attribution methodologies include transaction costs in the stock selection effect by default. Asset allocation effects are only measured by reference to the category index and the overall benchmark, with no allowance for transaction costs. Asset allocation decisions when implemented clearly generate transaction costs. These costs can be significant particularly for illiquid assets, such as emerging markets, and should be allocated to the asset allocator, not the stock selector.

Evolution of performance attribution methodologies

The evolution of performance attribution methodologies is shown in Figure 5.6. Evolution down the figure is not necessarily in chronological order but represents my preferences and my interpretation of key contributions and insights.

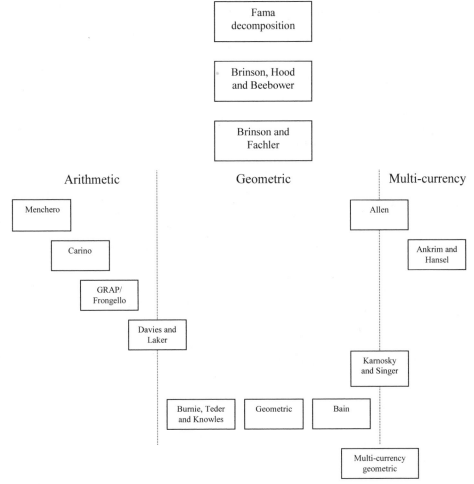

Figure 5.6 Evolution of performance attribution methodologies.

The key stages are Brinson and Fachler in 1985, Karnosky and Singer in 1994 and the three geometric methodologies apparently developed in isolation: (1) Burnie, Knowles and Teder, (2) Bain and (3) the geometric methodology (shown in detail in Appendix A). The arithmetic smoothing methodologies are interesting but are ultimately unnecessary; Karnosky and Singer, although appearing at first sight to be arithmetic, is actually geometric because of the use of continuously compounded returns. The multi-currency geometric methodology is that detailed in Appendix B.

REFERENCES

Allen, G.C. (1991) Performance attribution of global equity portfolios. *Journal of Portfolio Management*, Fall, 59–65.

Ankrim, E. and Hensel, C. (1992) Multi-currency performance attribution. *Russell Research Commentary*.

Bacon, C.R. (2002) Excess returns – arithmetic or geometric. *Journal of Performance Measurement*, Spring, 23–31.

Bain, W.G. (1996) The WM Company. *Investment Performance Measurement*, Woodhead Publishing.

Brinson, G. and Fachler, N. (1985) Measuring non-US equity portfolio performance. *Journal of Portfolio Management*, Spring, 73–76.

Brinson, G., Hood, R. and Beebower, G. (1986) Determinants of portfolio performance. *Financial Analyst Journal*, July/August, 39–44.

Brinson, G., Singer, B. and Beebower, G. (1991) Determinants of portfolio performance. II: An update. *Financial Analysts Journal*, May/June, 40–48.

Burnie, J.S., Knowles, J.A. and Teder, T.J. (1998) Arithmetic and geometric attribution. *Journal of Performance Measurement*, Fall, 59–68.

Campisi, S. (2000) Primer on fixed income performance attribution. *Journal of Performance Measurement*, Summer, 14–25.

Carino, D. (1999) Combining attribution effects over time. *Journal of Performance Measurement*, Summer, 5–14.

Davies, O. and Laker, D. (2001) Multiple-period performance attribution using the Brinson model. *Journal of Performance Measurement*, Fall, 12–22.

EIPC (2002) *Guidance for Users of Attribution Analysis*. European Investment Performance Council.

EIPC (2004) *Guidance on Performance Attribution Presentation*. European Investment Performance Council.

Frongello, A. (2002) Linking single period attribution results. *Journal of Performance Measurement*, Spring, 10–22.

GRAP (1997) *Synthèse des modèles d'attribution de performance*. Groupe de Recherche en Attribution de Performance, Paris [in French].

Illmer, S. and Marty, W. (2003) Decomposing the money-weighted return. *Journal of Performance Measurement*, Summer, 42–50.

Karnosky, D. and Singer, B. (1994) *Global Asset Management and Performance Attribution*. Research Foundation of the Institute of Chartered Financial Analysts.

Kirievsky, L. and Kirievsky, A. (2000) Attribution analysis: Combining attribution effects over time made easy. *Journal of Performance Measurement*, Summer, 49–59.

McLaren, A. (2001) A geometric methodology for performance attribution. *Journal of Performance Measurement*, Summer, 45–57.

Menchero, J. (2000) An optimized approach to linking attribution effects over time. *Journal of Performance Measurement*, Fall, 36–42.

Spaulding, D. (2003) Holdings vs. transaction-based attribution – an overview. *Journal of Performance Measurement*, Fall, 52–56.

van Breukelen, G. (2000) Fixed income attribution. *Journal of Performance Measurement*, Summer, 61–68.

6
Performance Presentation Standards

There are three ways of losing money – horses, women and taking the advice of experts:
   Horses – that is the quickest;
   women – that is the most pleasant; but
   taking the advice of experts – that is the most certain.

Apocryphally attributed to M. Pompidou (Hymans and Mulligan, 1980)

WHY DO WE NEED PERFORMANCE PRESENTATION STANDARDS?

The Association for Investment Management and Research (AIMR) sponsored the creation of the Global Investment Performance Standards (GIPS) to provide an ethical framework for the calculation and presentation of the performance history (or track record) of asset management firms. GIPS are voluntary standards based on the fundamental principles of full disclosure and fair representation of performance returns.

The need for the standards first became apparent in the United States in the mid-1980s. Pension funds in seeking firms to manage their assets would obviously see a large number of presentations from asset managers, the overwhelming majority of which presented above-average performance, begging the question "where are the below-average managers?" The answer, unfortunately, was that some of the below-average managers were presenting above-average returns.

Asset managers were very selective about the investment track records they presented to potential clients. Most marketing managers would be well aware over which time period they performed best and would consequently "cherry-pick" the best period to show performance. Often, single representative accounts would be used to calculate the firm's track record. Invariably, the representative account would be one of the better performing accounts for that investment strategy. If the representative account was performing badly a rationale would be found to choose a new one. Managers might also be selective in the choice of calculation methodology as demonstrated in Chapter 2. Often the performance track records presented by asset managers were not a fair and honest representation of the performance they had delivered to their existing clients.

The result was the creation of the AIMR Performance Presentation Standards (AIMR-PPS) in 1987, voluntary performance guidelines for the North American market. In the United Kingdom in 1992 the National Association of Pension Funds

(NAPF) produced its own guidelines for balanced pension funds. My interest in the standards developed at this time; I wished to bring my firm, a London-based subsidiary of a large US bank, into compliance with both the AIMR-PPS and the NAPF guidelines. It proved impossible to achieve both. The AIMR-PPS and the NAPF guidelines shared the same ethical objectives, yet in certain regards they were contradictory. With responsibility for a variety of European offices I could envisage the nightmare scenario of a separate set of contradictory standards in each European office; it was clear a set of global standards was required.

ADVANTAGES FOR ASSET MANAGERS

The advantages of a global standard for clients are obvious; clients can select asset managers based on good-quality information with a certain level of confidence that the numbers presented are a fair and honest representation of that firm's track record. For their own protection, pension fund trustees should only hire asset managers who are compliant with the standards. Non-compliance with the standards may suggest a weaker commitment to ethical standards or weak internal controls insufficient to claim compliance. If performance measurement controls are not best practice, that may be an indication that other controls within the firm are weak.

For asset managers the advantages are less obvious and of course there is the cost of compliance to be offset; however, in my view the following advantages significantly outweigh the cost of compliance:

(i) *Marketing advantage*

Clearly, in the early stages of a standard an asset manager can gain a marketing advantage by claiming compliance with a good-quality standard. In the US it has now become a marketing disadvantage not to be compliant, a situation that will arise in Europe at some stage.

Many pension funds will not welcome firms into the selection process if they are not compliant, and in some circumstances, if their claim of compliance is not independently verified. Any trustee is taking the risk of future criticism or legal action by selecting an asset manager who does not comply with performance presentation standards, if subsequently things go wrong and it is established that the original presentations were misleading.

(ii) *Level playing field – international passport*

The standards are designed to encourage global competition and eliminate barriers to entry. In effect, GIPS allow asset managers to market their track record worldwide with the knowledge they are subject to the same standards as local competitors.

The pressure to present misrepresentative performance is not so great if asset managers are confident their competitors are operating to the same standard.

(iii) *Increased professionalism*

To achieve compliance a firm must have good-quality performance measurement processes and procedures in place and a commitment to the ethical presentation of performance track records. This naturally increases the profile and importance of performance measurers in the firm.

(iv) *Risk control*

The standards require a basic level of risk control. Managers are required to investigate outliers in their track record to justify that accounts are being managed within the composite guidelines. This is good business practice, identifying poor-performing accounts early, ensuring good performance is real and ensuring the entire firm is aware and understands the investment objectives and guidelines for each account.

(v) *Business efficiency and data quality*

Establishing effective procedures and improving performance measurement systems obviously requires investment, however doing things right first time is obviously more efficient than calculating performance incorrectly and wasting time and resources investigating and correcting errors. Clearly, it's very inefficient if individual portfolio managers are wasting their time ensuring returns are calculated correctly.

THE STANDARDS

GIPS are ethical standards for investment performance presentation to ensure fair representation and full disclosure of a firm's performance track record. The core of the standard is here reproduced in Appendix E.

GIPS require firms to include all discretionary portfolios in "composites" defined according to similar style or investment strategy. A composite should be representative of the firm's performance with that investment strategy. All accounts managed to that strategy including lost accounts must be included, thus eliminating the practice of cherry-picking good-performing accounts.

Firms initially have complete flexibility to define their own composites. This flexibility allows firms to differentiate their product offering and encourages the development of new products.

The firm must decide between narrowly or widely defined composites. Widely defined composites will include minor variations in strategy; for example, the firm might conclude that the return series of a global equity account with a restriction disallowing investment in Australia is very similar to an unrestricted global equity account and therefore both accounts could co-exist in a widely defined global equity composite. Widely defined composites are easier to administer and allow the asset manager to present composites with larger assets under management. Narrowly defined composites are smaller and, because small changes of strategy must be closely monitored, more difficult to administer; however, the dispersion of returns within the composite will be narrower indicating tighter investment controls.

GIPS require at least 5 years of performance history initially, presented annually, increasing to 10 years as the data become available. This avoids the cherry-picking of time periods and provides some information about the consistency of performance. I would recommend the presentation of quarterly performance information, although this is not required.

Some flexibility in the choice of calculation method is allowed but from 1 January 2001 portfolios must be valued at least monthly. Time-weighted returns that adjust for cash flow are required.

Once a firm has met all of the required elements of GIPS the firm may claim compliance. It is the firm that claims compliance, the claim is not specific to an individual presentation or composite; in effect, the firm is making a claim of adhering to the ethical standards that form GIPS.

The standards are divided into five sections:

(i) *Input data*

The standards provide a blueprint for the consistency of input data crucial for effective compliance and full and fair comparisons of investment performance.

(ii) *Calculation methodology*

The standards mandate the use of certain calculation methodologies utilizing the time-weighted approach. True time weighting and linked modified Dietz are the two most common acceptable methodologies. Approximations using benchmarks such as the analyst's test, index substitution and the regression method are not acceptable. Internal rates of return are only acceptable for venture capital/private equity. Valuations will be required at the time of each cash flow from 1 January 2010; in effect, true time-weighted returns.

Time-weighted returns are favoured in GIPS because of the need for comparability. For fair comparison the impact of cash flows must be removed. Requiring valuations at the point of cash flow increases the theoretical level of accuracy and removes the opportunity to game returns by self-selecting the approximate methodology most advantageously impacted by cash flow. At present the standards require firms to adopt a policy for the treatment of external cash flow. For example, for managers using linked monthly modified Dietz as standard, if the cash flow is above a certain level (say, 10% of portfolio assets), then managers are required to change to a true time-weighted return by valuing the assets at the point of cash flow and chain-linking the sub-period returns within the month.

(iii) *Composite construction*

A composite is an aggregation of a number of portfolios into a single group that represents a particular investment strategy or objective.

Composite returns are asset-weighted using beginning period weights, beginning period weights plus day-weighted cash flows or simple aggregation. Equal weighting would allow smaller portfolios (more easily manipulated) to disproportionately impact the performance of the composite.

Appropriate documentation, such as the investment management agreement or other communication with the client, must support the inclusion of any portfolio in a composite. Every portfolio must belong to at least one composite (to avoid the performance record of a poor-performing account being lost); therefore, composite definitions may overlap.

(iv) *Disclosures*

Disclosures allow firms to provide more information relevant to the performance presentation. The standards include both required and recommended disclosures. If in doubt the asset managers should add disclosure to assist the user of the performance presentation.

(v) *Presentation and reporting*

Finally, after gathering input data, calculating returns, constructing composites and determining appropriate disclosures firms must present data within the GIPS guidelines.

The standards are not so explicit at present, but I would recommend all clients be provided with a compliant presentation initially, even if the client is not concerned by the standards. A firm cannot pick and choose when it is compliant; the claim of compliance should mean that all performance presentations are a fair and honest representation of performance.

VERIFICATION

Verification is the review of the firm's performance measurement processes and procedures by an independent third party or "verifier". Verification tests:

(i) Whether the firm has complied with all the composite construction requirements firm-wide.
(ii) Whether the firm's processes and procedures are designed to calculate and present performance in compliance with the GIPS.

Verification is not yet mandatory but is strongly encouraged. Verification not only brings credibility to the claim of compliance but goes a long way to improve the performance measurement process and provides assurance to the board that its claim of compliance is accurate.

Compliance is non-trivial; claiming compliance without verification is high risk. An erroneous claim of compliance could cause both significant reputational damage and major problems with regulators. I would recommend that verification be undertaken at least annually.

The cost of verification will be determined not only by the number of composites and portfolios but also the complexity of the business, the perceived quality of controls and the quality of performance measurement systems. Verification can cost from as little as a few thousand dollars to hundred of thousands of dollars for large, complex businesses.

Verifiers need only be independent of the asset manager, have a good understanding of the standards and relevant practical experience. The asset manager must consider the quality of the verifier not only in terms of attaching their name to performance presentations but in the assurance given to the firm that the claim is accurate and the effectiveness of the verification process.

I see no conflict of interest in verification firms providing pre-compliance consultancy; I would certainly recommend that firms bring verifiers into the initial compliance process at a very early stage.

INVESTMENT PERFORMANCE COUNCIL

The GIPS committee was a single-issue committee set up to write the standards; after publication in 1999 the committee disbanded itself. The objectives the committee set were:

(i) To obtain worldwide acceptance of a standard for the calculation and presentation of investment performance in a fair, comparable format that provides full disclosure.
(ii) To ensure accurate and consistent investment data for reporting, record keeping, marketing and presentation.
(iii) To promote fair, global competition among investment firms for all markets without creating barriers to entry for new firms.
(iv) To foster the notion of industry self-regulation on a global basis.

On publication the standards were well received; however, a standard can only be successful in the long run if it is promoted and if it has the ability to respond to changes in market practice, correct errors in the standards and to provide interpretation where required. The Investment Performance Council (IPC) was established by AIMR to manage the development and the promulgation of the GIPS standards.

The IPC consists of a number of investment professionals gathered from a wide range of disciplines, regions and investor groups.

The IPC holds four meetings per year; two in person and two via telephone conference call, all open to the public. Between these meeting the IPC tasks various permanent subcommittees and single-issue, temporary, technical subcommittees to do much of the work. All proposals discussed by the IPC are circulated to the public for comment prior to adoption into the standard. There are three permanent standing subcommittees.

Country Standards Subcommittee (CSSC)

The GIPS committee failed to foresee that individual countries keen to adopt GIPS would take GIPS and add additional requirements suitable to their local markets; in effect, "GIPS plus". Often, these local requirements were higher standards already well accepted in these countries. Extra requirements may lead to undesirable barriers to entry in these countries. To control this process and ensure that no artificial barriers to entry are erected, the IPC established the Country Standards Subcommittee to oversee the transition of all local standards to the GIPS as well as the ongoing evolution of the GIPS over time.

The IPC encourages countries without a standard to adopt GIPS as their local standard. Some countries have opted to adopt a "translation of GIPS" (or TG) into their local language. The CSSC checks each TG thoroughly before recommending the IPC endorse the local standard.

Other countries have chosen to adopt a "country version of GIPS" (or CVG) which includes a limited number of additions to GIPS deemed acceptable by the IPC and therefore not considered a barrier to entry. Local country sponsors must provide a transition plan for the elimination of these differences over a specified time period. The CSSC manages the approval process before ultimately recommending the CVG to the IPC for approval.

As at 31 March 2004, local standards endorsed by the IPC are shown in Table 6.1.

Other countries are being processed by the CSSC currently.

Table 6.1 IPC-endorsed standards (31 March 2004)

CVGs	TGs	English version
United States and Canada	Austria	Belgium
United Kingdom	Denmark	New Zealand
Japan	Norway	Portugal
Switzerland	Hungary	
Australia	The Netherlands	
Italy	France	
Ireland	Poland	
South Africa	Luxembourg (English, French and German)	
	Spain	

The GIPS committee took an early decision not to include some of the more complex areas, such as real estate, private equity and derivatives, in the original standards with the intention of including them at a later date.

The CSSC is overseeing the first major rewrite of the standard: *Gold GIPS. Gold GIPS* includes sections on real estate and private equity and is intended to include many of the best practices worldwide, thus eliminating the need for many CVGs. Issued for public comment until 1 August 2004 all stakeholders in the standards are encouraged to respond with comments. Both positive and negative comments are encouraged; if only negative comments are received it is all too easy for the IPC to respond and change a requirement that is disliked by, say, less than 5% of practitioners who nevertheless feel strongly enough to voice their opposition.

Gold GIPS is intended to be finalized and published in its final form in early 2005 with an effective date of 1 January 2006.

Verification Subcommittee

The Verification Subcommittee serves as a forum for promoting consistency in verification as well as the general application of the GIPS.

Global verification firms in particular are in a good position to ensure that there is no divergence of practice worldwide and that the claim of compliance in one country means much the same as the claim of compliance in another. Verifiers are able to identify areas in which many firms are struggling to comply with the standards; if these areas do not add much value, then there is the opportunity to change the standards to encourage maximum uptake.

The writers of the standards face a constant dilemma between not making the standards too onerous, encouraging firms to participate and providing sufficient protection for the users of the standards.

Interpretation Subcommittee

The Interpretation Subcommittee has the responsibility of ensuring the integrity, consistency and applicability of the standards; in effect, it is the safety valve of standards. Errors, issues of interpretation or responses to new developments or market trends can be addressed by the Interpretation Subcommittee issuing "guidance statements".

Guidance statements

Guidance statements are formal additions to the standards. Asset management firms and verifiers are required to understand their content and keep up to date with the standards. AIMR provides an email alert facility providing notification of new guidance statements. Information on GIPS, the IPC, guidance statements and how to subscribe to the email alert can be found on AIMR's website at *http://www.aimr.org/ standards*. A selection of the more controversial guidance statements are discussed in more detail in the following subsections.

Definition of firm

The standards require firm-wide compliance to ensure poor-performing accounts have not been excluded from the performance track record. Once the firm has been defined, the exercise of allocating accounts to composites can begin; this determines the universe of portfolios to be allocated.

The firm definition must be meaningful, rational and fair. The definition cannot be used narrowly to exclude poor-performing product areas. The standards recommend the broadest, most meaningful definition.

A firm may be defined as:

- An entity with the appropriate national regulatory authority overseeing the entity's investment management activities.
- An investment firm, subsidiary or division held out to clients or potential clients as a distinct business unit.
- Up to 1 January 2005 only, all assets managed to one or more base currencies.

The last option is a throwback to the original AIMR-PPS; UK firms keen to participate in the AIMR standards successfully argued they need only bring their US$ assets into compliance. This option will not be available after 1 January 2005.

Although the broadest definition is recommended, it is acceptable to define a number of firms within the same organization provided they meet the above criteria, with a view of combining into one firm at a later date. Not all firms within a single organization need be compliant simultaneously, allowing part of the organization time to work on bringing its firm into compliance. This flexibility is often used geographically, although it should never be used to exclude an underperforming part of the business.

Carve-outs

A carve-out is a subset of a portfolio's assets used to create a track record for a narrower mandate from a portfolio managed to a broader mandate. Carve-outs are permitted so that firms that manage assets to a particular strategy in a broader portfolio can demonstrate competency in that strategy, even though they do not manage stand-alone portfolios in that strategy.

By their very nature carve-out returns offer greater potential to mislead than stand-alone portfolios. Carve-outs by definition are portions of a larger portfolio, the criteria for which are determined by the firm. Because cash tends to act as a drag on performance (over the long term we would expect markets to outperform cash), if cash is not included in the calculation of the carve-out, the return may not be representative of what would have been achieved by a stand-alone portfolio. The standards require that cash is allocated consistently to carve-outs and at some future point will require that carve-outs be managed with their own cash balance.

Cash is one problem, there are others:

(i) *Concentration*

Because carve-outs are parts of larger portfolios they tend to contain a smaller number of securities than a stand-alone portfolio and, consequently, are potentially riskier.

(ii) *Currency*

If the larger portfolio contains a currency overlay strategy it is very difficult, if not impossible, to isolate the currency allocation of the carve-out.

(iii) *Asset allocation*

Within the larger portfolio, asset allocation "bets" are taken within the context of the overall benchmark, not the implied benchmark, of the carve-out. In other words, the carve-out may not be managed in the same way as a stand-alone portfolio.

(iv) *Bet size*

Bet sizes are exaggerated with carve-outs – particularly if the carve-out is a small percentage of the overall strategy.

(v) *Composite administration*

Allocation of portfolios to composites becomes significantly more difficult and expensive. For stand-alone portfolios it is easy to identify the number of accounts and changes to investment guidelines. However, if carve-outs are used, then all carve-outs managed to that strategy must be allocated to that composite – the firm must demonstrate that all carve-out strategies are included and that procedures are in place to identify changes to carve-out strategies within larger portfolios.

I would strongly recommend that firms avoid the use of carve-outs and, if absolutely required, only use if stand-alone portfolios are not available. I believe it is very difficult to demonstrate that the performance of a carve-out is representative of stand-alone performance.

Portability

The performance track record belongs to the firm, not an individual. The standards take the view that performance is generated by many factors (e.g., the support and guidance of senior management, the research function, the dealing department, feed-back from colleagues, the performance team, the asset allocation committee, etc., etc.) and therefore all the drivers of performance are not portable. The portfolio manager may be the major contributor, but could the same performance have been delivered by that manager in a different environment?

In most cases the performance results of a prior firm cannot be used to represent the historical record of a new affiliation or a new firm. Performance information of a prior firm can be shown as supplemental information.

Prior performance can be linked with the performance of the new firm if all the following conditions apply:

(i) Substantially all the investment decision makers are employed by the new firm.
(ii) The staff and decision-making process remains intact.
(iii) The new firm discloses that the performance results from the old firm are linked with results from the new firm.
(iv) The new firm has records that document and support the reported performance.
(v) And, with regard to a specific composite, substantially all the assets from the original firm's composite transfer to the new firm.

The standard is written to ensure portability is difficult to achieve and is most likely to occur in the event of a merger or acquisition.

Supplemental information

Supplemental information is defined as any performance-related information included as part of a compliant performance presentation that supplements or enhances the required and/or recommended disclosure and presentation provisions of GIPS.

Supplemental information is a powerful aid for firms that want to enhance the quality of their presentation by providing more information. Supplemental information must satisfy the spirit and principles of GIPS, must not contradict a compliant presentation and must be clearly labelled as supplemental since it is not covered by verification.

Examples of supplemental information include attribution, *ex ante* risk analysis of a representative account and risk-adjusted performance.

Supplemental information must not be used to bypass the GIPS presentation standards, although the standards in no way restrict any information being presented that is specifically requested by the client.

ACHIEVING COMPLIANCE

Achieving compliance is a non-trivial exercise; performance measurers alone cannot achieve compliance, senior management must buy in to the exercise from the start.

To increase the chance of success I would recommend establishing a steering committee chaired by the project sponsor and tasked with monitoring progress, allocating resources, ensuring co-operation within the firm and addressing specific issues.

A sound project plan is absolutely essential. As GIPS compliance projects can easily drift, for a relatively complex business at least 1 year should be allowed to achieve compliance. A new relatively simple business may achieve compliance in a short period, but 6 months would be a very aggressive target for most businesses. Allow plenty of contingency in the project plan which should also include time to educate the entire firm about what it means to be compliant. Many firms achieve compliance and verification but fail ultimately because client-facing individuals within the firm are unaware of their new responsibilities.

The most common issues firms struggle with are:

(i) *Definition of firm*

The firm definition determines the boundaries of the firm for establishing total firm assets – discretionary and non-discretionary.

The firm will have to justify its definition in terms of how it presents itself to the public. The firm will also have to demonstrate that all accounts that fall within the firm definition have been identified. Fee income is a useful indicator that an account existed and is particularly useful for demonstrating to verifiers that all accounts have been identified.

(ii) *Definition of composite*

The firm will have almost complete flexibility to define composite guidelines initially, but once defined it is difficult to make changes.

My recommendation would be to start with narrow definitions – it is a relatively easy process to define a new composite later that encompasses a number of narrow composites. Firms are required to disclose the composite creation date to illustrate that the composite may have been created retrospectively.

(iii) *Lack of data*

The performance claim must be supported by relevant data, which at a minimum will require periodic valuations and cash flows. Often, one of the toughest barriers to compliance is the lack of data, particularly from accounts that are now closed.

MAINTAINING COMPLIANCE

Having achieved compliance, maintaining compliance is not that straightforward. Compliance is not only calculating the correct returns and maintaining the correct composites but also, crucially, presenting information in the correct format to prospective clients. In essence, the claim of compliance by an asset manager means that performance presented by that asset manager is a fair and honest representation of performance. This requires that the entire firm is educated about the meaning of the claim of compliance.

To help maintain compliance I would certainly appoint an individual responsible for ensuring the integrity for the firm's performance presentations and establish a quarterly review process in addition to an annual verification.

I should emphasize the views expressed in this book are entirely my own and are not the formal view of the IPC. The environments in asset manager firms are so different and the flexibility built into the standards so great that it is very difficult to provide generic advice or rules that are suitable for all. However, if asset managers take as their touchstone the requirement to provide a fair and honest representation of the firm's track record they won't go far wrong. The standards help to lay down good practice and point the way to best practice. The foundations established by adopting the standards and establishing strong procedures and good-quality controls will not only strengthen the performance measurement analysis within the firm but strengthen the firm itself.

REFERENCE

Hymans, C. and Mulligan, J. (1980) *The Measurement of Portfolio Performance*. Kluwer.

Appendix A
Simple Attribution

A.1 ATTRIBUTION METHODOLOGY

The following methodology has been developed for use with single-currency portfolios.

A.1.1 Scenario

Suppose we have a portfolio invested in n asset classes or industrial sectors. Then, suppose that the performance of this portfolio is measured against a benchmark.

A.1.2 Portfolio returns

Let the weight of the portfolio in the ith asset class be w_i, where $\sum w_i = 1$, and let the return of the portfolio assets in the ith asset class be r_i. Now the total portfolio return is:

$$r = \sum w_i r_i$$

A.1.3 Benchmark returns

Let the weight of the benchmark in the ith asset class be W_i where $\sum W_i = 1$, and let the return of the benchmark for the ith asset class in the base currency of the portfolio be b_i. Now the total benchmark return is (as it is in the base currency of the portfolio):

$$b = \sum W_i b_i$$

A.1.4 Semi-notional returns

We define the semi-notional return of the ith asset class as $w_i b_i$. Now the total semi-notional return is:

$$b_S = \sum w_i b_i$$

A.1.5 Relative performance

We define the performance of the portfolio relative to the benchmark as:

$$\frac{1+r}{1+b} - 1$$

and it is this relative performance that we attribute in this methodology. We attribute it to two factors: stock selection and country allocation.

A.2   STOCK SELECTION

The term "stock selection" is used to describe the relative performance of the portfolio to the benchmark within a particular asset class. Intuitively, this seems to be the portfolio total return, r, relative to the semi-notional total return, b_S (remembering that b_S is the sumproduct of portfolio weights with the benchmark returns, so any difference between b_S and r is by definition due to stock selection).

We attribute relative performance to stock selection in the ith asset class as follows:

$$w_i\left(\frac{1+r_i}{1+b_i}-1\right)\left(\frac{1+b_i}{1+b_S}\right)$$

So the total stock selection is:

$$\sum_{i=1}^{n} w_i\left(\frac{1+r_i}{1+b_i}-1\right)\left(\frac{1+b_i}{1+b_S}\right) = \sum \frac{w_i[(1+r_i)-(1+b_i)]}{1+b_S}$$

$$= \sum \frac{w_i r_i - w_i b_i}{1+b_S}$$

$$= \frac{\sum w_i r_i - b_S}{1+b_S}$$

$$= \frac{1+\sum w_i r_i - (1+b_S)}{1+b_S}$$

$$= \frac{1+r}{1+b_S}-1$$

A.3   ASSET ALLOCATION

The term "asset allocation" is used to describe the effect of the relative weighting of the portfolio to the benchmark (or "bet") within a particular asset class.

We attribute relative performance to asset allocation in the ith asset class as follows:

$$(w_i - W_i)\left(\frac{1+b_i}{1+b}-1\right)$$

So, the total asset allocation is:

$$\sum_{i=1}^{n}(w_i - W_i)\left(\frac{1+b_i}{1+b}-1\right) = \sum(w_i - W_i)\left(\frac{1+b_i-1-b}{1+b}\right)$$

$$= \sum \frac{w_i b_i - W_i b_i - w_i b + W_i b}{1+b}$$

$$= \frac{\sum w_i b_i - \sum W_i b_i}{1+b} \quad \left(\text{because } \sum w_i = \sum W_i = 1\right.$$

$$\left. \Rightarrow \sum(W_i - w_i)b = 0\right)$$

$$= \frac{\sum w_i b_i - \sum W_i b + \sum W_i b_i - b}{1 + b}$$

$$= \frac{1 + \sum [(w_i - W_i)b_i + \sum W_i b_i] - (1 + b)}{1 + b}$$

$$= \frac{1 + b_S}{1 + b} - 1$$

A.4   SUMMARY

We now have attributed relative performance to the following factors:

$$\text{Stock selection} \quad \frac{1 + r}{1 + b_S} - 1$$

$$\text{Asset allocation} \quad \frac{1 + b_S}{1 + b} - 1$$

We can then see that these factors compound to give:

$$\left(\frac{1 + b_S}{1 + b} \right) \left(\frac{1 + r}{1 + b_S} \right) - 1 = \frac{1 + r}{1 + b} - 1$$

Thus, we have now accounted for all of our relative performance with no residuals (i.e., no "other" term). Once more, because these terms are geometric the relationship holds true over time.

Appendix B
Multi-currency Attribution Methodology

The following methodology has been developed for use with multi-currency portfolios.

B.1 SCENARIO

Suppose we have a portfolio invested in n asset classes with some asset classes having currencies other than the base currency of the portfolio. Then, suppose that the performance of this portfolio is measured against a benchmark.

B.1.1 Portfolio returns

Let the weight of the portfolio in the ith asset class be w_i, where $\sum w_i = 1$, and let the return of the portfolio assets in the ith asset class in local currency be r_{Li} and in the base currency of the portfolio be r_i. Now the total portfolio return is in local currency:

$$r_L = \sum w_i r_{Li} \quad \text{(or weighted average local return)}.$$

and in the base currency of the portfolio:

$$r = \sum w_i r_i$$

B.1.2 Benchmark returns

Let the weight of the benchmark in the ith asset class be W_i, where $\sum W_i = 1$, and let the return of the benchmark for the ith asset class in local currency be b_{Li}, in the base currency of the portfolio be b_i and hedged into the base currency be b_{Hi}. Now the total benchmark return is in local currency:

$$b_L = \sum W_i b_{Li}$$

and in the base currency of the portfolio:

$$b = \sum W_i b_i$$

B.1.3 Semi-notional returns

We define the semi-notional return of the ith asset class in the local currency as $w_i b_{Li}$ and with any deviation from the index weightings ("bet") hedged into the base currency as $b_{SHi} = (w_i - W_i)b_{Hi} + W_ib_{Li}$. Now the total semi-notional return is in the local currency:

$$b_L = \sum w_ib_{Li}$$

and with any deviation from the index weighting ("bet") hedged into the base currency:

$$b_{SH} = \sum \{(w_i - W_i)b_{Hi} + W_ib_{Li}\}$$

B.1.4   Relative performance

We define the performance of the portfolio relative to the benchmark as:

$$\frac{1 + r}{1 + b} - 1$$

and it is this relative performance that we attribute in this methodology. We attribute it to three main factors: stock selection, country allocation and currency effects.

B.2   STOCK SELECTION

The term "stock selection" is used to describe the relative performance of the portfolio to the benchmark within a particular asset class. Intuitively, this seems to be the portfolio total local return, r_L, relative to the semi-notional total local return, b_{SL} (remembering that b_{SL} is the sumproduct of portfolio weights with the benchmark returns, so any difference between b_{SL} and r_L is by definition due to stock selection).

We attribute relative performance to stock selection in the ith asset class as follows:

$$w_i \left(\frac{1 + r_{Li}}{1 + b_{Li}} - 1 \right) \left(\frac{1 + b_{Li}}{1 + b_{SL}} \right)$$

So, the total stock selection is:

$$\sum_{i=1}^{n} w_i \left(\frac{1 + r_{Li}}{1 + b_{Li}} - 1 \right) \left(\frac{1 + b_{Li}}{1 + b_{SL}} \right) = \sum \frac{w_i[(1 + r_{Li}) - (1 + b_{Li})]}{1 + b_{SL}}$$

$$= \sum \frac{w_ir_{Li} - w_ib_{Li}}{1 + b_{SL}}$$

$$= \frac{\sum w_ir_{Li} - b_{SL}}{1 + b_{SL}}$$

$$= \frac{1 + \sum w_ir_{Li} - (1 + b_{SL})}{1 + b_{SL}}$$

$$= \frac{1 + r_L}{1 + b_{SL}} - 1$$

B.3   Asset allocation

The term "asset allocation" is used to describe the effect of the relative weighting of the portfolio to the benchmark (or "bet") within a particular asset class. Within this effect we include the cost of hedging the "bet" back to base currency, reasoning that this is a cost that should be borne by the decision maker making the bet. In effect, we are saying that if the asset allocator causes a currency position in the portfolio, then that position must be notionally hedged back to the neutral benchmark exposure. The cost (or benefit) is reflected in the asset allocation calculation by using a fully hedged index to measure the impact.

We attribute relative performance to asset allocation in the ith asset class as follows:

$$(w_i - W_i)\left(\frac{1 + b_{Hi}}{1 + b_L} - 1\right)$$

So, the total asset allocation is:

$$\sum_{i=1}^{n}(w_i - W_i)\left(\frac{1 + b_{Hi}}{1 + b_L} - 1\right) = \sum(w_i - W_i)\left(\frac{1 + b_{Hi} - 1 - b_L}{1 + b_L}\right)$$

$$= \sum\frac{w_i b_i - W_i b_{Hi} - w_i b_L + W_i b_L}{1 + b_L}$$

$$= \frac{\sum w_i b_{Hi} - \sum W_i b_{Hi}}{1 + b_L} \quad \left(\text{because } \sum w_i = \sum W_i = 1 \Rightarrow\right.$$

$$\left.\sum(W_i - w_i)b_L = 0\right)$$

$$= \frac{\sum w_i b_{Hi} - \sum W_i b_{Hi} + \sum W_i b_{Li} - b_L}{1 + b_L}$$

$$= \frac{1 + \sum[(w_i - W_i)b_{Hi} + \sum W_i b_{Li}] - (1 + b_L)}{1 + b_L}$$

$$= \frac{1 + b_{SH}}{1 + b_L} - 1$$

B.4   CURRENCY EFFECTS

B.4.1   Naive currency performance

The difference between the base currency return of the portfolio and the weighted average local return must by definition be the total currency effect. Therefore, the currency return of the portfolio r'_C is:

$$r'_C = \frac{1 + r}{1 + r_L} - 1$$

Similarly, the currency return of the benchmark b'_C is:

$$b'_C = \frac{1 + b}{1 + b_L} - 1$$

Therefore, the naive currency attribution within the portfolio is the difference between the portfolio currency and the benchmark currency:

$$\frac{1+r'_C}{1+b'_C} - 1 = \left(\frac{\dfrac{1+r}{1+r_L}}{\dfrac{1+b}{1+b_L}}\right) - 1 \quad \text{or} \quad \frac{1+r}{1+r_L} \times \frac{1+b_L}{1+b} - 1$$

This is defined as naive because it makes no allowance for the transfer of the cost of hedging (discussed in asset allocation above) or compounding effects between market or currency returns. It does not reflect the currency effect from the perspective of the "currency overlay manager".

B.4.2 Measured currency returns

We can also derive the "measured" currency return from the bottom-up using currency exposures and returns.

We define the currency return of the benchmark in the ith currency as:

$$c_i = \frac{1+b_i}{1+b_{Li}} - 1$$

Because most commercial international indexes use the WM Reuters 4 o'clock closing exchange rates this currency return can be derived from spot rates:

$$c_i = \frac{S_i^{t+1}}{S_i^t} - 1$$

where: S_i^t = the spot rate of currency i at time t.

Defining the benchmark forward rate of a forward currency contract as:

$$f_i = \frac{S_i^{t+1}}{F_i^{t+1}} - 1$$

where: F_i^{t+1} = the forward exchange rate of currency i at time t for conversion through a forward contract at time $t+1$.

Note the interest-rate differential in currency i:

$$d_i = \frac{F_i^{t+1}}{S_i^t} - 1$$

The currency return is therefore:

$$\frac{S_i^{t+1}}{S_i^t} = \frac{S_i^{t+1}}{F_i^{t+1}} \times \frac{F_i^{t+1}}{S_i^t} = (1+f_i) \times (1+d_i)$$

Note that the hedged index return is the combined effect of local return with the interest-rate differential:

$$b_{Hi} = (1+b_{Li}) \times (1+d_i) - 1 \quad \text{or} \quad b_{Hi} = \frac{1+b_i}{1+f_i} - 1$$

We define the total measured currency return of the benchmark as:

$$b_C = \sum W_i c_i + \sum \tilde{W}_i f_i$$

where: $\tilde{W}_i$ is the benchmark weight of forward currency contracts in currency.

The slight difference between b_C and b'_C is caused by compounding between market returns and currency. This difference is measured by:

$$\frac{1 + b_C}{1 + b'_C} - 1$$

We define the currency return of the portfolio in ith currency as:

$$c'_i = \frac{1 + r_i}{1 + r_{Li}} - 1$$

Currency returns in portfolios differ from benchmark currency returns because transactions naturally occur at spot rates different from closing spot rates.

Forward currency returns in portfolios also differ from benchmark forward currency returns. If we let the forward currency return of the portfolio in the ith currency be f'_i, we can define the total measured currency return of the portfolio as:

$$r_C = \sum w_i c'_i + \sum \tilde{w}_i f'_i$$

where: $\tilde{w}_i$ is the benchmark weight of forward currency contracts in currency i.

Similarly, there is a slight difference between r_C and r'_C measured by:

$$\frac{1 + r_C}{1 + r'_C} - 1$$

B.4.3 Compounding effects

Comparing the impact of compounding in the portfolio with that of the benchmark, the combined impact is measured by:

$$\left(\frac{\dfrac{1 + r'_C}{1 + r_C}}{\dfrac{1 + b'_C}{1 + b_C}} \right) - 1 \quad \text{or} \quad \frac{1 + r'_C}{1 + r_C} \times \frac{1 + b_C}{1 + b'_C} - 1$$

This factor measures the impact of currency and market compounding invisible to the currency overlay manager, but nevertheless an effect within the total portfolio.

This factor may be shown separately or more commonly combined with the currency effect, particularly if the currency overlay manager is not independent of the investment decision process.

B.4.4 Currency attribution

We define the semi-notional currency return of the portfolio as:

$$c_S = \sum w_i c_i + \sum \tilde{w}_i f_i$$

Note that the semi-notional currency return applies benchmark currency or spot returns to actual physical portfolio weights and benchmark currency forward returns to the actual portfolio forward currency weights.

We define the semi-notional currency return of the portfolio including the cost of hedging as:

$$c_{SH} = \sum W_i c_i + \sum [(\tilde{w}_i + w_i - W_i) f_i]$$

B.4.4.1 Currency timing

Currency timing is used to describe the difference between the real portfolio currency returns and benchmark currency returns caused by intra-day foreign exchange and forward foreign exchange trades at spot and forward rates different from that assumed in the benchmark. Currency timing is analogous to stock selection:

$$w_i \left(\frac{1 + c_i'}{1 + c_i} - 1 \right) \left(\frac{1 + c_i}{1 + c_S} \right)$$

and including forward contracts:

$$w_i' \left(\frac{1 + f_i'}{1 + f_i} - 1 \right) \left(\frac{1 + f_i}{1 + c_S} \right)$$

The total currency timing effect:

$$\frac{1 + r_C}{1 + c_S}$$

B.4.4.2 Currency allocation

Currency managers generate currency exposure by using currency forward contracts or currency options whose price is derived from these forward currency contracts. They are priced by reference to spot rates and interest-rate differentials between the two currencies. A forward currency contract will therefore generate two exposures: one long and one short.

It follows that the currency manager can only generate a currency position by use of forward currency contracts and is therefore always exposed to interest-rate differentials. To measure the impact of any currency bet we must use currency forward rates, not spot rates, to determine the impact of that currency bet. Currency allocation is analogous to asset allocation selection:

$$(w_i + \tilde{w}_i - W_i'' - \tilde{W}_i) \left(\frac{1 + f_i}{1 + b_C} - 1 \right)$$

So, the total currency allocation performance is:

$$\frac{1 + c_{SH}}{1 + b_C} - 1$$

The total currency effects from the currency overlay perspective are:

$$\frac{1+r_C}{1+c_S} \times \frac{1+c_{SH}}{1+b_C} - 1$$

B.4.5 Cost of hedging

The "cost of hedging" represents the cost or benefit of hedging the asset allocator's decisions back to the "neutral" currency benchmark. The cost of hedging from the currency overlay perspective is:

$$\frac{1+c_S}{1+c_{SH}} - 1$$

The cost of hedging from the asset allocator s perspective is:

$$\frac{1+b_{SH}}{1+b_{SL}} - 1$$

The asset allocator's perspective, including the compounding with market returns which causes a very slight mismatch, is measured by:

$$\left(\frac{\dfrac{1+c_S}{1+c_{SH}}}{\dfrac{1+b_{SH}}{1+b_L}}\right) - 1 \quad \text{or} \quad \frac{1+c_S}{1+c_{SHC}} \times \frac{1+b_L}{1+b_{SH}} - 1$$

This impact is so small it can be ignored, unless you prefer to avoid all residuals.

B.4.6 Total currency effects

Combining all the currency effects in the portfolio we get:

$$\underbrace{\frac{1+r_C}{1+c_S} \times \frac{1+c_{SH}}{1+b_C}}_{\text{Currency overlay}} \times \underbrace{\frac{1+b_{SL}}{1+b_{SH}} \times \frac{1+c_S}{1+c_{SH}}}_{\text{Hedging mismatch}} \times \underbrace{\frac{1+r'_C}{1+r_C} \times \frac{1+b_C}{1+b'_C}}_{\text{Compounding}} - 1$$

which simplifies to:

$$\frac{1+b_{SL}}{1+b_{SH}} \times \frac{1+r'_C}{1+b'_C} - 1$$

The naive currency effect adjusted for the cost of hedging.

B.5 SUMMARY

We now have attributed relative performance to the following factors:

$$\text{Stock selection} \quad \frac{1+r_L}{1+b_{SL}} - 1$$

$$\text{Asset allocation} \quad \frac{1 + b_{SH}}{1 + b_L} - 1$$

$$\text{Total currency effects} \quad \frac{1 + b_{SL}}{1 + b_{SH}} \times \frac{1 + r'_C}{1 + b'_C} - 1 \quad \text{or} \quad \frac{1 + b_{SL}}{1 + b_{SH}} \times \frac{1 + r}{1 + r_L} \times \frac{1 + b_L}{1 + b} - 1$$

We can then see that these factors compound to give:

$$\underbrace{\frac{1 + r_L}{1 + b_{SL}}}_{\text{Stock}} \times \underbrace{\frac{1 + b_{SH}}{1 + b_L}}_{\text{Asset}} \times \underbrace{\frac{1 + b_{SL}}{1 + b_{SH}}}_{\text{Hedging cost transferred}} \times \underbrace{\frac{1 + r}{1 + r_L} \times \frac{1 + b_L}{1 + b}}_{\text{Naive currency attribution}} - 1 = \frac{1 + r}{1 + b} - 1$$

Thus, we have now accounted for all of our relative performance with no residuals (i.e., no "other" term). Once more, because these terms are geometric the relationship holds true over time.

Appendix C
EIPC Guidance for Users of Attribution Analysis*

DEFINITION

Return attribution is a technique used to analyse the sources of excess returns of a portfolio against its benchmark into the active decisions of the investment management process.

PREAMBLE

Return attribution is becoming an increasingly valuable tool not only for assessing the abilities of asset managers and identifying where and how value is added but also for facilitating a meaningful dialogue between asset manager and client.

In this guidance we have chosen the term "return attribution" rather than the more common "performance attribution" to emphasize the distinction between return and risk, on the one hand, and to encourage the view of performance as a combination of risk and return, on the other hand.

Risk and risk attribution are equally valuable tools for assessing the abilities of asset managers; however, in this note we have focused on the attribution of historic returns.

Over the years many different forms of attribution techniques have been developed with varying degrees of accuracy. Additionally, attribution results may be presented in a variety of different formats, which in some cases may lead to different conclusions being drawn.

The following list of questions has been provided to assist the user of attribution analysis to gain the maximum value from the presentation.

QUESTIONS:

1. Does the attribution model follow the investment decision process of the asset manager?

   Comment: Attributing factors that are not part of the asset manager's decision process add little value. It is essential the attribution process quantifies the actual decisions made by the asset manager.

---

* Reproduced with permission from the European Investment Performance Committee.

2. Is the benchmark appropriate to the investment strategy?

    Comment: Does the benchmark adequately reflect the investment strategy and hence the investment decision process? Has it been used consistently over time? Is this the formal benchmark for the account?

3. Has the benchmark or investment style changed during the period of analysis?

    Comment: Benchmark changes and changes in style and restrictions should be disclosed. It is not appropriate to attribute using a current benchmark if changes have occurred. The attribution should reflect the benchmark assigned at the time and attribution effects should be compounded consistently.

4. Has the attribution model changed during the period of analysis?

    Comment: Changes and the rationale for changes should be disclosed.

5. Does the model generate an unexplained performance residual?

    Comment: Many attribution models generate residuals or balancing items. Essentially, all factors of the investment decision process are attributable. Residuals may bring into question the quality of the analysis and bring into doubt any conclusions that may be drawn from it.

6. If a residual is generated is it:

    i. Shown separately as a residual, balancing, timing or transaction item?
    ii. Ignored?
    iii. Allocated between other factors?

    Comment: Because a large residual may be difficult to explain it may be renamed, ignored or even allocated to other factors. It is important to establish how the residual has been treated by the asset manager. It is not good practice to ignore residuals.

7. Is interaction specifically calculated?

    Comment: Interaction is a defined factor in early (classical) attribution models. It represents the combined impact (or cross product) of stock and asset selection. It is often used when asset managers wish to derive the stock selection effect assuming the portfolio asset allocations are in line with the benchmark. Interaction is the remainder stock selection effect caused by asset allocations not in line with the benchmark.

8. If interaction is calculated is it:

    i. Shown separately?
    ii. Ignored?
    iii. Allocated to another factor?
    iv. Allocated to other factors consistently?

    Comment: Like residuals, large interaction effects are difficult to explain. They are often allocated to other factors or ignored. It is important to establish if interaction has been consistently applied to the same factor (i.e., stock selection) over time. It is not good practice to ignore residuals.

9. Is the attribution model arithmetic or geometric (multiplicative)?

Comment: There are two common forms of expressing excess return: arithmetic $r - b$ and geometric $(1 + r)/(1 + b) - 1$. Different attribution models will be required to quantify arithmetic and geometric excess returns (r = portfolio return, b = benchmark return).

10. If the model used is arithmetic, has a smoothing algorithm been used to allocate residuals to other factors?

Comment: Arithmetic models are deficient for multi-period analysis, generating residuals over time. Smoothing algorithms have been developed in some cases which allocate in a systematic way this residual over time. The type of smoothing algorithm should be disclosed. Some geometric models are also deficient and hence should disclose any smoothing algorithm.

11. Is the attribution based on buy/hold snapshots or are transactions included?

Comment: Stock level attribution in particular is data-intensive. As an alternative, buy/hold attributions may be performed based on holdings at the beginning of the period. Clearly, such attributions will not reconcile with real portfolio returns. Transactions and associated costs may be a significant factor in the portfolio return and are ignored in buy/hold type analysis.

12. How are the weights of the elements of attribution defined?

Comment: All methods rely on allocating weights to the sectors to be attributed. Only weight measures that ensure the weighted sum of returns is equal to the portfolio return will be accurate.

13. Is the model genuinely multi-currency? What FX rates are used for the portfolio and benchmark?

Comment: Currency effects should only be allocated if the asset manager has a separate currency allocation process. Forward currency effects should be calculated reflecting the fact that local returns cannot be achieved – only base currency or hedged. If the timing of FX rates are different from the portfolio and benchmark this should be disclosed. Most international benchmarks use consistent FX rates.

14. How are asset allocation decisions outside of the benchmark treated?

Comment: Any "bet" taken outside the benchmark will require an index to measure the impact of this decision. The choice of index will change the allocation between stock selection and asset allocation. The asset manager's approach should be determined and should be tested to ensure the approach taken is consistent with the investment process.

15. Are transaction costs included within stock selection or asset allocation, or are transaction costs treated as a separate attributable factor?

Comment: Typically, all transaction costs are implicitly included in the calculation of stock level performance. However, asset allocation decisions may generate transaction costs which should be allocated to asset allocation. Some models allocate a notional transaction cost to asset allocation. Consideration should be given to attributing the impact of transactions in isolation and measuring the impact of dealing or the contribution of the dealing department.

16. Are the returns to be attributed net or gross of fees?

    Comment: If the returns are net of fees compared with a benchmark not adjusted for fees it is possible that the stock selection impact will include fees.

17. Is cash specifically included in the attribution? If so has a cash benchmark been determined?

    Comment: The user should establish whether the attribution reflects all the assets within the portfolio. If cash is included, has an appropriate cash benchmark been selected? The exact use of cash (excluded, systematically allocated to sectors or managed) should be disclosed. Since cash is lowly correlated with most assets and often not included in the benchmark it is frequently one of the larger "bets" in the portfolio and hence a contributor to relative performance.

18. Does the attribution include gearing or leverage and if so is the attribution based on an all-cash analysis?

    Comment: If the asset manager is employing gearing this should be attributed according to the investment decision process. Is the gearing at portfolio or asset level? Gearing should be disclosed.

19. Are derivatives included in the analysis? If yes, how?

    Comment: Just like any other asset class the impact of derivatives should be calculated in line with the investment decision process. It may not be appropriate to isolate the impact of derivatives alone. Attribution effects should be based on the economic exposure of derivatives if that accurately reflects the investment decision process.

20. Is the attribution derived directly from the asset manager's records? Is there a difference between the return used in the attribution and the formal portfolio return?

    Comment: It is important to determine the source of the attribution data, is it from the asset manager, custodian or another third party? Differences between the attribution calculated return and formal return should be identified. If top-level returns (portfolio and benchmark) can be reconciled to third parties, then is it appropriate to use the asset manager's attribution model? (Third parties' attribution models may not follow the asset manager's decision process.)

21. Which methodology is used to calculate portfolio returns?

    Comment: The return calculation methodology (time-weighted or money-weighted) will determine the accuracy of the attribution results and the weights used to determine factor allocations. In a similar way that large cash flows affect return calculations, large cash flows both external and internal between sectors in a portfolio may impact attribution calculations. Typically, more frequent return calculations lead to more accurate attribution results.

22. If the attribution base is not a benchmark what is the rationale for this choice?

Comment: Attributions can be performed against composites, representative accounts, model funds, carve-outs and peer groups. This should be disclosed together with the methodology used and the rationale for this type of presentation.

Appendix D
European Investment Performance Committee – Guidance on Performance Attribution Presentation*

SECTION 1 INTRODUCTION

Performance attribution has become an increasingly valuable tool not only for assessing asset managers' skills and for identifying the sources of value added but also for facilitating a meaningful dialogue between investment managers and their clients.

Like any other performance presentation, a presentation of performance attribution results provides meaningful information to the user only to the extent the user understands the assumptions and concepts underlying this presentation. That's why it is crucially important that the presentation of attribution results is provided in a way that does not mislead the users and contains all necessary disclosures to explain the underlying assumptions and concepts.

Given the aforementioned, the European Investment Performance Committee (EIPC) has decided to take the initiative and to address the demand of the investment management industry for specific guidance with respect to presentation of return and risk attribution analysis. The first step was the issue of the EIPC Working Paper "Guidance for Users of Attribution Analysis" in early 2002. The following Guidance on Performance Attribution Presentation represents the next milestone in this process and establishes a reporting framework, which provides for a fair presentation of return and risk attribution results with full disclosure. EIPC acknowledges that this Guidance is not the final step in this process and will have to be developed further to address any new matters arising in future.

Except for definition of some general terminology, the Guidance does not address methodological issues with respect to calculation of attribution results, nor attempts to present any prescriptive definitions. EIPC believes that setting any standard on performance attribution should primarily contribute to increasing the understanding of attribution through the necessary disclosures and transparency of the methodology and investment process. For details on various performance attribution methods and concepts, users should refer to the dedicated performance literature available. Being a "disclosure guidance", the Guidance can be generally applied to all types of investment portfolios (equity, fixed income or balanced).

The Guidance does not require investment managers to present return and risk attribution results. However, if investment managers do present attribution analysis, they are encouraged to provide full disclosure and to apply the provisions of the

---

* Reproduced with permission from the European Investment Performance Committee

Guidance. As the importance of a particular piece of information may vary depending on the situation, EIPC believes that differentiation in the disclosures between required and recommended may be too subjective.

EIPC regards it as the responsibility of users of performance attribution to duly inform themselves about performance attribution concepts and, when presented with performance attribution results, to ask relevant questions to understand the underlying assumptions and methods. Not doing this may lead to misinterpretations and misjudgment of the quality of investment managers presenting the attribution results.

The Guidance was approved by EIPC in January 2004. EIPC proposes that this Guidance be adopted by the Investment Performance Council (IPC) as a guidance for the investment management industry.

SECTION 2   DEFINITIONS

The purpose of the following definitions is to provide the user with an explanation on the terminology as it is used in this Guidance. The Guidance does not attempt to establish any absolute or dogmatic definitions and recognises that there may be various views and interpretations of these matters within the investment management industry.

Performance attribution   (1) Performance attribution techniques are generally understood as a process of decomposition of return and risk into the investment management decisions in order to measure the value added by active investment management and to communicate the risk components of the investment strategy.

(2) For the purposes of this Guidance term "Performance Attribution" refers both to attribution of historic returns and to risk attribution (ex-ante and ex-post). The Guidance emphasises the distinction between return and risk and encourages the view of performance as a combination of risk and return. As a rule, terms "*Return attribution*" and "*Risk attribution*" are explicitly used in this Guidance.

Excess/active return   The difference between a periodic portfolio return and its benchmark return. This value may be calculated either as an arithmetic or a geometric difference. Also called *relative* return.

Return attribution   (1) Return attribution techniques are generally understood as a process of decomposition of active (historic) returns into the investment management decisions in order to identify the sources of return.

(2) Return attribution can be applied to absolute returns (absolute attribution) or to relative/excess returns, being the difference between the portfolio and benchmark return (relative attribution).

Return contribution	Return contribution techniques are generally understood as a process of decomposition of returns in order to measure the contribution of each particular segment of the portfolio to the portfolio overall return.
Risk attribution	For the purpose of this Guidance, the following elements of risk attribution analysis are defined:

Risk measurement

The process of measurement of a portfolio's risk in absolute (e.g. volatility, value-at-risk) or relative (e.g. tracking error) terms, both ex-post (historic) and ex-ante (predicted).

Risk attribution

The first step of risk attribution is the risk decomposition, i.e. identifying the sources of a portfolio's risk, both ex-post (historic) and ex-ante (predicted), both in absolute terms and relative to the selected benchmark. This process may include decomposition into sources of systematic and specific risk or into various factors (e.g. industry, style, country, currency, credit quality, etc.) affecting a portfolio's risk; as well as determination of contribution of individual securities to the overall portfolio risk.

The further step of risk attribution is the process of measurement of contribution of investment management decisions to the active portfolio risk (e.g. to the portfolio tracking error).

Risk attribution for the purposes of this Guidance only refers to the analysis of investment risk and not to operational or other types of business risks.

SECTION 3   GUIDING PRINCIPLES

Investment managers are required to apply the following principles when calculating and presenting return and risk attribution results:

- Return and risk attribution analysis must follow the investment decision process of the investment manager and measure the impact of active management decisions. It is essential that the attribution analysis reflects the actual decisions made by the investment manager. Return and risk attribution analysis must mirror the investment style of the investment manager.
- For the attribution of relative return and risk, a benchmark appropriate to the investment strategy must be used. The employed benchmark should be specified in advance and meet such criteria as investability, transparency and measurability.
- If investment managers are not able to produce return and risk attribution results that comply with the above guiding principles, they still may use these results for internal purposes but should refrain from presenting attribution to external users or use it for the purposes of soliciting potential clients.

SECTION 4   DISCLOSURES

A   Return attribution

The following disclosures are required to be provided, as long as they are applicable, when presenting return attribution results.

A.1   Investment process

A.1.1	Object of a return attribution analysis	Firms must disclose the object of a return attribution, e.g. a particular portfolio, a representative portfolio, a model portfolio, a group of portfolios (composite), etc., and the reasons for selecting this particular object.
A.1.2	Investment management process and investment style	Firms must disclose the main elements of their investment management process, including the key investment decision factors employed.

A.1.3	Benchmark	Firms must disclose the composition of the benchmark used for the return attribution purposes. Benchmark rebalancing rules must also be disclosed. If there has been any change in benchmark, the old benchmark(s) and date(s) of change(s) are to be disclosed.
		    In case of investments outside of the scope of the benchmark, firms must disclose the treatment of the impact of these investments, e.g. allocated to another attribution effect, presented separately, etc.
		    If the attribution is not based on a benchmark, firms must disclose the rationale for this.

A.2   Return attribution model

A.2.1	Return attribution model and attribution effects	Firms must disclose a description of the return attribution model.* Attribution effects derived (e.g. depending on the portfolio type: timing, security selection, currency effects, or income, duration, spread effects, etc.) must be clearly identified. If the attribution model has changed during the period of analysis, these changes and the rationale for them must be disclosed. In addition, the implications for the attribution history, if any, as a result of this change must be disclosed.

---

* If the model is one which has been documented in an industry publication, its name and source reference must be disclosed. If the model is a variation of a published model, the original name and source reference must be disclosed, as well as an explanation of the revisions which have been made. If the model is unpublished or proprietary, then a broad description of its details must be disclosed.

A.2.2	Excess/active returns	Firms must disclose whether periodic excess returns are derived using an arithmetic or a geometric method.
A.2.3	Presentation period	Firms must disclose what time period the attribution analysis covers and why this period has been chosen.
A.2.4	Frequency of return attribution analysis	Firms must disclose the frequency of calculation of attribution effects (e.g. daily, monthly basis, etc.).
A.2.5	Linking methodology	If the attribution report provides effects which were calculated for subperiods (e.g. days) and linked to present results for longer periods (e.g. a month), then the details of the linking methodology must be made available upon request. If a smoothing algorithm has been employed to allocate in a systematic way residual effects over time, the type of this algorithm is to be disclosed.
A.2.6	Buy-and-hold vs. transaction based approach	Firms must disclose whether the return attribution approach is buy-and-hold or transaction based.
A.2.7	Interaction effect and/or unexplained residuals	Some attribution models generate interaction effects or even unexplained residuals. Unexplained residuals may impair the quality of analysis and conclusions that may be drawn from it. If the model has an interaction term or an unexplained residual, details of its treatment must be disclosed, e.g. presented separately, ignored, allocated to other attribution effects, etc.
A.2.8	Derivatives	Firms must disclose to what extent derivatives are included and how they are treated in the return attribution analysis.
A.2.9	Effect of leverage	If leverage is employed, firms must disclose how leverage effects are attributed according to investment decision process.
A.2.10	Foreign currency effects	If investments in currencies other than the base currency of the portfolio are employed, treatment of foreign currency effects in terms of the currency management strategy must be disclosed.
A.2.11	Inclusion of cash	Firms must disclose whether cash is specifically included in the attribution analysis and whether a cash benchmark is determined. Firms also must disclose any difference in treatment of strategic cash allocation positions vs. temporary cash from realised income.
A.2.12	Transaction costs, fees	Firms must disclose the treatment of the impact of transaction costs, fees, etc. – e.g. allocated to a particular attribution effect, presented separately, etc.

A.3   Underlying input data

A.3.1	Portfolio returns	Firms must disclose:

- methodology and frequency of calculation of portfolio and portfolio segment returns,
- treatment of single performance components, such as management fees, custodian fees, taxes and transaction costs (gross vs. net treatment).

A.3.2	Benchmark returns	Firms must disclose:

- methodology of calculation of benchmark returns,
- any adjustments with respect to management fees,
- realised income positions, taxes etc., source of data.

Firms are encouraged to disclose any other specific details that may be important.

A.3.3	Leveraged portfolios	If the underlying portfolio includes discretionary leverage, the firm must disclose whether calculation of portfolio returns is performed on an actual or "all-cash" basis.*
A.3.4	Underlying valuation data	Firms must disclose if there are any differences with respect to sources and timing of prices of underlying securities between the portfolio and the benchmark.
A.3.5	Foreign exchange rates	Firms must disclose if the sources or timing of foreign exchange rates are different between the portfolio and the benchmark.
A.3.6	Income positions	Firms must disclose if realised income from dividends and coupons is considered after or before deduction of applicable withholding taxes both for the portfolio and the benchmark.

Firms are encouraged to disclose any additional matters they find useful or relevant for the users of attribution analysis.

B   Risk attribution

The following disclosures are required to be provided when presenting risk attribution analysis results.

B.1   Investment process

B.1.1	Object of risk attribution	Firms must disclose the object of risk analysis, e.g. a particular portfolio, a representative portfolio, a model

---

*For details regarding "all-cash" basis calculations refer, for example, to *AIMR-PPS Handbook*, 1997, App. B, p. 117.

portfolio, a group of portfolios (composite), and the reasons for selecting this particular object.

B.1.2	Investment management process and investment style	Firms must disclose the main elements of their investment management process, including the key investment decision factors employed.
B.1.3	Benchmark	Firms must disclose the composition of the benchmarks used for the risk attribution purposes. Benchmark rebalancing rules must also be disclosed. If there has been any change in benchmark, the old benchmark(s) and date(s) of change(s) are to be disclosed.

In case of investments outside of the scope or profile of the benchmark, firms must disclose the treatment of the impact of these investments.

If the attribution is not based on a benchmark, firms must disclose the rationale for this.

In case risk attribution is presented together with return attribution, the same benchmark as for return attribution should be used. If a different benchmark is used, the rationale for this must be disclosed.

B.2   Risk attribution model

B.2.1	Risk attribution model and attribution factors	Firms must disclose a general description of the risk attribution model, including description of the presented risk measures* and risk decomposition factors.

If the risk attribution model has changed during the period of analysis, these changes and the rationale for them are to be disclosed. In addition, the implications for the analysis history, if any, as a result of this change must be disclosed.

The risk attribution should, where possible, involve both ex-post and ex-ante analysis. This should also involve a reconciliation of the ex-post and ex-ante measures in order to assess the validity of the model.

B.2.2	Ex-ante risk measures	When presenting forward-looking risk measures, firms must provide a broad description with respect to the methods used to estimate portfolio holdings and/or likely magnitudes of relative returns for individual securities, sectors or markets and their correlation with each other.

---

* If the model is one which has been documented in an industry publication, its name and source reference must be disclosed. If the model is a variation of a published model, the original name and source reference must be disclosed, as well as an explanation of the revisions which have been made. If the model is unpublished or proprietary, then a broad description of its details must be disclosed.

Firms must also disclose the impact of the portfolio turnover and how this would influence their assumption regarding stability of the future portfolio asset structure.

B.2.3   Analysis period

When presenting risk measures, firms must disclose the reporting date of the analysis.

When presenting backward-looking risk measures, firms must disclose what time period the analysis covers and why this period has been chosen. In case ex-post risk attribution is presented together with return attribution, the analysis period should be the same as for the return attribution.

B.3   Underlying input data

B.3.1   Portfolio returns

Firms must disclose:

- methodology and frequency of calculation of portfolio and segment returns,

- treatment of single performance components, such as management fees, custodian fees, taxes, external cash flows and transaction costs (gross vs. net treatment).

B.3.2   Benchmark returns

Firms must disclose:

- methodology of calculation of benchmark returns,

- any adjustments with respect to management fees, realised income positions, taxes, etc.,

- source of data.

Firms are encouraged to disclose any other specific details that may be important.

B.3.3   Leveraged portfolios

If the underlying portfolio includes discretionary leverage, the firm must disclose whether calculation of portfolio returns is performed on an actual or "all-cash" basis.*

B.3.4   Underlying valuation data

Firms must disclose if there are any differences with respect to sources and timing of prices of underlying securities and foreign exchange rates between the portfolio and the benchmark.

B.3.5   Foreign exchange rates

Firms must disclose if the sources or timing of foreign exchange rates are different between the portfolio and the benchmark.

B.3.6   Income positions

Firms must disclose if realised income from dividends

---

* For details regarding "all-cash" basis calculations refer, for example, to *AIMR-PPS Handbook*, 1997, App. B, p. 117.

and coupons is considered after or before deduction of applicable withholding taxes.

Firms are encouraged to disclose any additional matters they find useful or relevant for the users of attribution analysis.

SECTION 5   RELATION TO THE GLOBAL INVESTMENT PERFORMANCE STANDARDS (GIPS™)

EIPC does not currently view this Guidance as a part of the Global Investment Performance Standards (GIPS™) compliance framework. However, the Guidance can obviously be considered as a part of a broader ethical code of conduct for investment managers. Firms claiming GIPS compliance and presenting performance attribution analysis are encouraged to follow this Guidance. However, users should be aware that some GIPS requirements may not always be applicable for attribution analysis purposes, e.g. return calculation methods for individual client reporting.

Attribution analysis results may also be presented as a supplemental information to a GIPS compliant performance presentation. If attribution analysis is presented as a part of a GIPS compliant performance presentation, users should also refer to the GIPS Guidance Statement on the Use of Supplemental Information for guidance.

ANNEX 1   EXAMPLE OF RETURN AND RISK ATTRIBUTION REPORT IN COMPLIANCE WITH THIS GUIDANCE

The sample attribution analysis report shown overleaf refers to an equity portfolio and is *an example* of how a performance attribution presentation in compliance with this Guidance could look like. This sample report is absolutely not intended to serve as a "best practice" benchmark to present performance attribution in terms of methodology or layout.

Disclosures

Investment process

Object of the attribution analysis	The return and risk attribution analysis is performed for Portfolio XYZ as an integral part of the periodic client reporting to company XYZ.
Investment management process and investment style	Portfolio XYZ is a discretionary equity mandate with reference currency EUR managed in an active way against the customised benchmark specified by company XYZ as described below. In addition, the following specific client guidelines apply: outperform the defined benchmark (basis EUR) by 2% p.a. over a rolling 2-year period with a tracking error of max. 3% p.a.

Investment Manager ABC

Return Attribution and Risk Attribution Report for Equity Portfolio XYZ as of 31.03.2001

Return and Risk Attribution Report for:	**PORTFOLIO XYZ**
Period:	**1.1.2000 - 30.03.2001**
Reference Currency:	**EUR**
Benchmark:	**Customised (refer to Disclosures)**

Sector Overweights

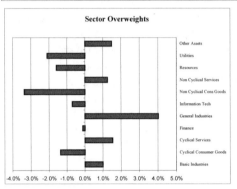

Return	
Portfolio	-4.45%
Benchmark	-2.89%
Active (Relative) Return	-1.56%

Return Attribution Analysis by Industry Sector	
Asset Allocation	-0.79%
Stock Selection	-0.52%
Other Effect	-0.25%
Total	**-1.56%**

Return Attribution Analysis by Region	
Asset Allocation	0.09%
Stock Selection	-2.74%
Other Effect	1.09%
Total	**-1.56%**

Attribution Analysis by Industry Sector

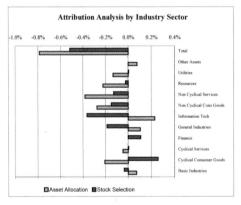

■ Asset Allocation ■ Stock Selection

Risk Analysis (end of period)	Portfolio	Benchmark
Number of Securities	99	576
Number of Currencies	2	2
Portfolio Value	227'447'728	
Total Risk (ex-ante)	15.76%	15.31%
- Factor Specific Risk	15.53%	15.20%
- Style	4.91%	4.29%
- Industry	11.95%	11.80%
- Stock Selection Risk	2.72%	1.83%
Tracking Error (ex-post)	2.29%	
Tracking Error (ex-ante)	2.35%	
Value at Risk (at 97.7%)	10'878'425	
R-squared	0.98	
Beta-adjusted Risk	15.59%	15.31%
Predicted Beta	1.02	
Predicted Dividend Yield	2.22	2.37

Attribution Analysis by Region

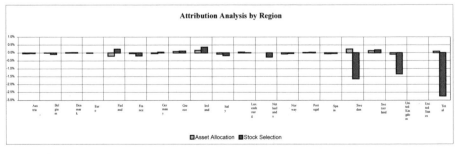

■ Asset Allocation ■ Stock Selection

Investment Manager ABC applies a top-down investment approach by actively modifying the portfolio asset allocation and taking active decisions with respect to stock selection. Foreign currency positions are not actively hedged. The inception date of portfolio XYZ is 1.1.2000.

Benchmark

The benchmark for portfolio XYZ is given as follows:

- EUR Cash Index Z   5%
- EUR Stock Index X   60%
- World Stock Index Y   35%

A monthly rebalancing is applied.

Results from investments in single stocks outside of the scope of the benchmark are allocated to the stock selection effect.

There were no changes in the benchmark since inception of the mandate.

Attribution model

Return attribution model

Return attribution is performed under the *Brinson–Fachler* method. Details and explanations to this model are available upon request. Returns are attributed to asset allocation (timing) and stock selection effects and presented according to the industry sector and region. Please refer also to disclosure "Interaction effect and/or unexplained residuals".

There has been no change in the model since inception of the portfolio.

Excess/active returns

Periodic excess returns are derived using an arithmetic method.

Presentation period

The return attribution and risk attribution analyses cover the period from 1.1.2000 to 31.03.2001 and is performed within the regular quarterly since-inception reporting.

Frequency of return attribution analysis

The attribution effects are calculated on a monthly basis.

Linking methodology

The monthly attribution effects are multiplicatively linked to show the attribution results for the whole presentation period. No smoothing algorithms are employed to systematically allocate the residual effects over time. Details on the methodology are available upon request.

Treatment of transactions	The return attribution model is based on a "buy-and-hold" approach. However, as transactions in the portfolio usually occur at the beginning of the month and the attribution effects are calculated on a monthly basis, portfolio manager ABC believes that potential distortions should be minimal.
Interaction effect and/or unexplained residuals	The model generates a residual effect due to multiplicative linking of arithmetically derived attribution effects over time. This effect is presented separately as "Other effect". The model does not generate any other unexplained residuals.
Derivatives	Derivatives are not employed in this portfolio.
Use of leverage	Leverage is not employed in this portfolio.
Inclusion of cash	According to the defined portfolio benchmark, cash represents a strategic position and is specifically included in the attribution analysis against a specified cash benchmark index. There is no difference in treatment of the strategic cash allocation position comparing to temporary cash from realised income as the realised income cash is deemed to be immaterial.
Foreign currency positions	Foreign currency positions are not hedged into the portfolio reference currency. Foreign exchange effects of these positions are included in the return attribution analysis within the stock selection effect.
Transaction costs and fees	Returns are calculated net of transaction costs and gross of fees. The impact of transaction costs vis-à-vis the benchmark return is not calculated specifically as the model is not transaction based. The model implicitly includes transaction costs on a cash level.
Risk attribution analysis	The presented risk attribution analysis includes both ex-post and ex-ante risk measurement and risk decomposition. Ex-post analysis includes calculation of the historical annualised tracking error. Ex-ante analysis includes calculation of the predicted total risk of the portfolio (annualised volatility) and its decomposition into factor-specific (style and industry) and stock selection components. In addition ex-ante annualised tracking error and value-at-risk (VaR) measures are presented. The predicted VaR measure is calculated on the basis of the parametric (variance/covariance) method. The methodology and assumptions used for calculation of ex-ante (predicted) risk measures are

developed and implemented in the proprietary model of company WWW, broad details of which are available upon request. For the purposes of the ex-ante risk analysis, an assumption is taken that the portfolio strategic asset structure remains stable (with monthly rebalancing) over time.

While reasonable care is exercised when predicting risk parameters, users of this report should be aware of inherent limitations of such forecast methods as well as of the assumptions underlying the calculation of risk measures (such as normality of return distributions, etc.).

A periodic reconciliation of the ex-post and ex-ante measures is performed on a quarterly basis to assess the model risk. The historic reconciliation results (since portfolio inception) show that an average model error lies within the bandwidth of 200–300 b.p.

Underlying input data

Underlying portfolio returns

The underlying portfolio returns are calculated in EUR on a monthly basis according to the true time-weighted rate of return method and under application of the total-return concept. Returns are calculated net of transaction costs and withholding taxes on interest and dividend income and gross of management and custodian fees.

The underlying portfolio data are derived from the accounting records of Investment Manager ABC. The source of securities prices and foreign exchange rates is data provider ZZZ.

Benchmark returns

The underlying benchmark returns are calculated on a monthly basis under application of the total-return concept and monthly rebalancing. The benchmark returns are calculated on the basis of EUR as reference currency. The source of the benchmark data is data provider ZZZ.

Appendix E
The Global Investment
Performance Standards*

II CONTENT OF THE GLOBAL INVESTMENT PERFORMANCE STANDARDS

GIPS is divided into five sections that reflect the basic elements involved in presenting performance information: Input Data, Calculation Methodology, Composite Construction, Disclosures, and Presentation and Reporting:

1. *Input Data*: Consistency of input data is critical to effective compliance with GIPS and establishes the foundation for full, fair, and comparable investment performance presentations. The Standards provide the blueprint for a firm to follow in constructing this foundation.
2. *Calculation Methodology*: Achieving comparability among investment management firms' performance presentations requires uniformity in methods used to calculate returns. The Standards mandate the use of certain calculation methodologies (e.g., performance must be calculated using a time-weighted total rate of return method).
3. *Composite Construction*: A composite is an aggregation of a number of portfolios into a single group that represents a particular investment objective or strategy. The composite return is the asset-weighted average of the performance results of all the portfolios in the composite. Creating meaningful, asset-weighted composites is critical to the fair presentation, consistency, and comparability of results over time and among firms.
4. *Disclosures*: Disclosures allow firms to elaborate on the raw numbers provided in the presentation and give the end user of the presentation the proper context in which to understand the performance results. To comply with GIPS, firms must disclose certain information about their performance presentation and the calculation methodology adopted by the firm. Although some disclosures are required of all firms, others are specific to certain circumstances, and thus may not be applicable in all situations.
5. *Presentation and Reporting*: After constructing the composites, gathering the input data, calculating returns, and determining the necessary disclosures, the firm must incorporate this information in presentations based on the guidelines set out in GIPS for presenting the investment performance results. No finite set of guidelines can cover all potential situations or anticipate future developments in investment industry structure, technology, products or practices. When appropriate, firms have

the responsibility to include in GIPS compliant presentations information not covered by the Standards.

The standards for each section are divided between requirements, listed first in each section, and recommended guidelines. Firms must follow the required elements of GIPS to claim compliance with GIPS. Firms are strongly encouraged to adopt and implement the recommendations to ensure that the firm fully adheres to the spirit and intent of GIPS. An example of a GIPS compliant presentation for a single composite is included as Appendix A.

Although GIPS may be translated into many languages, if a discrepancy arises between the different versions of the standards, the English version of GIPS is controlling.

1 Input data

1.A   Requirements

1.A.1   All data and information necessary to support a firm's performance presentation and to perform the required calculations must be captured and maintained.

1.A.2   Portfolio valuations must be based on market values (not cost basis or book values).

1.A.3   Portfolios must be valued at least quarterly. For periods beginning January 1, 2001, portfolios must be valued at least monthly. For periods beginning January 1, 2010, it is anticipated that firms will be required to value portfolios on the date of any external cash flow.

1.A.4   Firms must use trade-date accounting for periods beginning January 1, 2005.

1.A.5   Accrual accounting must be used for fixed income securities and all other assets that accrue interest income.

1.A.6   Accrual accounting must be used for dividends (as of the ex dividend date) for periods beginning January 1, 2005.

1.B   Recommendations

1.B.1   Sources of exchange rates should be the same between the composite and a benchmark.

2 Calculation methodology

2.A   Requirements

2.A.1   Total return, including realized and unrealized gains plus income, must be used.

2.A.2   Time-weighted rates of return that adjust for cash flows must be used. Periodic returns must be geometrically linked. Time-weighted rates of return that adjust for daily-weighted cash flows must be used for periods beginning January 1, 2005. Actual valuations at the time of external cash flows will likely be required for periods beginning January 1, 2010.

2.A.3 In both the numerator and the denominator, the market values of fixed income securities must include accrued income.

2.A.4 Composites must be asset-weighted using beginning-of-period weightings or another method that reflects both beginning market value and cash flows.

2.A.5 Returns from cash and cash equivalents held in portfolios must be included in total return calculations.

2.A.6 Performance must be calculated after the deduction of all trading expenses.

2.A.7 If a firm sets a minimum asset level for portfolios to be included in a composite, no portfolios below that asset level can be included in that composite.

2.B Recommendations

2.B.1 Returns should be calculated net of non-reclaimable withholding taxes on dividends, interest, and capital gains. Reclaimable withholding taxes should be accrued.

2.B.2 Performance adjustments for external cash flows should be treated in a consistent manner. Significant cash flows (i.e., 10% of the portfolio or greater) that distort performance (i.e., plus or minus 0.2% for the period) may require portfolio revaluation on the date of the cash flow (or after investment) and the geometric linking of subperiods. Actual valuations at the time of any external cash flows will likely be required for periods beginning January 1, 2010.

3 Composite construction

3.A Requirements

3.A.1 All actual, fee-paying, discretionary portfolios must be included in at least one composite.

3.A.2 Firm composites must be defined according to similar investment objectives and/or strategies.

3.A.3 Composites must include new portfolios on a timely and consistent basis after the portfolio comes under management unless specifically mandated by the client.

3.A.4 Terminated portfolios must be included in the historical record of the appropriate composites up to the last full measurement period that the portfolio was under management.

3.A.5 Portfolios must not be switched from one composite to another unless documented changes in client guidelines or the redefinition of the composite make it appropriate. The historical record of the portfolio must remain with the appropriate composite.

3.A.6 Convertible and other hybrid securities must be treated consistently across time and within composites.

3.A.7 Carve-out returns excluding cash cannot be used to create a stand-alone composite. When a single asset class is carved out of a multiple asset portfolio and the returns are presented as part of a single asset composite, cash must be allocated to the carve-out returns and the allocation method must be disclosed.

Beginning January 1, 2005, carve-out returns must not be included in single asset class composite returns unless the carve-outs are actually managed separately with their own cash allocations.

3.A.8   Composites must include only assets under management and may not link simulated or model portfolios with actual performance.

3.B   Recommendations

3.B.1   Separate composites should be created to reflect different levels of allowed asset exposure.

3.B.2   Unless the use of hedging is negligible, portfolios that allow the use of hedging should be included in different composites from those that do not.

4   Disclosures

4.A   Requirements

The following disclosures are *mandatory*:

4.A.1   The definition of "firm" used to determine the firm's total assets and firmwide compliance.

4.A.2   Total firm assets for each period.

4.A.3   The availability of a complete list and description of all of the firm's composites.

4.A.4   If settlement-date valuation is used by the firm.

4.A.5   The minimum asset level, if any, below which portfolios are not included in a composite.

4.A.6   The currency used to express performance.

4.A.7   The presence, use, and extent of leverage or derivatives including a description of the use, frequency, and characteristics of the instruments sufficient to identify risks.

4.A.8   Whether performance results are calculated gross or net of investment management fees and other fees paid by the clients to the firm or to the firm's affiliates.

4.A.9   Relevant details of the treatment of withholding tax on dividends, interest income, and capital gains. If using indexes that are net-of-taxes, firms must disclose the tax basis of the composite (e.g., Luxembourg based or U.S. based) versus that of the benchmark.

4.A.10   For composites managed against specific benchmarks, the percentage of the composites invested in countries or regions not included in the benchmark.

4.A.11   Any known inconsistencies between the chosen source of exchange rates and those of the benchmark must be described and presented.

4.A.12   Whether the firm has included any non-fee-paying portfolios in composites and the percentage of composite assets that are non-fee paying portfolios.

4.A.13   Whether the presentation conforms with local laws and regulations, that differ from GIPS requirements and the manner in which the local standards conflict with GIPS.

4.A.14   For any performance presented for periods prior to January 1, 2000 that does not comply with GIPS, the period of non-compliance and how the presentation is not in compliance with GIPS.

4.A.15   When a single asset class is carved out of a multiple asset portfolio and the returns are presented as part of a single asset composite, the method used to allocate cash to the carve-out returns.

4.B Recommendations

The following disclosures are *recommended*:

4.B.1   The portfolio valuation sources and methods used by the firm.
4.B.2   The calculation method used by the firm.
4.B.3   When gross-of-fee performance is presented, the firm's fee schedule(s) appropriate to the presentation.
4.B.4   When only net-of-fee performance is presented, the average weighted management and other applicable fees.
4.B.5   Any significant events within the firm (such as ownership or personnel changes) which would help a prospective client interpret the performance record.

5   Presentation and reporting

5.A   Requirements

5.A.1   The following items must be reported:

(a) At least five years performance (or a record for the period since firm inception, if inception is less than five years) that is GIPS compliant; after presenting five years of performance, firms must present additional annual performance up to ten years. (For example, after a firm presents five years of compliant history, the firm must add an additional year of performance each year so that after five years of claiming compliance, the firm presents a ten year performance record.)

(b) Annual returns for all years.

(c) The number of portfolios and amount of assets in the composite, and the percentage of the firm's total assets represented by the composite at the end of each period.

(d) A measure of the dispersion of individual component portfolio returns around the aggregate composite return.

(e) The standard Compliance Statement indicating firmwide compliance with the GIPS.

(f) The composite creation date.

5.A.2   Firms may link non-GIPS compliant performance to their compliant history, so long as firms meet the disclosure requirements of Section 4 and no non-compliant performance is presented for periods after January 1, 2000. (For example, a firm that has been in existence since 1990 that wants to present its entire performance history *and* claim compliance as of January 1, 2000, must present performance history that meets the requirements of GIPS at least from

January 1, 1995, and must meet the disclosure requirements of Section 4 for any non-compliant history prior to January 1, 1995.)

5.A.3   Performance for periods of less than one year must not be annualized.

5.A.4   Performance results of a past firm or affiliation can only be linked to or used to represent the historical record of a new firm or new affiliation if:

(a) a change only in firm ownership or name occurs, or

(b) the firm has all of the supporting performance records to calculate the performance, substantially all the assets included in the composites transfer to the new firm, and the investment decision-making process remains substantially unchanged.

5.A.5   If a compliant firm acquires or is acquired by a non-compliant firm, the firms have one year to bring the non-compliant firm's acquired assets into compliance.

5.A.6   If a composite is formed using single asset carve-outs from multiple asset class composites the presentation must include the following:

(i) a list of the underlying composites from which the carve-out was drawn, *and*

(ii) the percentage of each composite the carve-out represents.

5.A.7   The total return for the benchmark (or benchmarks) that reflects the investment strategy or mandate represented by the composite must be presented for the same periods for which the composite return is presented. If no benchmark is presented, the presentation must explain why no benchmark is disclosed. If the firm changes the benchmark that is used for a given composite in the performance presentation, the firm must disclose both the date and the reasons for the change. If a custom benchmark or combination of multiple benchmarks is used, the firm must describe the benchmark creation and re-balancing process.

5.B   Recommendations

5.B.1   The following items should be included in the composite presentation or disclosed as supplemental information:

(a) Composite performance gross of investment management fees and custody fees and before taxes (except for non-reclaimable withholding taxes).

(b) Cumulative returns for composite and benchmarks for all periods.

(c) Equal-weighted means and median returns for each composite.

(d) Volatility over time of the aggregate composite return.

(e) Inconsistencies among portfolios within a composite in the use of exchange rates.

5.B.2   Relevant risk measures, such as volatility, tracking error, beta, modified duration, etc., should be presented along with total return for both benchmarks and composites.

III VERIFICATION

The primary purpose of verification is to establish that a firm claiming compliance with GIPS has adhered to the standards. Verification will also increase the understanding and professionalism of performance-measurement teams and consistency of presentation of performance results.

The verification procedures attempt to strike a balance between ensuring the quality, accuracy, and relevance of performance presentations and minimizing the cost to investment firms of independent review of performance results. Investment firms should assess the benefits of improved internal process and procedures, which are as significant as the marketing advantages of verification.

The goal of the GIPS committee in drafting the verification procedures is to encourage broad acceptance of verification.

A Scope and purpose of verification

1. Verification is the review of an investment management firm's performance measurement processes and procedures by an independent third-party "verifier." Verification tests:

    A. Whether the investment firm has complied with all the composite construction requirements of GIPS on a firmwide basis, and

    B. Whether the firm's processes and procedures are designed to calculate and present performance results in compliance with the GIPS standards.

    A single verification report is issued in respect of the whole firm; GIPS verification cannot be carried out for a single composite.

2. Third-party verification brings credibility to the claim of compliance, and supports the overall guiding principles of full disclosure and fair representation of investment performance. Verification is *strongly encouraged* and is expected to become mandatory (but no earlier than 2005). Countries may require verification sooner through the establishment of local standards.

3. The initial minimum period for which verification can be performed is one year of a firm's presented performance. The recommended period over which verification is performed will be that part of the firm's track record for which GIPS compliance is claimed.

4. A verification report must confirm that:

    A. the investment firm has complied with all the composite construction requirements of GIPS on a firmwide basis, and

    B. the firm's processes and procedures are designed to calculate and present performance results in compliance with the GIPS standards.

    Without such a report from the verifier, the firm cannot claim that its claim of compliance with GIPS has been verified.

5. After performing the verification, the verifier may conclude that the firm is not in compliance with GIPS, or that the records of the firm cannot support a complete verification. In such situations, the verifier must issue a statement to the firm clarifying why a verification report was not possible.

6.   A principal verifier may accept the work of a local or previous verifier as part of the basis for the principal verifier's opinion.

7.   The minimum GIPS verification procedures are described in Section III(B) Required verification procedures.

B   Required verification procedures

The following are the *minimum* procedures that verifiers must follow when verifying an investment firm's compliance with GIPS. Verifiers must follow these procedures prior to issuing a verification report to the firm.

1   Pre-verification procedures

A.   *Knowledge of the Firm.* Verifiers must obtain selected samples of the firm's investment performance reports, and other available information regarding the firm, to ensure appropriate knowledge of the firm.

B.   *Knowledge of GIPS.* Verifiers must understand the requirements and recommendations of GIPS, including any updates, reports, or clarifications of GIPS published by the Investment Performance Council, the AIMR sponsored body responsible for oversight of the Global Investment Performance Standards.

C.   *Knowledge of the Performance Standards.* Verifiers must be knowledgeable of country-specific performance standards, laws, and regulations applicable to the firm, and must determine any differences between GIPS and the country-specific standards, laws, and regulations.

D.   *Knowledge of Firm Policies.* Verifiers must determine the firm's assumptions and policies for establishing and maintaining compliance with all applicable requirements of GIPS. At minimum, verifiers must determine the firm's following policies and procedures of the firm:

    i.   Policy with regard to investment discretion. The verifier must receive from the firm, in writing, the firm's definition of investment discretion and the firm's guidelines for determining whether accounts are fully discretionary;

    ii.   Policy with regard to the definition of composites according to investment strategy; the verifier must obtain the firm's list of composite definitions with written criteria for including accounts in each composite;

    iii.   Policy with regard to the timing of inclusion of new accounts in the composites;

    iv.   Policy with regard to timing of exclusion of closed accounts in the composites;

    v.   Policy with regard to the accrual of interest and dividend income;

    vi.   Policy with regard to the market valuation of investment securities;

    vii.   Method for computing time-weighted portfolio return;

    viii.   Assumptions on the timing of capital inflows/outflows;

    ix.   Method for computing composite returns;

    x.   Policy with regard to the presentation of composite returns;

    xi.   Policies regarding timing of implied taxes due on income and realized capital gains for reporting performance on an after-tax basis;

    xii. Policies regarding use of securities/countries not included in a composite's benchmark;

    xiii. Use of leverage and other derivatives; and

    xiv. Any other policies and procedures relevant to performance presentation.

E.   *Knowledge of Valuation Basis for Performance Calculations.* Verifiers must ensure that they understand the methods and policies used to record valuation information for performance calculation purposes. In particular, verifiers must determine that:

    i.   The firm's policy on classifying fund flows (e.g., injections, disbursements, dividends, interest, fees, taxes, etc.) is consistent with the desired results, and will give rise to accurate returns;

    ii.   The firm's accounting treatment of income, interest, and dividend receipts is consistent with cash account and cash accruals definitions;

    iii.   The firm's treatment of taxes, tax reclaims, and tax accruals is correct, and the manner used is consistent with the desired method (i.e., gross- or net-of-tax return);

    iv.   The firm's policies on recognizing purchases, sales, and the opening and closing of other positions are internally consistent, and will produce accurate results; and

    v.   The firm's accounting for investments and derivatives is consistent with GIPS.

2   *Verification procedures*

A.   *Definition of the Firm.* Verifiers must determine that the firm is, and has been, appropriately defined.

B.   *Composite Construction.* Verifiers must be satisfied that:

    i.   the firm has defined and maintained composites according to reasonable guidelines in compliance with GIPS;

    ii.   all of the firm's actual discretionary fee-paying portfolios are included in a composite;

    iii.   the manager's definition of discretion has been consistently applied over time;

    iv.   at all times, all accounts are included in their respective composites and no accounts that belong in a particular composite have been excluded;

    v.   composite benchmarks are consistent with composite definitions and have been consistently applied over time;

    vi.   the firm's guidelines for creating and maintaining composites have been consistently applied; and

    vii. the firm's list of composites is complete.

C.   *Non-Discretionary Accounts.* Verifiers must obtain a listing of all firm portfolios and determine on a sampling basis whether the manager's classification of the account as discretionary or non-discretionary is appropriate by referring to the account's agreement and the manager's written guidelines for determining investment discretion.

D.   *Sample Account Selection.* Verifiers must obtain a listing of open and closed accounts for all composites for the years under examination. Verifiers may check compliance with GIPS using a selected sample of a firm's accounts. Verifiers should consider the following criteria when selecting the sample accounts for examination:

i.   number of composites at the firm;

ii.   number of portfolios in each composite;

iii.   nature of the composite;

iv.   total assets under management;

v.   internal control structure at the firm (system of checks and balances in place);

vi.   number of years under examination; and

vii.   computer applications, software used in the construction and maintenance of composites, the use of external performance measurers, and the calculation of performance results.

This list is not all-inclusive and contains only the *minimum* criteria that should be used in the selection and evaluation of a sample for testing. For example, one potentially useful approach would be to choose a portfolio for the study sample that has the largest impact on composite performance because of its size, or because of extremely good or bad performance. The lack of explicit record keeping, or the presence of errors, may warrant selecting a larger sample or applying additional verification procedures.

E.   *Account Review.* For selected accounts, verifiers must determine:

i.   whether the timing of the initial inclusion in the composite is in accordance with policies of the firm;

ii.   whether the timing of exclusion from the composite is in accordance with policies of the firm for closed accounts;

iii.   whether the objectives set forth in the account agreement are consistent with the manager's composite definition as indicated by the account agreement, portfolio summary, and composite definition;

iv.   the existence of the accounts by tracing selected accounts from account agreements to the composites;

v.   that all portfolios sharing the same guidelines are included in the same composite; and

vi.   that shifts from one composite to another are consistent with the guidelines set forth by the specific account agreement or with documented guidelines of the firm's clients.

F.   *Performance Measurement Calculation.* Verifiers must determine whether the firm has computed performance in accordance with the policies and assumptions adopted by the firm and disclosed in its presentations. In doing so, verifiers should:

i.   recalculate rates of return for a sample of accounts in the firm using an acceptable return formula as prescribed by GIPS (i.e., time-weighted rate of return); and

ii.   take a reasonable sample of composite calculations to assure themselves of the accuracy of the asset weighting of returns, the geometric linking of returns to produce annual rates of returns, and the calculation of the dispersion of individual returns around the aggregate composite return.

G.   *Disclosures.* Verifiers must review a sample of composite presentations to ensure that the presentations include the information and disclosures required by GIPS.

H.   *Maintenance of Records.* The verifier must maintain sufficient information to support the verification report. The verifier must obtain a representation letter from the client firm confirming major policies and any other specific representations made to the verifier during the examination.

C   Detailed examinations of investment performance presentations

Separate from a GIPS verification, an investment management firm may choose to have a further, more extensive, specifically focused examination (or performance audit) of a specific composite presentation.

Firms cannot make any claim that a particular composite has been independently examined with respect to GIPS unless the verifier has also followed the GIPS verification procedures set forth in Section B. Firms cannot state that a particular composite presentation has been "GIPS verified" or make any claim to that affect. GIPS verification relates only to firmwide verification. Firms can make a claim of verification after a verifier has issued a GIPS verification report.

To claim verification of a claim of compliance with the Standards, a detailed examination of a composite presentation is not required. Examinations of this type are *unlikely* to become a requirement of GIPS or become mandatory.

Bibliography

Adams, A.T, Bloomfield, D.S.F., Booth P.M. and England, P.D. (1993) *Investment Mathematics and Statistics*. Graham & Trotman.

AIMR (1999) *The Global Investment Performance Standards*. Association for Investment Management and Research.

AIMR (2001) *AIMR Performance Presentation Standards (AIMR-PPS)*. Association for Investment Management and Research.

AIMR (2002). *The Global Investment Performance Standards (GIPS) Handbook*. Association for Investment Management and Research.

Allen, G.C. (1991) Performance attribution of global equity portfolios. *Journal of Portfolio Management*, Fall, 59–65.

Amenc, N. and Le Sourd, V. (2003) *Portfolio Theory and Performance Analysis*. John Wiley & Sons.

Ankrim, E. and Hensel, C. (1992) Multi-currency performance attribution. *Russell Research Commentary*, November.

Bacon, C.R. (2002) Excess returns – Arithmetic or geometric. *Journal of Performance Measurement*, Spring, 23–31.

BAI (1968) *Measuring the Investment Performance of Pension Funds for the Purpose of Inter Fund Comparison*. Bank Administration Institute.

Bain, W.G. (1996) *Investment Performance Measurement*. Woodhead Publishing.

Bogle, J.C. (1994) *Bogle on Mutual Funds*. Irwin.

Bogle, J.C. (1999) *Common Sense on Mutual Funds*. John Wiley & Sons.

Brinson, G. and Fachler, N. (1985) Measuring non-US equity portfolio performance. *Journal of Portfolio Management*, Spring, 73–76.

Brinson, G., Hood, R. and Beebower, G. (1986) Determinants of portfolio performance. *Financial Analyst Journal*, July/August, 39–44.

Brinson, G., Singer, B. and Beebower, G. (1991) Determinants of portfolio performance. II: An update. *Financial Analysts Journal*, May/June, 40–48.

Brown, P.J. (2002) *Constructing and Calculating Bond Indices*. Gilmour Drummond Publishing.

Burnie, J.S., Knowles, J.A. and Teder, T.J.. (1998) Arithmetic and geometric attribution. *Journal of Performance Measurement*, Fall, 59–68.

Butler, C. (1999) *Mastering Value at Risk*. Financial Times Prentice Hall.

Byrne, R. (1996) *The 2,548 Best Things Anybody Ever Said*. Galahad Books.

Campisi, S. (2000) Primer on fixed income performance attribution. *Journal of Performance Measurement*, Summer, 14–25.

Carino, D. (1999) Combining attribution effects over time. *Journal of Performance Measurement*, Summer, 5–14.

Davies, O. and Laker, D. (2001) Multiple-period performance attribution using the Brinson model. *Journal of Performance Measurement*, Fall, 12–22.

Dietz, P.O. (1966) *Pension Funds: Measuring Investment Performance*. Free Press.

Dembo, R.S. and Freeman, A. (1998) *Seeing Tomorrow Rewriting the Rules of Risk*. John Wiley & Sons.

Donald, D.W.A. (1981) *Compound Interest and Annuities-Certain*. Heinemann.

Dunbar, N. (2000) *Inventing Money*. John Wiley & Sons.

Elton, E.J. and Gruber, M.J. (1991) *Modern Portfolio Theory and Investment Analysis* (4th edn). John Wiley & Sons.

Fabozzi, F. (1999) *Duration, Convexity, and Other Bond Risk Measures*. Frank J. Fabozzi Associates.

Fama, E. (1972) Components of investment performance. *Journal of Finance*, **27**(3), June.

Feibel, B.J. (2003) *Investment Performance Measurement*. John Wiley & Sons.

Fischer, B. (2000) *Performance Analyse in der Praxis*. Oldenbourg [in German].

Frongello, A. (2002) Linking single period attribution results. *Journal of Performance Measurement*, Spring, 10–22.

Gibson, R.C. (1996) *Asset Allocation*. McGraw-Hill.

Golub, B.W. and Tilman, L.M. (2000) *Risk Management*. John Wiley & Sons.

Goodwin, T. (1998) The information ratio: More than you ever wanted to know about one performance measure. *Russell Research Commentary*.

GRAP (1997) *Synthèse des modèles d'attribution de performance*. Groupe de Recherche en Attribution de Performance [in French].

Haight, G.T. and Morrell, S.O. (1997) *The Analysis of Portfolio Management Performance*. McGraw-Hill.

Hussain, A. (2000) *Managing Operational Risk in Financial Markets*. Butterworth-Heinemann.

Hymans, C. and Mulligan, J. (1980) *The Measurement of Portfolio Performance*. Kluwer.

Illmer, S. and Marty. W. (2003) Decomposing the money-weighted return. *Journal of Performance Measurement*, Summer, 42–50.

ICAA (1971) *The Standards of Measurement and Use for Investment Performance Data*. Investment Counsel Association of America.

Jensen, M. (1969) Risk, the pricing of capital assets, and the evaluation of investment portfolios. *Journal of Business*, **42**(2), April.

Jorion, P. (1997) *Value at Risk*. Irwin.

Karnosky, D. and Singer, B. (1994) *Global Asset Management and Performance Attribution*. Research Foundation of the Institute of Chartered Financial Analysts.

Kirievsky, L. and Kirievsky, A. (2000) Attribution analysis: Combining attribution effects over time made easy. *Journal of Performance Measurement*, Summer, 49–59.

Knight, J. and Satchell, S. (2002) *Performance Measurement in Finance Firms, Funds and Managers*. Butterworth-Heinemann.

McLaren, A. (2001) A geometric methodology for performance attribution. *Journal of Performance Measurement*, Summer, 45–57.

Menchero, J. (2000) An optimized approach to linking attribution effects over time. *Journal of Performance Measurement*, Fall, 36–42.

Modigliani, L. (1997) Risk-adjusted performance. Part 1: The time for risk measurement is now. *Morgan Stanley's Investment Perspectives*, February.

Neubert, A.S. (1998) *Indexing for Maximum Investment Results*. Glenlake Publishing.

Reilly, F.K. (1989) *Investment Analysis and Portfolio Management*. Dryden Harcourt, Brace, Jovanovich.

Smith, K. and Tito, D. (1969) Risk return of ex-post portfolio performance. *Journal of Financial and Quantitative Analysis*, **IV**(4), December.

Sortino, F.A. and Satchell, S.E. (2001) *Managing Downside Risk in Financial Markets.* Butterworth-Heinemann.

Spaulding, D. (1997) *Measuring Investment Performance.* McGraw-Hill.

Spaulding, D. (2003) *Investment Performance Attribution.* McGraw-Hill.

Spaulding, D. (2003) Holdings vs. transaction-based attribution: An overview. *Journal of Performance Measurement,* Fall, 52–56.

Swensen, D.F. (2000) *Pioneering Portfolio Management.* Free Press.

Zask, E. (2000) *Global Investment Risk Management.* McGraw-Hill.

Index